About Island Press

Since 1984, the nonprofit organization Island Press has been stim-ulating, shaping, and communicating ideas that are essential for solving environmental problems worldwide. With more than 1,000 titles in print and some 30 new releases each year, we are the nation's leading publisher on environmental issues. We identify innovative thinkers and emerging trends in the environmental field. We work with world-renowned experts and authors to develop cross-disciplinary solutions to environmental challenges.

Island Press designs and executes educational campaigns, in conjunction with our authors, to communicate their critical mes-sages in print, in person, and online using the latest technologies, innovative programs, and the media. Our goal is to reach targeted audiences—scientists, policy makers, environmental advocates, urban planners, the media, and concerned citizens—with infor-mation that can be used to create the framework for long-term ecological health and human well-being.

Island Press gratefully acknowledges major support from The Bobolink Foundation, Caldera Foundation, The Curtis and Edith Munson Foundation, The Forrest C. and Frances H. Lattner Foundation, The JPB Foundation, The Kresge Foundation, The Summit Charitable Foundation, Inc., and many other generous organizations and indi-viduals.

The opinions expressed in this book are those of the author(s) and do not necessarily reflect the views of our supporters.

STRATEGIC
CORPORATE
CONSERVATION
PLANNING

STRATEGIC CORPORATE CONSERVATION PLANNING

A Guide to Meaningful Engagement

MARGARET O'GORMAN

ISLANDPRESS   Washington | Covelo | London

Island Press is a trademark of The Center for Resource Economics.

Library of Congress Control Number: 2019946445

All Island Press books are printed on environmentally responsible materials.

Manufactured in the United States of America
10 9 8 7 6 5 4 3 2 1

Keywords
business drivers, community engagement, conservation partnerships,
corporate citizenship, corporate conservation, corporate conservation
plan, corporate lands, corporate social responsibility, corporate STEM
education, corporate sustainability, ecological remediation, environmental education, nature-based climate solutions, nature-based solutions,
pollinator gardens, social license to operate, strategic conservation plan,
sustainability key performance indicator

For MIKE
For my mom, MARY

—

For every corporate conservationist bending and breaking the rules to get the job done.

CONTENTS

—

PREFACE

—

My journey to understanding how essential it is to build healthier relationships between business and the environment began when I was working at the Pinelands Preservation Alliance (PPA) in New Jersey. PPA's mission is to protect 1.1 million acres of ecological significance in a state scarred by its industrial history, dominated by suburban sprawl, and subjected to constant pressure from development of all types. New Jersey is an ideal place to begin to understand the needs and opportunities for ecological action in settings that are not pristine, not protected, and not wilderness.

To learn about environmental issues in New Jersey is to learn in a place where no corner of the state has been left untouched by humans, and it is to learn about the legacy of industry across a state industrialized since the first European migrants arrived on its bountiful shores. To know environmental issues in New Jersey is to know the Ciba Geigy plant in Tom's River, where illegally dumped pollutants leached into residents' groundwater for decades causing irreparable harm to human health, as well as environmental damage that will take decades to clean up. It is to know the Passaic River, where more than seventy companies are responsible for the highly toxic chemicals dumped there and found in the sediments today. To know New Jersey's environmental past and present is to know the complicated relationship between business and nature that exists both in the Garden State and across the rest of the world. It is to know places both pristine and broken, ugly and beautiful, industrial and postindustrial. In Liberty State Park, it is to see that toxic places can be fixed. In the New Jersey Pine Barrens, it is to understand that patterns of abusive land use can be regulated but must be forever guarded against. In the amazing biodiversity of New Jersey, it is to celebrate that nature can thrive and indeed recover in a human-dominated landscape that was, in the late 1980s, home to just a single pair of bald eagles, where today over 100 productive pairs are resident.

In 2012, when I started working with the private sector to advance a model of environmental engagement focused on conservation implementation, my worldview broadened to embrace a different aspect of the corporate relationship to nature. Listening to a quarry manager at Vulcan Material's Calica quarry in Playa Del Carmen, Mexico, I heard about the joys of dynamic reclamation (which means not waiting until the quarry has been fully excavated before starting the ecological reclamation, but instead restoring as the excavation moves across the site). Visiting Fighting Island in the Detroit River, I learned about a conservation partnership between the US Fish and Wildlife Service and BASF, the global chemical company, which has resulted in the first spawning sturgeon the river has seen in decades. I met an employee from an Exxon oil refinery in Billings, Montana, who was brimming with pride for a restoration project that not only created functional wetlands out of gravel pits but also connected school children to STEM education. Again and again, I have seen or learned about conservation efforts happening on corporate lands that were meeting global conservation objectives, satisfying a corporate business need, and connecting employees and community members with a shared sense of meaning.

Reconciling the view of the corporate polluter with the view of the corporate ecologist is not easy, but it can be done. The reconciliation happens across time and scale. The view of the polluting overlord is formed by the actions of the past and observed at a large corporate scale. That's not to say that the polluting overlord is an extinct concept. Sad to say, it's not. Legal and illegal pollution is still happening today (especially in developing countries) but not at the reckless and dangerous scale of yesteryear. A better corporate relationship with nature and communities is evolving. It's a new relationship that is local, personal, and based in the present while focused on the future.

This evolution still has a long way to go. One of the biggest threats to global biodiversity is from corporate action, clearing forests for crops. The main driver of climate change is fossil fuel extracted and burned by industry. The very model of capitalism that the global economy is based on is predicated on corporate success, which is ultimately based on exploiting the planet's finite resources. The challenge is how to keep shifting away from the destructive corporate actions and mindsets of the past, from lax materials management and poor environmental performance toward a place where respect for nature is mainstreamed into operations, considered in daily decisions, and included in corporate goals, reports, and plans. The challenge is to get to a place where nature is not just a "risk" or an "externality" but a true and deeply held value and where action for nature is the norm and not the exception.

This book is an effort to nudge us all along that journey by presenting a pragmatic, accessible, and affordable way to engage companies in ecological stewardship action on their lands that meet a business need and deliver a conservation result. In 2004, Mark Rose, the chief executive officer of Fauna and Flora International, stated: "Perhaps the single most influential group when it comes to determining the future of the planet is the corporate sector. The land area under corporate management is vast. The extent to which people depend on businesses for their incomes and livelihoods is overwhelming. Single companies are wealthier than entire groups of governments." Much should be expected of companies both large and small as we address our global environmental crises and transition to a different model of being. Within this transition, companies cannot be excluded from expectations for better lands management, better ecological restoration, or better natural-resources stewardship efforts—however great or small their potential contribution may be.

Today, nongovernmental organizations' (NGOs') intersections with the private sector have focused on talking, planning, and the creation of new frameworks, coalitions, and initiatives. From one world capital to another, from one global conference to the next, we start and sustain important conversations—but we also need to elevate the value of real change *on the ground*. This book is a contribution to advancing and valuing actual change on the ground. It seeks not to ignore the larger conversations, frameworks, and initiatives but to promote action and encourage engagement as the conversations continue to take place. It seeks to offer frank and pragmatic direction as an option for private-sector landowners and their NGO partners.

We need to value action as much as we do words. We need to celebrate prosaic practical approaches as much as we do complicated methodologies. We need to commend simple solutions, to embrace pragmatism, and to applaud getting things done.

But to get to meaningful engagement, we need to reframe how those of us working in natural-resources conservation view the corporate world. Christine Bader, writing in *The Evolution of a Corporate Idealist*, explains how, with the issue of human rights, there is a spectrum of engagement ranging from those who raise hell about human rights violations, naming and shaming corporate wrongdoers, to those who work quietly and iteratively inside companies to make them adopt better practices. The same spectrum exists in the environmental community, where "deep green groups" take direct action against corporate malpractice both past and present, while others work close to and within the corporate sphere to advance practices for better land management and biodiversity protection. The community will be stronger when it acknowledges this continuum and begins to see the myriad benefits of groups that quietly and carefully engage with the corporate sector. Far from dining with the devil, engagements with the corporate sector are opportunities for creative problem-solving and impactful change.

We also have to accept that few companies will implement biodiversity projects solely for biodiversity outcomes—and we need to be okay with that. In fact, we have to be okay with it because we won't succeed in mainstreaming conservation into industry otherwise. Business needs a business reason to take action. In addition, to address both the biodiversity and climate-change crises, we need to move beyond "either/or" and focus instead on "and/and." The door to action should be open to all possibilities at all scales.

Nobel laureate Wangari Maathi famously says that you don't need a diploma to plant a tree. She talks about the importance of simple action, saying, "You can make a lot of speeches, but the real thing is when you dig a hole, plant a tree, give it water, and make it survive. That's what makes the difference." She advocates simplicity and action. As a species we seem to distrust simplicity, but it is in the simple act of digging the hole and planting the tree that change happens, and it is by repeating these simple acts that change becomes permanent.

Figure 0-1: A simple act of conservation—digging a hole and planting a tree. (Used with permission from General Motors.)

Effecting conservation change on corporate lands—or any lands—starts with a simple act. There are many ways to get to that act, to that moment when a human or a machine moves earth and begins to make a positive difference for nature. This book seeks to get to the act—that is, to create effective conservation programs—by understanding the importance of a company's business needs and the opportunities of a company's land holdings, by overcoming the challenges of working in an ever-churning corporate space, and by connecting the dots from corporate headquarters to the hole in the ground where the tree is about to be planted.

Our world is warming from greenhouse-gas emissions and it is becoming impoverished by the increasing pace of species extinction. Both nature and the private sector are central to both of these challenges. With a shift in thinking and some fresh approaches, we can help create a world where nature is integrated into management practices and considered necessary for business success. My hope for this book is to extract some of the ingredients of successful engagements with the private sector in conservation planning and action, and to present them as a recipe that can be adapted by NGO partners and corporations in order to meet different needs and adapt to different situations. Ultimately, this book aims to inspire readers to act and, through action, to incite enthusiasm for more conservation projects on more corporate lands. The potential for impact lies in the myriad lands held by companies across the world. We just have to recognize the potential (even in the most unlikely of places) and begin to create change from it.

Margaret O'Gorman

01 AN EVOLVING RELATIONSHIP

—

You can't go back and change the beginning but you can start where you are and change the ending.

—C.S. LEWIS

It's a hot July day in the Midwest. Clear blue water laps at fine sandy soil, while the air hums with insects and a kestrel hovers overhead. In one direction, the Indiana dunes recede into the distance. These dunes, a complex of four discrete systems receding by age from the shores of Lake Michigan, represent an ecological progression from open beaches to stable oak forests. As a rare remaining natural place in the region, they provide recreation space for the residents of Chicago and northwest Indiana. On this summer day, the dunes are teeming with people playing ball, chasing pets, corralling children, and generally enjoying a day out at the Indiana Dunes National Park. In the near distance, the waters of Lake Michigan play host to sailboats, motorboats, and paddleboards.

In contrast to this scene of twenty-first-century leisure, a small group gathers on another shore nearby. It's silent but for the humming insects, protected from any interruption because it's privately owned. Turning away from the water, the view reveals a distant blast furnace being fed iron ore and other ingredients needed to start a process that will eventually turn out sheets of steel to be used in cars and other products.

The group of people gathered on the lakeshore on the grounds of this active steel mill, owned by steel-making giant Arcelor Mittal, are there not to make steel but to continue ecological restoration work that has been ongoing at this location for almost a decade. Across the sprawling facility in Burns Harbor, Arcelor Mittal employees and conservation partners have restored an oak savanna in a re-created dune habitat that is being actively managed through

1

the use of selective thinning and prescribed burns to ensure the best possible outcomes for biodiversity. Along the shoreline, coastal bird habitat has been created by removing debris and regrading surfaces to recover ecological functionality. The presence of insects and birds belies the land's past as a dumping grounds formerly filled with forty-foot-high piles of slag, a by-product of the steel-making process.

The work at Burns Harbor is just one example of the evolving relationship between corporations—making products that improve our lives but impact the environment—and nature. Today, with notable exceptions such as industrial agriculture, the curve is bending toward a better relationship with nature as past transgressions are corrected and those involved in future developments seek to better understand and mitigate impacts on nature. This transformation has been driven by customers and stakeholders who are increasingly engaged in the ethics and operations of the corporate world; by national and subnational governments that have built agencies and regulations to curb corporate excesses; and industry itself, adopting evolving corporate citizenship approaches to replace the outdated profit-only models of corporate growth.

The transformation at the Burns Harbor plant is part of that evolution. It took leadership, planning, time, money, and partnerships. The results show that sound environmental outcomes and social benefits can be realized from corporate conservation efforts.

Conservation partners such as the Shirley Heinz Land Trust, the Field Museum, and the Wildlife Habitat Council, and education partners such as the Dunes Learning Center and the Mighty Acorns program as well as the Portage School system all work together with Arcelor Mittal and the employees on-site to provide input into restoration priorities, carry out implementation, support monitoring efforts, and leverage the lands for education and recreation. Together, the company and the community are united to help reconnect this place with other industrial lands into a greener asset for all in the Calumet Region of northwest Indiana. In the late 1930s this region was one of the greatest industrial centers of the world; but before industry arrived it was home to a fantastic wilderness of swamps and swales and sand hills and dunes that were among the most interesting natural phenomena in North America.[1]

The partnership project at Arcelor Mittal's Burns Harbor facility makes a variety of contributions at multiple levels. First, it contributes to a landscape approach to increase habitat connectivity in a heavily fragmented landscape. It also contributes to Arcelor Mittal's corporate sustainability vision to be a trusted user of air, land, and water. It aligns with the objectives of the company's conservation and education partners and provides them with a location for implementing high-quality projects. By realizing these co-benefits, the restoration project at Burns Harbor is an example of a strategic corporate conservation effort where site-based implementation contributes to local and regional environmental and education objectives as well as global corporate citizenship goals.

The Corporation as a Citizen

Milton Friedman, the Nobel Prize–winning economist, famously stated that the sole responsibility of business toward society was the "maximization of profits to the shareholders." This ethos enabled a corporate culture that long excused bad actions as being good for business, and it allowed communities, both human and otherwise, to be exploited in the name of profit, leaving a legacy of broken places. But, predating Friedman's free-market philosophies, ideas about a better relationship between society and nature were powerfully described in *Social Responsibility of the Businessman*. Written by H. R. Bowen, an economist and academic, it described the obligations of business to operate according to a model that today is called corporate social responsibility (CSR). Bowen suggested that policies, decisions, and actions should reflect societal values and meet societal objectives. As Bowen argued, "those who own property have the duty of using and administering it, not exclusively for their own purpose, but in ways that will serve the needs of the whole society."[2]

Corporate social responsibility has now become a corporate norm, adopted by most enterprises regardless of sector, size, or market share and regardless of ownership structure. Its ubiquity is due in part to the fact that CSR has a very broad range of meanings. It can cover a variety of approaches and deliver a diversity of results both for business and society. Since the 1950s, CSR has also birthed a number of related corporate approaches such as sustainability, resiliency, and shared value creation. CSR and these related approaches can be gathered under a "corporate citizenship" banner that provides various frameworks for companies to engage in both the world and the communities in which they operate.

Like the corporate world itself, corporate citizenship has many expressions. At its worst, it can be a mere façade, a spun story full of symbols but lacking substance. Greenwashing is an example of dishonest corporate citizenship where benefits come only to the brand and not to people or the planet. Greenwashing reflects no material change. It is a superficial environmentalism that is all style and no significance, and focuses on a small number of criteria and neglects all others.[3] A notable example of greenwashing occurred in 2012, when Mazda created a co-branded campaign with the movie *The Lorax*, which brought Dr. Seuss's beloved children's book character, an environmentalist curmudgeon called the Lorax, to animated life. When Mazda used the character to promote the sale of cars, claiming them to be "Certified Truffula Tree Friendly," outrage ensued not only from environmentalists but also from auto industry pundits and brand experts.

If greenwashing is corporate citizenship at its worst, the best corporate citizenship can impact lives in systematic and sustainable ways. When Hurricane Maria caused the longest power blackout in US history on the island of Puerto Rico, Tesla Motors acted quickly to install its solar technology at sensitive locations such as hospitals. This act of corporate citizenship not only allowed Tesla to acquire social capital for its brand, but it also gave the company a market advantage, as Puerto Rico considered rebuilding its grid around distributed renewables.

Within corporate citizenship there is a spectrum of depth of engagement, from cursory or reactive outreach to meaningful, planned, and strategic efforts. The most shallow engagement is through arm's-length corporate philanthropy in which a business provides financial support to nonprofits, schools, and other community groups through dedicated sources of funding generally aligned to the core mission of the business. Contributions can be direct grants, donations that match employee giving, or in-kind support of materials or human resources. For example, in 2011, Apple started matching employees' contributions and in just three years realized $50 million for local charities in the United States. In 2018, it increased its match to two dollars for every one dollar an employee donated up to a maximum of $1,000. These donations are significant, but they have necessitated no material change in policies, processes, or approaches from the company.

At the opposite end of the engagement spectrum is the newest addition to the corporate citizenship toolbox, shared value creation. In 2011, Michael Porter and Mark Kramer, writing in the *Harvard Business Review*, suggested that business needed to step out of its outdated value-creation model and embrace a new approach that generates economic value and also creates value for society.[4] Shared value creation is about considering the costs and benefits of designing for society, blurring the lines between for-profit and not-for-profit enterprises.

An early example of shared value creation is the food company Newman's Own, which sends 100 percent of its profits to charitable organizations. More recently, Nestlé, the multinational food and drink company, has invested in education and technology to allow its coffee farmers to increase productivity and reliability, benefitting both Nestlé's bottom line and farmers' quality of life.[5] In recent years, shared value creation has led to a new type of business designation. A business can register as a benefit corporation in thirty-three states in the United States; elsewhere, a business can apply for independent B Corp certification, which signifies a business whose mission includes positive social impact as well as profit. One of the leading certified B Corp brands in the United States is Method, a household cleaning products company with a social and environmental benefit mission integrated with a business mission that allows it to make decisions based on environmental and social outcomes, not just financial ones. The company has adopted evaluation criteria for both product and packaging that examines aspects beyond simple compliance with regulations. It scores the biodegradable quality of its products, the recycling content in its packaging, the sustainability of its supply chain, and eleven other criteria with an internal tool called Compass of Clean. For every product, a score is generated and the company then works to improve the score by addressing each of the criteria through measures such as sourcing local ingredients, including more plant-based ingredients, and increasing the recycled and recyclable qualities of the packaging.

Shared value creation and other corporate citizenship efforts acknowledge the importance of the community, both the local community at a facility or operation and the global community connected through a value chain and the consumer. Today, the community is now considered a key stakeholder and a significant contributor to the success of a business and its ability to operate. Consumers have also become a factor to business success beyond being mere customers. In *The Big Pivot: Radically Practical Strategies for a Hotter, Scarcer, and More Open World*, author Andrew Winston draws a compelling picture of how corporate transparency is being driven by customers' need for more information, which itself is being fueled by the ease with which such information is shared and with which individuals can organize for or against corporate actions or products. Winston cites transparency as a major force moving corporations toward citizenship and meaningful action.

But transparency will only take a company and its citizenship efforts so far. Perceptions and storytelling are both very powerful forces that give some companies stellar reputations for corporate citizenship efforts and leave others with a significant gap between their actions and how the public sees them. A 2014 report from the Conference Board showed a widening gap between action and perception; the report author highlighted a trend whereby actual performance in the corporate citizenship realm of "sustainability" is increasing even as perception of sustainability performance by specific stakeholders is declining.[6]

This gap between perception and reality can be explained as a failure to communicate effectively, or as unmet expectations, or growing cynicism, or an inability to differentiate between true CSR and lip service. Interestingly, businesses such as BP, Shell, and BHP with strong sustainability practices, that is, with sustainability reality scores well above the mean, languished with low sustainability perception scores, while businesses such as Apple, Google, and Amazon had high perception scores even though they scored significantly below the mean for actual practice.

These differences illustrate the difficulties that legacy industries have in gaining acceptance of their citizenship efforts as well as the "pass" given to beloved brands whose products and services seem physically distant from the "dirty" business of extraction and processing, and decades removed from the long-ago practices of toxic-waste mismanagement.

Opportunities for enhanced lands management and ecological restoration can help to raise sustainability scores for both legacy industries and newer companies. Older companies with low perception scores can advance highly visible ecological remediation efforts and other natural-resources stewardship programs on their lands and leverage the projects and outcomes to inform the story about their environmental impacts. Newer companies with low practice scores can signal an understanding of their products' impacts on the planet by committing to ecological stewardship activities on all the lands they control, promoting biodiversity-based design at corporate campuses and integrating nature around static facilities such as server farms and promoting biodiversity action along the value chain.

Corporate Citizenship and Environmental Efforts

Corporate citizenship efforts can generally be grouped around three pillars: environmental stewardship, social initiatives, and governance. The Conference Board report measured performance against these three pillars, and the environmental pillar returned the lowest mean scores for both practice and perception. The environment, beyond regulatory compliance, is rarely the first choice for corporate citizenship initiatives. Investments in social initiatives like literacy or health are usually adopted first in a company's journey toward better citizenship. Environmental initiatives are adopted later, due to a number of political, business, and operational reasons. For some companies with legacy land liabilities and lingering discontent and controversy from formerly impacted community members and consumers, the environment may represent a third rail that creates a reluctance to engage in conservation. For other companies, ecological stewardship efforts may seem to be too complicated and unrelated to the bottom line or mission of the organization. Many companies, especially small or mid-sized enterprises, simply do not have

Figure 1-1: Biodiversity exists where business operates like this northern map turtle at a BASF property in Rensselaer, New York. (Used with permission from BASF.)

the resources to undertake conservation initiatives on their lands. Involvement of the private sector in the environment beyond regulated action was not part of the early iterations of corporate social responsibility, and natural-resources stewardship continues to be a trailing concern today. For many business, the connection is not obvious.

And yet all business, regardless of distance from source, has an impact on biodiversity. Everything we design, build, buy, and sell has its origin somewhere in the natural world, whether it's extracted from the ground or grown in the soil. Every product that exists in today's global economy impacts the environment, from its creation to its eventual disposal. This impact on the planet has long gone unacknowledged by society as well as government and business leaders.

A recent comprehensive accounting of corporate social responsibility goals was carried out by Andrew Winston to support his findings in *The Big Pivot*. PivotGoals.com lists over 380 companies that have published corporate citizenship goals and categorizes the types of goals that have been established and subsequently reported upon. The absence of nature-related goals in this list is very obvious. Of 380-plus companies on the website, and almost 4,000 goals associated with them, only 59 companies have published biodiversity or nature-based goals. Fewer than ten of these companies publish goals that go beyond the goal of "having a plan." Companies still have a long way to go when it comes to their nonregulatory (beyond compliance) relationship with nature. In a more recent study from 2018, Prue Addison, a former research fellow at Oxford University exploring the intersection of business and biodiversity, and her colleagues found that within the top 100 companies in the Fortune 500, only 31 companies made specific commitments to biodiversity.[7]

Reviewing the companies that do set biodiversity-related goals shows that the further a company's products and activities are from direct impact, the less likely it is to view biodiversity as a material risk and the less likely it is to have a specific commitment to biodiversity protection. Because of their impacts, extractive industries have some of the most sophisticated approaches to biodiversity protection and goals that go beyond mere compliance with regulation. Their impacts are direct and highly visible, and stakeholders and watchdogs are robust in pursuing compliance in this sector. In other industry sectors such as apparel, household products, or consumer electronics, the brands maintain an arm's-length public-relations relationship with nature, at best investing in its protection through philanthropic investments that appeal to their customers and at worst using nature in marketing and brand awareness without any concern or commitment for its well-being.

The Evolution Starts Here

While nobody can deny the positive impact of corporate goods and services, it is also true that industrialization has impacted much of our planet in ways both reversible and not. One of the most obvious places the private sector can start to reverse its relationship with nature is where industry has caused some of the most serious harm in the ecosystems degraded and contaminated by industrial processes.

These imprints on the planet are the lasting legacy of a relationship based on exploitation unfettered by good governance. All around the world, former mines, manufacturing sites, and waste dumps are now toxic sites dangerous to human health and the environment overall. These are places where people cannot live, work, or play, where ecological functions are seriously impaired and nature is destroyed. These places may have concentrated pockets of contamination or pollution dispersed across a wide area. Some of these places are famous, like Love Canal, a residential development in New York State built on land contaminated with eleven known cancer-causing compounds, or Chernobyl, site of a nuclear reactor in Ukraine that poisoned an entire region following an industrial accident. Others are known only within the communities fighting for the cleanup. Every such site tells a sorry saga of lax management, mismanagement, or no management at all.

But today in these broken places, business, government, and community are working together to remediate the damage and restore the ecosystems. Such efforts, while fractious, complex, and drawn-out, are a sign that the relationship between nature and business is evolving, amends are being made, and wounds are being healed. Since nobody can change the beginning, companies and communities are now working to change the ending.

How Boeing Is Changing the Ending

When Steve Shestag was growing up in the Simi Hills of southern California in the 1970s and '80s, he knew about the Santa Susana Field Laboratory (SSFL). He knew that it was a polluted place where fuels that sent rockets to the moon were developed and tested. Now, more than thirty years later, Steve works for the Boeing Company, one of the parties responsible for cleaning up SSFL, and has discovered a deeper legacy at the site that is the very definition of a silver lining. In a twist of fate, the damage done to the site saved the historical and environmental assets from destruction by making the land unavailable to developers during the building boom that saw the suburbs of Los Angeles sprawl over the hills and valleys of Ventura County throughout the 1980s and '90s.

Today, SSFL is a place out of time. It has an incredible density of archaeological artefacts, with one of the best-preserved, most-unmolested collections of pictographs in the country. The results of archaeological studies suggest that it was once a place of ritual for local tribes to gather on the winter solstice, when sunlight flows through a slit in the rock to illuminate a pictograph. In addition, SSFL provides the last corridor for wildlife movement that connects the Santa Monica Mountains, to the south, to the Sierra Madre ranges of the Los Padres National Forest, to the north—a critical connection in a fragmented and increasingly fire-prone landscape. Once a place where fuels were tested and nuclear power was developed, SSFL is now home to an incredible array of both plant and animal species, including local populations that are under pressure, elsewhere, from development and human activity. What initially harmed SSFL now helps preserve it.

The story of SSFL's early days echoes every contaminated site across the world—lax management, mismanagement, and no management. The story of how SSFL was rescued offers hopeful lessons about the kind of impact that citizen activists, government attention, and an evolution in the corporate mindset can have.

The SSFL landscape was harmed during the 1940s, '50s, and '60s, a time before the Environmental Protection Agency (EPA) existed or regulations to protect human health and the environment had been created. At SSFL, researchers developed the fuels that allowed humans to escape our planetary boundaries for the first time. While the technological innovations were groundbreaking, the management of materials and waste was retrograde. An alphabet soup of chemicals has been found at the site, including a variety of radionuclides, trichloroethylene (TCE), perchloroethylene (PCE), metals, and petroleum hydrocarbons disposed with no thought for process or safety.

The damage started during the Cold War when North American Aviation (NAA) was commissioned by the US government to build a rocket big enough to carry a cruise missile to the Soviet Union. NAA and its subsidiary Rocketdyne concentrated on research and development of rockets and rocket fuel throughout the 1950s and '60s, becoming the largest builder of US rocket engines by 1965.

Rocketdyne tested the fuels for rockets at SSFL, chosen for its location distant from Los Angeles and other major populated areas at the time. While Rocketdyne was testing its fuels, another division established the first commercial nuclear power plant in the United

States. Over time, ten nuclear reactors were built on the land. Many important innovations in space exploration and energy technology began at SSFL, all without a concern for pollution or other negative impacts.

In 2000, John Luker was working on a film crew making a documentary about SSFL when he realized the site was a mile from his front gate. Fascinated, he began learning more and exploring as a vigilante trespasser. Now he is an outspoken supporter of the remediation efforts being undertaken on the site, as well as the possibilities for this unique site to be protected for the future. When John talks about the places at the site where, for eighteen years, chemical waste was disposed of by burning in open pits twice a week, he wonders who ever thought it was a good idea. As he says, "Just about everything bad this country produced in the twentieth century went into the ground at this place."

Today Rocketdyne and NAA no longer exist, thanks to a series of corporate mergers and acquisitions. But SSFL still exists, and the responsibility for it now sits with the Boeing Company, NASA, and the US Department of Energy. Each entity is responsible for a different part of the site. The cleanup of the 2,580-acre site is overseen by the California Department of Toxic Substances Control.

As part of the cleanup, the Boeing Company has had to remove contaminated soil and install state-of-the-art bioswales and erosion controls. Today it continues to pump contaminated groundwater to a water-treatment facility to remove the dangerous chemicals. In 2016, Boeing placed an easement on the property to protect it from development in perpetuity, allowing it to remain a critical wildlife corridor and a site with high natural and cultural value.

Today, the majority of SSFL lands are undeveloped and contain a number of important natural communities such as chaparral and oak woodland. Three important threatened vegetation communities in the state—Ventura coastal sage scrub, Southern California walnut woodland, and southern willow scrub—also occur there. The site's biodiversity is notable: 360 species of plants, 170 vertebrate species, and an as-yet-uncounted variety of invertebrate species have been identified. The undeveloped nature of the location and the variety of natural communities means the site functions as a key connection in a fragmented landscape, allowing animals such as mountain lions to move through the Simi Hills. Its importance as a place of nature within dense suburban residential development cannot be understated. In 2018, SSFL was 60 percent burned in the Woolsey fire, but not before its lands provided important connectivity for species fleeing the fire across a heavily developed landscape. Air-quality studies at the time found no radiation of hazardous materials was released during the fire.

Today, under the leadership of Steve Shestag and a dedicated team at the site, SSFL welcomes 2,000 visits a year, hosts numerous research projects, and partners with a wide variety of nongovernmental organizations (NGOs), including the Pollinator Partnership and Monarch Watch, to help preserve the site as an amenity for the community. But it wasn't quick or easy to get to where it is today. John Luker recounts battles: between Boeing and the activists; between the government and the activists; between the government and Boeing and even between warring factions of activists.

So how did things begin to go right? John identifies a period of about five years when change occurred and he knew that SSFL was on its way to becoming a community asset. It was a culture change at Boeing, a pivot by the company as corporate leadership recognized that stonewalling and secrecy were not working. Instead, they chose to promote transparency and engagement. As John says, "Boeing changed from the Cold Warriors who were protecting America and keeping our secrets safe, to environmental stewards . . . trying to protect this environment and make it safe for people to enjoy." John points to culture change, transparency, access, and information as the keys to allowing him to evolve from advocate against Boeing to advocate for SSFL and a cheerleader for its potential. Steve Shestag also considers the evolution in leadership at the Boeing Company to be key, and he cites an innovation in collaboration that allowed partners external to the company to be engaged, allowing them to bring real value to the company's efforts to improve the outcomes.

The Need for Action

If what happened at SSFL is the story of every contaminated site, the evolution of the company and its partners is increasingly the story of successful cleanups. SSFL shows that with transparency, collaboration, time, and money, even the most polluted property has potential to become an asset—even if it's not obvious at first. SSFL is an example of a corporate evolution where change in corporate culture resulted in ecological restoration that has transformed the land, perception of the land, and the community's relationship with it.

Across the world, the relationship between business and nature has evolved in the same way, mostly driven by government and activist involvement. It continues to evolve today, as communities and customers become better educated and engaged, and compel corporations to repair their relationships with nature, clean up past mistakes, avoid new ones, and maintain a neutral or positive impact within their own operations and across the fences that separate them.

While this progress is encouraging, there still need to be significant changes in the corporate sector's mindset for the private sector to systematically make a net positive contribution to the natural world—that is, to essentially mainstream nature-based decisions into their operations. It is necessary to right the wrongs of the past but also to contribute positively to the ongoing issues of the present.

Action across many fronts is needed. While some measures of the health of natural communities show improvements in certain parts of the world, habitat degradation and biodiversity loss continue apace across the world, especially in developing countries in the southern hemisphere where industrial agricultural practices are driving species to the brink of extinction. In the developed world, unsustainable land use and our everyday throwaway relationship with nature drives declines in common species, disrupting natural systems and impacting ecological integrity in ways that may seem small and singular—but when they are aggregated, they drive powerful impacts on natural populations from backyards to wilderness areas.

All indicators point toward an unceasing diminishment of the world's biodiversity, or, as George Monbiot writes in the *Guardian*, "The world is greying, its wealth of color and surprise and wonder fading." Today the main drivers for extinctions and loss of biodiversity are land clearances for agriculture, black-market trade in wildlife for superstitious uses, and the spread of invasive species and disease, as well as the impacts of a changing climate. The International Union for Conservation of Nature's (IUCN) Red List, the global list of species at risk of extinction, grows longer with every new assessment. The lungs of the planet—its forests—continue to be destroyed for agricultural uses. Valuable wetlands that provide ecological and economic value are being lost at alarming and accelerating rates, and our oceans are under siege from plastic pollution and coral-killing acidification. In 2018, the World Wildlife Fund's Living Planet Report recorded a 60 percent decline in the size of the populations of mammals, birds, fish, reptiles, and amphibians in the past forty years, caused mostly by human activity—a calamity that is occurring quietly and without fanfare. In 2019, the latest global assessment of biodiversity published by the Intergovernmental Panel on Biodiversity and Ecosystem Services (IPBES) made headlines with its assertion that one million species will become extinct if we don't change our impact on the planet. The fact that this report made headline news was in itself newsworthy, as biodiversity collapse has long been happening in the shadows of other global crises.

A paper published in *Frontiers in Ecology and Evolution* found that coverage of climate change by the media between 1991 and 2016 was eight times that of biodiversity during the same time period. The study, titled "Our House Is Burning: Discrepancy in Climate Change vs. Biodiversity Coverage in the Media as Compared to Scientific Literature," found that scientific output on the two issues was not reflected in commensurate media coverage (i.e., lower media interest was not driven by less scientific output). Rather, media coverage of climate change has been largely driven by specific occurrences like dramatic, telegenic weather events. No media channel is dispatching intrepid reporters to the scene of the slow erasure of a species.[8]

The lack of attention paid to biodiversity and the absence of an urgent reaction to the loss of nature is not limited to any sector public or private. Carlos Manuel Rodriguez, Costa Rica's minister of environment, said in 2018 during the Fourteenth Conference of the Parties (COP14) to the Convention on Biological Diversity (CBD), "Humans spend more money buying ice cream that we spend on biodiversity conservation." In country after country, investments in protection of natural heritage represent a tiny fraction of GDP. In the United States, less than 1 percent of the federal budget is allocated to the agencies charged with protecting the nation's natural resources. In 2019, at Ireland's first national conference on biodiversity, the minister responsible for the country's natural heritage proudly stated that she was doubling funding for local biodiversity efforts to all of €1 million. At that conference, the president of Ireland, Michael D. Higgins, underscored both the urgency and lack of attention to biodiversity, saying that if we were coal miners we would be up to our knees in dead canaries right now.

With only 13.9 percent of biodiversity found on publicly owned lands, privately owned lands are critical if we are to arrest and reverse current trends in species loss and ecosystem degradation.[9] Business has a role to play in natural-resources conservation and has a duty from its historical relationship with nature to do so. There is great potential for biodiversity action lying within the landholdings that companies already own, but the corporate sector is responding slowly to the crisis, mostly in ad hoc ways, eschewing strategic integration of nature-based action for one-off programs, offsets, and philanthropy. While philanthropy, in the absence of public investment, remains critical to support governmental and NGO efforts, more robust and strategic engagement with the NGO community at local, regional, and national scales is needed to spur action for a sustainable relationship with nature. While business can be implicated in almost every downward trend of the planet's natural resources, it can also help reverse these trends through improved processes, materials, and practices.

From Site-Specific Work to Multimillion-Dollar Initiatives

When companies engage with biodiversity efforts, they tend to do so in two contrasting approaches to nature, neither of which is integrated or sustainable or designed to be replicated. By understanding these approaches and their limitations, it becomes easier to see beyond the status quo, to advocate for different methods, and to design better outcomes.

The first and most common engagement between the private sector and the natural world is through nonstrategic, site-specific, short-to-medium-term activities. This type of engagement tends to provide the site with community-focused benefits but no value at the corporate level, because the action cannot be incorporated into a larger corporate framework.

This approach frequently features the following nature-based activities: organizing an annual Earth Day expo on-site; getting employees engaged in the cleanup of a stream or beach; sponsoring charitable events that support environmental NGOs; or opening lands for outdoor recreation such as fishing. These events focus on the activity rather than the impact and are inspired by personal community relationships rather than strategic drivers. They tend to be low-cost, low-impact, and short-lived—usually the first to go following budget cuts, personnel changes, or changing relations with the community.

At the other end of the spectrum of business and biodiversity engagement lies the multimillion-dollar, high-profile corporate-level initiative that engages few employees and even fewer community members. The impact of this work is more likely to drive the creation of new frameworks for engagement rather than conservation on the ground. These initiatives are finite, focused, and expensive. They are presented at mega-conferences and in TED talks. They spawn press releases and reports and are labeled as unique or as pilot partnerships. They are lauded by insiders. They are also rarely replicated or scaled in any meaningful way. These unique efforts start with the best of intentions to drive change at the C-suite. But unless they are developed with an operational plan, as discussed in this book, change at the C-suite may indeed happen, but action on the ground will not.

There is a vast middle ground approach that some companies are taking and that this book will explore further. These kinds of projects integrate biodiversity into a strategic conservation plan that allows a site-based effort to contribute to a local or regional conservation objective while also supporting a corporate business goal. Efforts like this recognize that all corporate conservation action must be locally based but that value can be realized at a landscape scale and at corporate HQ through planning and smart alignments.

Industries that have the most direct and visible impacts on nature were among the first to address biodiversity in this systematic

Figure 1-2: A roadrunner coexists with a Chevrolet truck at the General Motors proving ground in Yuma, Arizona. (Used with permission from General Motors.)

way, mainstreaming it into development and operations beyond environmental remediation and regulatory requirements. Driven by external stakeholders, especially international environmental NGOs, financial initiatives such as the Equatorial Lending Principles, and other programs such as the UN Global Compact, companies such as LafargeHolcim, Rio Tinto, and others started to develop approaches to address biodiversity loss at their mines and quarries in the late 1990s. At that time, these initiatives generally set a no net loss / net positive impact (NNL/NPI) goal for biodiversity companywide.

The companies established frameworks for measuring biodiversity before, during, and after operations through painstaking stakeholder input and ecological assessments. They encouraged site managers to consider biodiversity impacts throughout the life cycle of the site and mitigate impacts through operational change, habitat management, and reclamation that went beyond compliance. Many companies made resources available to drive change on the ground.

While these strategic planning efforts are not a panacea, they have driven systematic change in thinking and communication about biodiversity across the industry sectors. In 2004, Rio Tinto made a much-lauded commitment to achieve net positive impact (NPI) on biodiversity across all of its operations. After twelve years, Rio Tinto backed away from the broad NPI goal, having learned over the course of its commitment to the goal that it was impossible to achieve such a positive impact company-wide. Rio Tinto's transparency is admirable, and its admission that NPI is impossible was likely a difficult one to make. The Rio Tinto story reflects the challenges inherent in reconciling ambitious environmental goals with corporate realities. It also underscores the importance of having a strategic plan to make sure that efforts are yielding results, and that a new approach could be needed if the initial concept isn't working. Rio Tinto is now focused on a site-level approach that considers the unique context of each site and allows for great flexibility in site management. Rio Tinto's openness to adopting and adapting new approaches while retaining a focus on reducing harm to biodiversity is an important evolutionary step for the private sector.

Planning for Success in Corporate Conservation

As the Rio Tinto example shows, it is not always easy for a company to transition to a better relationship with society or nature—for a variety of reasons. Companies of all sizes battle the forces of culture, leadership, and financial expectation as they seek to drive change. In addition, companies struggle to embed a culture of nature into operations already dealing with health and safety priorities and into corporate offices focused on quarterly-results calls and a plethora of disclosure and reporting deadlines.

But there are ways to overcome these challenges and engage companies from many different sectors with natural-resources stewardship projects across their entire landholdings. This book seeks to illustrate the various elements that create the enabling environment for strategic, long-lived, and meaningful corporate conservation.

There are number of key contributors to success, collected in table 1-1, that will be explored throughout the book and expanded

Table 1-1: Checklist for Success

Checklist for Success

☐ Has a business reason been identified?

☐ Is it integrated into other corporate citizenship efforts?

☐ Can the conservation project be aggregated with others to provide value to corporate?

☐ Is it aligned with local or regional conservation priorities?

☐ Is it pragmatic in terms of resources, outcome expectations, and potential expenses?

☐ Is it sensitive to operational constraints and regulations?

---

upon with case studies and examples in the following chapters. They include

- the importance of framing a strategic corporate conservation plan with one of sixteen common business reasons;
- the co-benefits to be realized from integrating biodiversity action with employee engagement, community-outreach efforts, or other corporate citizen programs;
- the necessity to aggregate site-based conservation implementation into a corporate goal or objective; and
- the power of aligning the efforts with existing regional or local conservation priorities.

The project at Arcelor Mittal's Burns Harbor steel-making facility in Indiana ticks all the boxes of strategic corporate conservation as listed in table 1-1. The extensive restoration effort is voluntary and it meets a business need for Arcelor Mittal, contributing to the company's corporate objective to be a good steward of land and water.

With the restoration of the historic dune and swale ecosystems that are closely associated with the Great Lakes and rare in the industrialized regions, and with the lakeshore restoration, the project is also contributing to the Great Lakes Restoration Initiative, a multi-agency plan to restore the largest freshwater system in world. By bringing school groups on-site for education and environmental action, it is also making a difference to efforts by the Field Museum in Chicago and others to reconnect the communities of the Calumet Region to local natural resources.

To support its corporate stewardship commitment, Arcelor Mittal has made substantial philanthropic investments in the Sustain Our Great Lakes grant program administered by the National Fish and Wildlife Foundation, funding other NGOs in the region in restoration and land-preservation efforts. The work on-site at Burns Harbor brings this corporate goal close to home for the company and its employees. A walking trail through the oak savannah and other parts of the restoration project contains signs that promote heart-healthy lifestyles and illustrate the conservation value of the effort, giving employees a sense of ownership. At Burns Harbor, the priority is to make steel and contribute to the success of the business, and do so in a way that keeps its employees safe. Burns Harbor has strategically and creatively developed conservation actions that work with—not against—these operational imperatives, and by so doing it has made an investment that will last and flourish.

Operational sensitivity and pragmatism are two key factors for successful implementation. As Rio Tinto learned in its attempts to seek a company-wide net positive impact, "allowing sites to tackle their own contexts on a case-by-case basis is more viable in the long run than applying a blanket NPI target." Any natural-resources stewardship efforts, whether for a small pollinator garden or a large quarry reclamation, that ignore operational priorities will fail.

This approach is increasingly being understood and utilized by business. From an Indiana-based steel-making facility to a corporate campus in Pittsburgh, Pennsylvania, a toxic site being cleaned up in California, an auto-manufacturing plant in Spain, or a petrochemical plant in South Africa, operationally sensitive site-based conservation efforts are contributing to landscape-scale objectives, providing measurable business value and connecting employees and communities to positive action.

There are many routes to bringing strategic conservation into a company and to further evolve the old relationship from corporate conqueror to corporate caretaker. Understanding the elements that propel the evolution will not only help companies and their conservation partners build the strongest-possible programs but will also contribute to addressing the global biodiversity crisis by realizing real conservation value.

02 UNDERSTANDING BUSINESS DRIVERS
—

To prosper over time, every company must not only deliver financial performance but also show how it makes a positive contribution to society.

—LAURENCE FINK, CHAIRMAN AND CEO, BLACKROCK, JANUARY 2018

When companies engage in meaningful conservation and stewardship projects beyond one-off pilot partnerships or arms-length philanthropic investments, they do so for a business reason. Arcelor Mittal's efforts at Burns Harbor were done to support its community-engagement efforts that secure its social license to operate in the Calumet Region. Without a supporting business reason, corporate conservation efforts are constantly at risk of losing support and being discontinued. Across business sectors and company size, there are a number of common business reasons (or drivers) to explain why companies engage in meaningful and integrated conservation efforts, strategically using nature.

These business drivers are an expression of the multiple ways to place nature-based efforts within a corporate framework. They show that conservation action can address a variety of business needs, contributing to numerous business challenges or opportunities. This chapter will explore these compelling motivations that bridge corporate priorities to conservation action and provide examples from across industry sectors. Whether working to implement a conservation action at a business with a single location or operation, or developing a strategic corporate conservation plan for a multinational corporation, identifying one or more business drivers will help to answer the question "Why?" and will bring more support and resources to the stewardship effort, creating a place for corporate conservation that is sustainable over time and across budget cycles.

Table 2-1: The common business concerns that can be addressed with conservation action

Corporate Categories	Business drivers that can be addressed with nature-based action
Operations	1. Mitigate biodiversity impacts. 2. Inform better remediation remedies. 3. Permit acquisition & renewal. 4. Secure social license to operate.
Management	1. Improve government relations. 2. Increase employee engagement. 3. Address climate change. 4. Implement nature-based solutions. 5. Improve lands management and realize cost savings. 6. Position for talent acquisition.
Citizenship	1. Inform reporting and disclosures. 2. Provide a sustainability goal and performance metric. 3. Create meaningful community engagement. 4. Frame corporate investment in education. 5. Satisfy SRI and shareholders. 6. Drive action along supply chain / circular economy.

While there is an entire professional community dedicated to encouraging companies to account for the dollar value of nature as it relates to the corporate balance sheet, a strong case can be made that business opportunities leveraging nature-based programs can benefit the bottom line in simpler and more pragmatic ways. Framing corporate conservation within a business need is not about putting a price tag on nature or about monetizing the ecological services provided by nature. These business drivers likely do not make a *direct* contribution to the profitability of a business but are instead indirect contributions to overall financial success and reputation. Nature-based efforts can, through smart and creative design, be extensively leveraged. Like the conservation project at Burns Harbor, they can contribute to site goals, corporate goals, and community goals.

The business drivers can be split into three categories of impact on a company: operational, business management, and corporate citizenship.

Operational Business Drivers

In a business, operations are where value creation happens. Operations is the manufacturing site, the quarry, or the power plant. Operations is different from marketing, financial management, and accounting or other corporate functions. Operations, unlike corporate headquarters, are more likely to impact the community with noise, dust, traffic, or other emissions that cannot be contained on-site. Operations are key to conservation action, as they tend to have bigger footprints and higher potential for meaningful action.

Many operations—particularly at manufacturing and extractive sites—are governed by regulations from a variety of agencies and institutions. These regulations are designed to protect the environment, consumers, and employees and to hold the business accountable for how they manage their processes, as well as how they use and dispose of raw materials, waste, and by-products. Businesses that have a direct impact on the natural world operate under regulations that address these impacts. The extractive, chemical, and building materials sectors operate under more-stringent environmental regulations than companies further along the supply chain. The energy sector maintaining rights of way for electricity distribution and transmission is responsible for compliance with land-management regulations that secure this critical infrastructure. Environmental regulations differ across the world but generally provide business with direction on how to avoid or mitigate their impacts. Some environmental regulations can cause companies to make poor decisions with respect to nature, as sometimes happens with utility companies and their perennial issues with tree maintenance. But there are many ways to make good decisions and use nature-based action to achieve and exceed compliance.

For example, a company such as Waste Management, whose operations include landfills (both open and closed), will be required by regulation to seed closed landfills for stability, drainage, and aesthetics. Local or states regulations may require a certain amount of natural cover, but the company can decide to go beyond compliance by choosing plants for their benefit to biodiversity. For legacy companies that are responsible for historic polluted locations that require remediation action mandated by the Environmental Protection Agency (EPA) or another regulatory agency, nature-based design can bring the sites back to productive community use faster. Choosing ecological remediation can enhance community and regulator relationships and can contribute cost-effective solutions to the mandated remedy.

Ecological approaches can also be used in risk-mitigation scenarios. Every company assesses and manages risk to predict probable negative impacts on the business. Risks come in all shapes and sizes across a range of probability and severity. Typical business risks include operational disruptions from natural disasters, financial uncertainties from volatile supplier prices, and strategic management errors. Environmental risks to business include reduced productivity from resource scarcity, fines and assessments on unpermitted biodiversity impacts, restricted access to lands from the presence of rare or protected species, and loss of social license to operate due to negative business and biodiversity interactions. All risks, if realized, could ultimately reduce credit scores, damage the brand, and increase the difficulty of doing business. Conservation efforts can be deployed in many risk-management scenarios, both those that are related to specific biodiversity actions and those that are not.

Traditionally, risk has been defined around economics and focused on direct or "material" business risk. But recent trends have seen the emergence of assessing nontraditional risk in environmental and social issues.[1] All businesses face biodiversity-associated risk, either directly or indirectly. The World Economic Forum (WEF) defines biodiversity risk as both a company's direct impact on biodiversity and also a company's relationship with biodiversity through its supply chain. Biodiversity was first identified by WEF as a serious global risk in 2010 with an associated potential cost of $30 billion. In 2019, the WEF's annual Global Risks Report found that "Biodiversity Loss and Ecosystem Collapse" as a business risk had an above-average likelihood of happening, with an above-average impact on the global economy. As an example of business-related risk from biodiversity loss, the Intergovernmental Science-Policy Platform on Biodiversity and Ecosystem Services (IPBES) report pointed out that, in 2019,

> Currently . . . $235 billion and $577 billion in annual global crop output is at risk as a result of pollinator loss. Moreover, loss of coastal habitats and coral reefs reduces coastal protection, which increases the risk from floods and hurricanes to life and property for the 100 million–300 million people living within coastal 100-year flood zones.[2]

The following business concerns that intersect with biodiversity are all essentially risk-mitigation activities—from direct impact on biodiversity to reducing risk of remediation liabilities and securing permits and social license to operate. Corporate conservation emphasizes the many uses of ecological stewardship action to mitigate or manage these environmental or social risks.

OPERATIONAL BUSINESS DRIVER 1: MITIGATE BIODIVERSITY IMPACTS

Mitigating the impact of operations on biodiversity is a key business driver for the extractive industries and others that realize value directly from the earth itself. Governments review environmental impact statements and can decline to give permits for operations if impacts are not mitigated. Watchdog and other advocacy organizations can create legal and reputational trouble if damage is done to biodiversity. Increasingly, banks and other financial institutions are measuring the impacts of developments on biodiversity and refusing investments that pose a high risk to biodiversity.

Because of the lack of consistency in regulatory governance across countries, states, and provinces, the international financial institutions that provide investment for private-sector development have emerged as powerful actors to equalize expectations on environmental standards, including biodiversity, on a global stage. In 2010, the International Finance Center launched the Equator Principles, a financial-industry benchmark for managing environmental and social risk in privately financed projects. These principles have driven change across multiple industries globally since their inception and are currently adopted by over ninety private lending institutions worldwide. Understanding that different countries and regions impose different regulations on business operations and that these regulations are implemented in different ways depending on the effectiveness of governments, the Equator Principles seek to mitigate these institutional weaknesses by imposing consistent expectations of those assuming the risk for the development—the financial institutions.

What this means is that the ninety signatories will not provide loans to development projects that won't or can't comply with the Equator Principles. Through the Equator Principles, protecting biodiversity becomes a financial decision. One of the performance standards in the Equator Principles (PS6) is specific to biodiversity and seeks to

- protect and conserve biodiversity;
- maintain benefits from ecosystem services; and
- promote sustainable management of living natural resources.

The latest guidance on the PS6, published in November 2018, requires no net loss of biodiversity in all areas of natural habitat, and net gains of biodiversity impacted by projects occurring where "critical habitat" for the species has been designated.[3] The Equator Principles and PS6 are largely responsible for driving the adoption of the Mitigation Hierarchy and corporate-wide no net loss/net positive impact (NNL/NPI) commitments. The mitigation hierarchy— avoid, minimize, restore, rehabilitate, and offset—helps frame impacts on biodiversity at the operational level. Implementation of PS6 and the mitigation hierarchy have not been consistent, and much criticism exists that the hierarchy merely provides an expedited pathway for destruction that allows offsets, that is, payment for protection for biodiversity in a location other than that being developed, without adequate governance to prove net positive impact.

For companies in industry sectors with the most obvious and immediate impacts on the environment—mining and other extractive industries—there is an increasing expectation that they adopt site-specific and corporate-wide frameworks to measure and manage impacts on biodiversity, in keeping with the mitigation hierarchy or NNL/NPI. By developing systems that can illustrate adherence to PS6, global companies can begin to think differently about biodiversity across their footprint, demonstrate a beyond-compliance mindset in developed economies and show leadership in developing economies with weaker environmental and social governance.

In the United States, another tool that business can use to address direct impacts on biodiversity is the habitat conservation plan (HCP). This tool is increasingly being used in the utility sector for risk abatement in order to address impacts to rare, protected, or imperiled species across a company's landholdings. This proactive planning approach provides a level of predictability to both the regulator and the regulated entity. Over the last decade, there has been significant growth in the number of companies across all sectors that have engaged in conservation planning driven by PS6, using the mitigation hierarchy and HCPs and adopting commitment to NNL/NPI outcomes. Moving these efforts and commitments from planning to implementation remains an ongoing challenge.

Some companies seek to mitigate their impacts with compensatory measures such as investing in land preservation through an offset program. A strategic corporate conservation approach seeks solutions on-site by considering the impacts of the operation and designing subsequent restoration and reclamation efforts for the greatest-possible biodiversity benefit.

The Lafarge Group, prior to its merger with Holcim, was a leader in sustainability for its work to address biodiversity on-site. The company understood that the cement industry has significant global environmental impacts and set out to address them. The Lafarge Group was a founding member of the Cement Sustainability Initiative (CSI), a group of cement companies partnering across the globe on biodiversity programs designed to go beyond compliance in countries with strong regulations and to demonstrate good environmental stewardship where no or lax regulation existed.

As a member of the CSI, the Lafarge Group built a strategic corporate-wide approach to addressing its impact on biodiversity at all of its operations. Working first with the World Wildlife Fund and then with a broader global advisory body, the company built a suite of tools and guidance documents to develop an approach to achieve a net positive impact on biodiversity across the entire company. Each site, regardless of its operations, was assessed and screened for negative impact on biodiversity as well as for the potential for positive restoration. A centralized management system was developed so that the impacts could be recorded and reported for the entire company

In the building materials industry, quarries supplying the raw materials for cement have the greatest biodiversity impact. Today, new quarries are only developed following stringent environmental assessments, but older quarries have few, if any, regulations attached. No two sites have the same impact or the same opportunity to mitigate it. Jim Rushworth, the former vice president for environment and community affairs at the Lafarge Group, tells how this corporate-wide approach encouraged plant managers to think about nature, provided corporate managers with centralized and consistent data, and created the opportunity for quarry closures to achieve higher levels of biodiversity outcomes than had been previously required. The Lafarge Group used nature-based approaches on-site to address biodiversity risk by minimizing disturbance but mostly by designing restoration projects with high biodiversity value, engaging nongovernmental organizations (NGOs) and community partners for long-term maintenance and ownership.

Nature-based restoration and reclamation can reduce biodiversity risk for existing or recently excavated sites. Nature-based remediation can have the same impact on lands that suffered a longer time ago.

OPERATIONAL BUSINESS DRIVER 2: REMEDIATION REMEDIES

Remediation of contaminated lands is a business concern that has a deep intersection with risk and reputation. Understanding and leveraging the opportunities of ecological remediation can provide a company with an effective approach to moving contaminated sites from financial liability to community asset.

Most companies operating in the United States today that have been around since the mid-twentieth century own or have responsibility for places that have been polluted by unregulated or illegal activities. The EPA database of designated Superfund sites lists over 1,000 such sites. These places are liabilities for the companies in financial as well as reputational terms. Companies that have responsibility for the pollution negotiate a remediation remedy with the government body overseeing the cleanup. In these cases, community stakeholders or trustees will be engaged to ensure that the final cleanup meets the community's standards and addresses their needs. For many such sites, nature is at risk from the contamination, but it can also be a mitigating factor to help address pollution. By integrating ecological end uses into a remedial design, a company can change its conversation with the community, improve its relationship with the agency, and move the site back to productive use faster.

Approaches to site remediation have evolved substantially since the early days of corporate cleanup efforts following the establishment of the EPA and the creation of the Superfund and Brownfields programs to address polluted sites across the United States. The Sustainable Remediation Forum (SURF), showed in its seminal white paper on the subject that environmental management has evolved significantly since the 1950s, when discarding waste in a negligent manner and ignoring pollution of air, soil, and water were standard practices. At first, the remediation profession promoted aggressive action including pumping, removal, and burning; today, remediation science, while still evolving, allows for less-invasive measures, such as natural attenuation and innovative use of engineering and technology. In addition, there is now greater community acceptance of creative remedies and proposed future conditions that may not be pristine but do not present a risk to the community.[4]

The non-technological, social aspects of the process have also evolved. Stakeholder engagement—a key facet of remediation design—has become more sophisticated, and companies with a culture of openness strive to provide meaningful opportunities for communities to engage in planning for future use whereby the best use is not always dictated by monetization through development or divestment. Many companies have been very effective in embracing more-innovative end uses that incorporate ecological goals, such as the former Milltown Reservoir site in Montana that is now a state park, or the DuPage County Landfill that is now a hiking trail and birding spot for residents in Warrenville, Illinois. For remediation to successfully incorporate ecological components or approaches, nature must be inserted into the conversation at the earliest stage. To make green approaches to remediation strategic and integrated, businesses must develop protocols, frameworks, or decision trees where natural benefits and ecological options are considered at each stage as the land is moved through remediation toward an end use for habitat and human recreation.

Success with one ecological remediation project leads to others. Bridgestone Americas, the tire and rubber company, used ecological approaches on a number of significant and high-profile remediation sites. The success of the approach led to more ecological remediation, which then led to implementation of conservation projects on non-remediation lands across the Bridgestone Americas operations in the United States and beyond and to the creation of a financial fund to support the efforts. Successful conservation in one aspect of business spurred conservation elsewhere.

It all started in Perryville, Cecil County, Maryland, at the site of a former quarry from the 1950s that was used as an industrial dump in the 1960s and where vinyl chloride was found to contaminate the ground water in the 1980s. When the quarry was listed as a Superfund site in 1987, the prescription for cleanup—i.e., the remedy as advanced by the EPA—was to remove all the topsoil from the site, install an engineered cap that would contain the contamination, and require ongoing maintenance and a system to pump contaminated groundwater from the site for treatment and discharge to a local stream. The cost was estimated to be in excess of $42 million. In addition, this remedy would have caused the site to be closed permanently, leaving the community with a blighted property in perpetuity.

Testing during the design phase of the remedy found that the concentrations of vinyl chlorides were declining due to biological processes called *natural attenuation*, meaning that the area of contamination was shrinking. Using these results and input from the community, Bridgestone asked EPA to reconsider its remedy so that the site could continue to recover through natural attenuation, retain its ecological function, and become an asset for the community. The revised remedy cost of $6 million represented substantial savings to the company. In addition, future costs of maintenance and risk of cap failure will both be lower. Today, the site is called the New Beginnings Woodlawn Wildlife Area. It has higher biodiversity values than the surrounding agricultural land, rapidly declining contamination that is regularly monitored by an external firm, and a public program that sees garden clubs, youth groups, and schools use the site for environmental education and ecological stewardship.

The success of the Woodlawn project spurred other projects across Bridgestone. When Tim Bent, who was director of environmental affairs for Bridgestone and who oversaw the Woodlawn cleanup, talks of his experience with this and other legacy remediation sites, he draws a direct line between the success at Woodlawn and the growth of a corporate-wide understanding that all parts of the businesses could benefit from natural-resources stewardship programs also. The success of Woodlawn in both cost savings and community relations spurred company leaders to make financial investments and send supportive messaging to allow and encourage similar programs on non-remediation sites that included the award-winning environmental education center called BEECH and 600-plus acres of forest restoration at a plant in Tennessee (to be profiled further in chapter 7), as well as a xeric shrubland restoration effort at a tire plant in Monterrey, Mexico, and many others.

Remediation efforts started in the United States under the Superfund program over thirty years ago. Since then, experience and research has shown that, contrary to the earlier intensive interventions, natural solutions are possible and in fact are more effective and efficient for many such sites. The use of ecological or sustainable approaches to remediation is becoming more common and acceptable to regulators and stakeholders, and also more frequently adopted by the responsible parties.

OPERATIONAL BUSINESS DRIVERS 3 & 4: PERMIT ACQUISITION AND RENEWAL, AND SOCIAL LICENSE TO OPERATE

Permits for new developments and formal licenses to operate a business are usually approved by government agencies at a variety of scales. The social license to operate (SLO) is an approval given by the community. Permit acquisition and renewal, as well as SLO, are always assessed as possible risks for any development projects, risks that, if realized, could lead to significant overruns in terms of time and money, or even cessation of the project overall.

The concept of the SLO is an emerging community issue that is becoming more influential thanks to increased action from civil society groups engaged with environmental justice and indigenous communities. At its simplest, SLO is obtained when a development application or operation has the ongoing approval of the community.[5] SLO drives companies to go beyond compliance and to remain in step with their stated sustainability efforts. SLO is only granted by a community, not by a governing body. It can be withdrawn at any time. There is no physical SLO, and the terms of it can change and evolve with the community's changing relationship with the company and operation. There is no formal communication that an SLO has been secured. SLO is essentially a metaphor for the acceptability of an operation to the community. The concept of SLO evolved from the UN's promotion of "free, prior, and informed consent" (FPIC) that recognizes that communities have the right to self-determination. In Kerala, India, lack of SLO forced Coca Cola to shut down a bottling company that stakeholders believed was exacerbating drought conditions in the region, while in the Philippines, Royal Dutch Shell and its partners saved as much as $72 million in project delays by securing community consent and an SLO for a natural gas extraction project by being transparent about the project plans.[6]

A long-running effort to exploit the Pebble Deposit in Alaska shows the power of SLO to impact a company before a single permit has been issued. The Pebble Deposit is one of the largest known gold and copper accumulations in the world. It is located in Bristol Bay, home to the largest sockeye salmon fishery in the world, valued at $1.5 billion annually. In 2005, Northern Dynasty Minerals, a company with no other mining assets, acquired the lease to the Pebble Deposit. In 2007, Anglo American, a diversified mining company with the well-known subsidiary De Beers, bought into the partnership. At that time Anglo American instituted a stakeholder engagement called the Pebble Mine Dialogue facilitated by the Keystone Policy Center. This dialogue was designed to explore whether an SLO could be secured and under what circumstances. The CEO of Anglo American stated at the outset that the company wouldn't develop the mine without support from the majority of the community. During the years of the dialogue, residents in the Lake and Peninsula Borough in the Bristol Bay region of Alaska approved a ballot initiative to forbid local permits to be granted to Pebble or any mine that would impact salmon fisheries. In 2013, Anglo American withdrew from the partnership with a $300-million write-down, and in that same year, Rio Tinto, a minority owner in Northern Dynasty, also withdrew from the partnership. Anglo American stated that its action was taken in order to "prioritize capital to projects with the highest value and lowest risk,"[7] but most observers agree that failure to secure SLO was a big driver for both companies' withdrawals and subsequent financial losses. The current market value of the Pebble Deposit is not in doubt, but the risk of an unsecured SLO was too high for Anglo American.

A community rarely has the power to withhold government permits or licenses. In the case of the Pebble Mine, permit applications are still being made despite the withdrawal of the two main companies and being fought by environmental advocacy groups such as the Theodore Roosevelt Conservation Partnership and others. But community does have the power to withhold or bestow social license to operate (SLO).

The Pebble Mine Dialogue was a formal approach to understanding whether an SLO would be forthcoming from the community. SLO can also be assessed by measuring the level of public distaste for the project through traditional activism activities such as protests, letters to newspapers etc. Without SLO, operations face risk from shutdown, delayed permits, increased inspections, increased action by advocacy groups, and, in extreme cases, blockades or protests. In the case of the Pebble Deposit, it cost millions before a single official license was given.

Natural-resources stewardship efforts can be leveraged to support applications for licenses, permits, and SLO. For most development proposals, environmental assessments are required to secure permits. As a best practice in developing them, stakeholders through community advisory groups or other forums should be provided with the genuine capacity to contribute.[8] During these assessments, local stakeholders augment consultants and science by highlighting local values from social, cultural, and environmental points of view. A small forest may have insufficient tree acreage to score high for protective action or preservation as an environmental resource, but it may have very high value to the community that uses it for recreation. If the company adopts values of community engagement in a sincere manner, the legitimacy of the process will be secured, and risk will be averted.[9] Understanding community values and priorities is a key component to both securing SLO and completing an honest environmental assessment.[10] Seeking to understand and address the local value of nature can be a powerful approach to mitigating risk and increasing a program's chances of acceptance by the community. Any developer, whether of infrastructure, residential properties, or industrial facilities who does not listen to a community or who minimizes the concerns and values of the community will realize the full risk inherent in its permit application, will see cost overruns, and will not secure their permit in a timely manner. While community advocacy against development proposals are often dismissed as NIMBYism (from "Not In My BackYard"), it should be respected, since it is the community members who will remain living, working, and playing there regardless of the outcome of the development application. Community members have a right to a say in how their communities are impacted. In the Simi Valley, the residents living around the Santa Susana Fuel Laboratory were rightly concerned about the impacts to their water and air from chemicals leaving the site. Today, many residents are cheerleaders for the effort to clean it up and secure it for its natural and cultural values.

In Normandy, France, the Lafarge Group worked very closely with the local town to develop a community-focused withdrawal and reclamation plan for an existing quarry during the quarry's productive life. The Lafarge Group was implementing dynamic restoration as part of its permit. As the operational needs of the quarry changed and as parts of the operation moved to new extraction areas, sections of the site were reclaimed and restored. In the case of the quarry in Normandy, Lafarge listened to the community when it said it wanted an apple orchard—a traditional land use in Normandy where apples are harvested to make the spirit known as Calvados. The community also valued access to nature, especially forests and wetlands—both scarce commodities in a heavily managed

Figure 2-1: The former Lafarge quarry in Normandy, France, is now a wetland and a site of high biodiversity value that constitutes a positive feature in the community. (Photo by author.)

agricultural landscape. The company presented these needs to the appropriate government agency when planning for the site's closure and asked that they be part of the closure plan. Today, the village has its community orchard, a diverse forest, and a beautiful marsh humming with insect life and providing habitat to a wide array of species. By attending to the community's needs, Lafarge secured their SLO for the length of operations and provided community value as it restored certain sections of land and opened and exploited others.

Securing SLO reduces risk and saves time and money for the company. As in the Lafarge example, ecological actions to secure SLO can provide benefits to not just the human community but to nature as well. Operations may be where the most biodiversity impact happens, but across the company, management has needs that it, too, can meet with smart conservation action.

Management Business Drivers

In the majority of companies, managers have responsibilities beyond a single regulated operation. They have responsibility for their employees, for relations with government, for maintenance of non-operational lands, and for the many reports and disclosures that a company is required to file. Many managerial concerns can be addressed with nature-based approaches that will contribute to the smooth running of the company. Because these concerns focus on issues other than direct impacts on biodiversity, the conservation approaches will be designed less around risk and remediation, and more around people, employees, communities, and budgets.

MANAGEMENT BUSINESS DRIVER 1: GOVERNMENT RELATIONS

Whether working with local, state, or federal government, companies with a proven commitment to nature can develop a better relationship with pertinent agencies based on conservation outcomes that go beyond compliance with regulations. By building relationships with natural-resources agencies through biodiversity planning and engagement, companies can engage in a key government relations practice that "the relationship be separate from the substance."[11] According to author Roger Fisher in *Getting to Yes*, successful government relations grow from integrity, relationships, and informed strategic engagement. Companies can leverage their natural-resources stewardship plans and activities to secure good relations with government agencies, be seen to be responsive players, add value to government agencies' nonregulatory mission, and, in the best-case scenario, leverage government programs for better outcomes.

All companies interact with governments at multiple scales. They deploy significant resources to protect their interests when new laws and regulations are being considered. Companies may interact with government on a regular basis through compliance inspections and other regulated activities. They may be in joint ventures with foreign national governments as a way to do business in a specific country. Companies may also engage with government for development and operational permits, setting rates, securing passage for goods, and providing stakeholder input as a member of the community. It is a fact of life in the twenty-first century that the private and the public sectors have close and interwoven relationships—sometimes to the benefit of society and sometimes to its detriment. These relationships are very important. According to a 2011 McKinsey study, *Managing Government Relations for the Future*, government ranks second only to customers in their ability to impact a company's bottom line. For CEOs, managing government relations always ranks as a top-three priority.

Government agencies also have their needs. Most departments charged with natural-resources management are severely under-resourced yet burdened with underfunded mandates to protect rare species, manage for game species, maintain lands and infrastructure, and carry out stewardship and education activities on their protected lands. In the United States alone, the Association of Fish and Wildlife Agencies (AFWA) has reported a $1.3 billion annual gap between the amount of money government agencies assign to natural-resources stewardship and the amount of money needed to both keep common species common and protect and repopulate rare and endangered species. This gap, which was identified by the Blue Ribbon Panel on Sustaining America's Diverse Fish & Wildlife Resources, a group of twenty-six business and NGO leaders convened by AFWA in 2016, represents 71 percent of the total money needed for effective biodiversity protection in the United States.

State Wildlife Action Plans, the blueprints for wildlife protection and management developed by every state wildlife agency in the United States, are full of unmet needs and not enough public lands on which to take action. Corporate lands can play a key role in implementing State Wildlife Action Plans by opening their lands for conservation or connecting their conservation efforts to those of nearby states and, in so doing, secure good relationships with the agencies.

Covia, a multinational mineral and materials company, has helped the Illinois Department of Natural Resources and the US Fish and Wildlife Service to monitor and manage the Magazine Mine site, one of the largest underground mines in Illinois, for bats. The site hosts about 60,000 Indiana bats, about one tenth of the entire population of this species, which is federally listed as endangered. Covia partners with both state and federal government agencies to manage the site for the species by stabilizing and securing the mine entrance for bats and against human disturbance, and by educating local school students about the special species that lives in the mine.

This mine is not part of Covia's current operations, yet the work on the site helps to build relationships between the company and state and federal government entities.

State wildlife agencies and state wildlife plans represent only a fraction of the opportunities for the private sector to help meet conservation needs. While advocates may cry foul about such partnerships, there are many examples of strong outcomes when the two sectors work honestly together toward an important conservation goal.

MANAGEMENT BUSINESS DRIVER 2: EMPLOYEE ENGAGEMENT

The term *employee engagement* is used in different ways according to different functions in an organization. The human resources (HR) department views employee engagement as any employee's willingness "to go above and beyond" for the company. Corporate social responsibility (CSR) and sustainability professionals view it as any employee's active participation in citizenship and sustainability initiatives. Regardless of the definition, employee engagement is now considered essential for bottom-line success, and the thinking around it is constantly evolving. A study of the global workforce in 2012 found that, for peak productivity and employee retention, employers needed to move beyond the HR definition of willingness "to go above and beyond" and move toward the CSR vision of an energized workforce operating with greater autonomy and meaningful support from leadership participating fully and eagerly in health and social wellness programs.[12] This type of engagement is called *sustainable employee engagement*. In an analysis of fifty global companies, Willis Towers Watson found a seventeen-point difference between operating margins of companies with low engagement scores and those with the highest "sustainable engagement" scores.[13] The study highlighted two ways to build sustainable engagement. The first is to provide employees with the tools and resources to do their jobs easily, whether through investments in technology or innovative management. The second is to create an environment that energizes employees by promoting physical, emotional, and social well-being.

There are many ways to create this environment of sustainable employee engagement, such as providing on-site gyms and fitness trackers to increase physical well-being, offering scheduling flexibility to support emotional well-being, and promoting volunteer days and other activities to support social well-being. Engaging employees in a company's sustainability efforts can be a very effective mechanism for promoting well-being at work. The Global Environmental Management Initiative (GEMI), in its "Quick Guide to Engaging Employees in Sustainability," advocates building engagement through ownership and finds that the most successful sustainability program results from individuals working together as a team toward a common goal.[14] Many companies view the business value of their conservation programs through this lens.

Since local appropriateness is a prerequisite to a successful conservation project, a sense of ownership can be easily secured with employees engaged in local action. In addition, by engaging employees in every aspect of the conservation project, from the choice of the project to its design, implementation, management, and monitoring, the company can create a team that embraces all levels of skills, depth of interest, and physical abilities to participate. Nature-based programs also have significant overlap with wellness programs, so projects can be designed to provide opportunities for activity both at implementation and afterwards, especially if walking trails are designed into the effort. The flexibility and accessibility of conservation projects makes them highly suitable as sustainable employee-engagement tools.

Owens Corning makes insulation, roofing, and fiberglass materials. Included in its sustainability goals is a biodiversity statement that contains a commitment for facilities to get involved in local nature projects. At its Granville, Ohio, Science & Technology Center, a wildlife team is made up from employees across the site. The team manages a pollinator garden, a prairie restoration, ponds, a community garden, and an actively managed program to provide nesting habitat for bluebirds.

Designed to engage employees, the wildlife team's efforts recently dovetailed with employee wellness initiatives to launch an annual Nature Day, with walks to the various conservation projects led by experts. The path is accessible all year-round to give employees an opportunity to exercise in nature whenever possible. In addition to Nature Day, the wildlife team provides education to employees on conservation actions they can take at home.

The efforts at Granville have been so effective in increasing employee engagement that Owens Corning has encouraged the wildlife team at Granville to share successes and lessons learned with other locations within the company, helping kick-start employee-led conservation activities at sites across the country, taking what was a one-off exercise and integrating it into the company's ethos and operations.

MANAGEMENT BUSINESS DRIVER 3: ADDRESS CLIMATE CHANGE

While industry is part of the climate-change problem, it is also a source of solutions. Global companies are making bold commitments for a carbon-neutral future through technological innovations and energy-transition investments. Nature, as a contributing factor to climate solutions of mitigation and adaptation, has not been part of the conversation. But this is changing. According to the Nature4Climate initiative, newly launched in 2018, nature can contribute 30 percent of the global emissions reductions needed to hold warming at 1.5°C, but it currently garners less than 1 percent of the coverage of all possible solutions. Nature can contribute to carbon sequestration through better restoration and management of forests, grasslands, and wetlands that can make a substantial contribution to keeping global warming to 1.5°C. Corporations with lands and innovative cultures can participate in this part of the solution.

In addition to mitigating carbon emissions, companies can mitigate impact by building nature-based resilience to climate change. In many cases, where energy infrastructure is at risk from climate-related storms or sea-level rise, nature-based solutions may be the best and most cost-effective ways to protect their investments and literally keep the lights on.

For the corporate world, climate change and its associated disruption is a significant business driver and a highly probable and highly impactful business risk. Nature-based action to address this risk is an accessible and practical solution. Chapter 8 in this book delves more deeply into the potential for the corporate world to create nature-based projects that meaningfully address aspects of climate change.

MANAGEMENT BUSINESS DRIVER 4: IMPLEMENT NATURE-BASED SOLUTIONS

While an appreciation of nature-based action for climate mitigation and adaptation is just dawning, the idea of nature-based solutions for other environmental problems has moved further into the mainstream. In many parts of the world, the green-infrastructure community of practice is well established, spurring the installation of rain gardens in a variety of locations to better manage stormwater and promoting natural engineered solutions to cool and shade buildings. Implementation is not yet universal, but adoption is growing. The private sector increasingly views nature-based solutions or green infrastructure as good for business and the environment.

Nature-based solutions that companies are increasingly adopting include vegetated or green buffers instead of concrete walls to protect against sound, dust, and other fugitive releases from their operations into the community. Companies are re-engineering flood-prone zones with rain gardens and other natural solutions to mitigate flooding and reduce local or state stormwater taxes.

In Detroit, the electric utility company DTE has made a commitment to remain and invest in the city, which has been hollowed out following a major demographic downturn. DTE has been head-quartered in the city for over 100 years and is now investing in the west side of the downtown area, near its headquarters. In 2014, it purchased and renovated a long-vacant, art-deco Salvation Army building in the neighborhood. The company restored the building, keeping many of its art deco features, and reopened it to house 140 employees in the newly named Navitas House. Navitas House stands in an area with a lot of concrete but little green space. During the renovation, DTE designed and installed bioswales—engineered structures to capture and passively treat rainwater on a 6,000-square-foot plot. These bioswales were also planted to create an urban habitat for birds and insects, thus realizing co-benefits. Because such "wild" green spaces are unusual in a city setting, DTE designed and installed signs throughout to provide employees and passers-by with information about the installation, adding an educational benefit to the effort.

MANAGEMENT BUSINESS DRIVER 5: REALIZE COST SAVINGS

Active and intensive management of land for a specific aesthetic is expensive. About $22 billion is spent annually on landscaping of commercial and industrial lands, with the largest portion spent on mowing and maintaining mostly formal landscapes, especially vast expanses of manicured grass that can be seen often in suburban areas where corporate headquarters sit in pastoral landscapes. Beyond cost, formal landscaping can also have a negative impact on biodiversity if nonnative species are used and if excessive chemicals are applied during maintenance. Moving to a less rigid aesthetic that embraces nature and native species will yield significant cost savings for a company as well as strong positive impacts on biodiversity, especially insects. Moving to natural landscaping saves on irrigation, chemical application, and mowing. Simply implementing *reduced* maintenance of existing landscaping can also have great benefit. Reduced-landscaping regimens are healthier for biodiversity, since less mowing provides for longer lives for plants and grasses used by pollinators and grassland birds, and reduced use of herbicides for weed control allows the growth of "weeds" that provide benefit to biodiversity. While the aesthetic of reduced-landscaping regimens may be anathema to the average American, the ecological benefit is real.[15] The multiplier effect across an entire corporate footprint makes this a worthwhile endeavor that can realize a significant cost saving.

Following the financial crash of 2008, General Motors (GM) was one of a number of car companies that, in 2009, filed for protection against bankruptcy and received government assistance during its restructuring. During that time, cost savings were key, so nonessential expenses were cut wherever possible. At GM's Technical Center, a National Historic Landmark building in Warren, Michigan, maintenance of the landscaping was deemed a nonessential expense and so reduced-landscaping regimens were put in place. A vegetated berm surrounds the Technical Center and acts as a buf-

Figure 2-2: GM's Technical Center is a nationally significant building designed by Eero Saarinen. It has adopted native planting but in a historically sensitive way. (Photo by author.)

fer for the neighborhood. During this time of tight budgets, the berm was left unmowed, allowing the seedbed to regenerate, resulting in multi-seasonal blooms, transforming the berm from a sterile green strip to a colorful, buzzing pollinator habitat. Overall, thirty-five acres that had previously been maintained on the site as a traditional corporate campus lawn were converted to no-mow zones, realizing substantial cost savings for the company but also increased biodiversity across the property. In addition, architect Eero Saarinen's formal landscape was replanted with native species but in a way that maintained the integrity of the historic site design, showing clearly that natives do not have to be "untidy" or "wild."

MANAGEMENT BUSINESS DRIVER 6: TALENT ACQUISITION

All companies invest in talent acquisition to ensure that future productivity and profitability is not placed in jeopardy by lack of qualified staff. Many such efforts build pipelines to educational establishments and develop programs and materials to attract top talent. Other such efforts are focused on the immediate community, educating members about opportunities to work at a specific operation. Conservation action on corporate lands can enhance corporate talent-acquisition strategies, including leveraging them for education. By showing community members the operations and introducing them to its employees, a company is showing what it looks like to work at that facility, possibly modeling STEM (science, technology, engineering, and mathematics) jobs to students and engaging them with the facility, less as just another physical location within their community and more as a potential workplace.

A generational shift in incoming employees' interests and motivations has long been a significant issue facing the private sector, especially in manufacturing and extractive industries. In the United States, as the baby boom generation moves toward retirement, the next large generation of workers, the millennial generation, has different views on traditional factory jobs or careers in what are considered dirty industries. Much has been written about the challenges that traditional recruiters face when seeking to attract and retain a generation of workers with different needs and drivers than the generation being replaced. The incoming workforce looks for a workplace that enables a life/work balance, is flexible to an individual's needs, understands the variety of work styles that can accomplish tasks, and is interested in doing good in addition to doing well. Corporate citizenship is important to the workforce of the future, and inclusive nature-based efforts on company lands can be used to show that a company is a good place to work and is also a good steward of the planet.

Workforce development happens where management merges into corporate citizenship when a business's continuity imperative is linked to a beyond-compliance activity. But it is not the only corporate citizenship opportunity that can leverage nature-based action.

Corporate Citizenship

Corporate citizenship is the extra mile a company goes to illustrate its standing as a member of the local community and the global society. Corporate citizenship efforts can be focused around sustainability and reporting on goals and actions for reducing energy use, emissions, and waste. They can also be focused around community, providing education programs, access to lands, or simply donations to local sports teams. Nature-based corporate citizenship efforts will be focused more on nonregulatory, voluntary actions rather than on specific operational impacts or management needs.

Many corporate citizenship efforts are today framed as corporate sustainability. Corporate sustainability has many definitions. It can be seen as the maturation of corporate social responsibility. It can also be viewed as eco-efficiency, driven by the need to cut costs through reduced resource use and in so doing to minimize impacts on the planet. In a third understanding, corporate sustainability is a suite of actions a company takes toward meeting financial and development goals as established by multilateral bodies such as the IFC and codified by such instruments as the UN Global Compact. (Chapter 3 further explores these issues and how they can drive conservation of natural resources within the larger global framework.)

CORPORATE CITIZENSHIP DRIVERS 1 AND 2: REPORTING AND DISCLOSURES, SUSTAINABILITY GOALS, AND PERFORMANCE METRICS

Companies that are publicly traded on stock exchanges around the world must comply with certain reporting requirements that differ across jurisdictions. In the United States, the Securities and Exchange Commission (SEC) requires financial reporting from companies on an annual and quarterly basis as well as reports on issues that may materially impact share price. In the European Union, nonfinancial statements are required to disclose the impacts of the business within an environmental, social, and governance (ESG) framework; the business model and its long-term sustainability; and current and future risks. This effort is designed to bring a company's stated strategy and its actual performance into a clearer light, encouraging companies to link their KPIs—the key performance indicators—to their strategic plans.

Beyond compliance with financial regulations, companies augment these required reports with CSR reports that aim to present the company's corporate citizenship through compelling stories and the data to back them up. Being a good corporate citizen is good for business and is increasingly expected by stakeholders, both internal and external. The rewards of corporate citizenship are not fully realized unless stakeholders are aware of it.[16] These reports are now considered essential items for both shareholders and stakeholders. The strongest CSR reports are audited by external bodies to verify the reported progress against stated goals.

Best practice requires that a company reports against a standard or a goal, that material issues are clearly highlighted, that anecdotes are illustrative, and that goals and metrics are SMART—that is, Specific, Measurable, Achievable, Relevant, and Time-constrained. Andrew Winston's *Pivot Goals* list 3,293 corporate citizenship goals being reported by the 250 top global companies. According to the Global Reporting Initiative (GRI), which claims to be the most widely adopted nonfinancial reporting mechanism in the world, 93 percent of the world's largest 250 companies report on their sustainability performance. Other reporting initiatives include the Dow Jones Sustainability Index (DJSI) that was launched in 1999, the Sustainability Accounting Standards Board (SASB), the Integrated Reporting Framework, ISO 2600 on social responsibility, and ISO 14001 on environmental management, not to mention an entirely new and separate set of reports around climate disclosure such as the Task Force on Climate-Related Financial Disclosures (TCFD). Conservation and stewardship programs can contribute both anecdotes and SMART metrics to a company's reporting efforts.

Most corporate sustainability efforts are a "race to zero" as companies seek to reduce carbon emissions, water use, waste production, and energy consumption, subtracting from the planet's burden. But natural-resources stewardship programs provide a company with an opportunity to report its handprint—the good it does for the environment. In addition, natural-resources efforts provide access to a company's sustainability efforts. Many employees, especially younger workers, want to contribute but can't do so, as many sustainability goals sit in highly technical areas such as materials management and energy conservation. Ecological stewardship programs can be accessible to all employees and provide hands-on opportunities for anyone seeking to make a positive impact. Finally, a sustainability goal focused on nature can engage all sites, regardless of their function. While certain corporate locations such as factories or mines will be able to contribute most to goals for energy reduction or waste reduction, all facilities, including office locations and distribution centers, can contribute to a sustainability goal for nature.

CORPORATE CITIZENSHIP DRIVER 3: COMMUNITY ENGAGEMENT

Community Engagement is closely linked to SLO but goes well beyond the transactional nature of SLO when it is considered within a corporate citizenship program. Meaningful community engagement approaches can help those communities that have historically borne an uneven burden from industrial processes, and all communities that can benefit from the corporate location in their midst.

Much community engagement consists of attempts to repair past ills created when industry established the nosiest, most-polluting operations in poorer communities where labor and land were cheaper and regulations often less rigorously enforced. This pattern of land use by the private sector, and the subsequent outcry by communities and activists in the United States, led in 1992 to the creation of the office of Environmental Equity at EPA. In 1994, President Bill Clinton signed Executive Order 12898, instructing all federal agencies to consider the harmful impacts of development projects on less affluent and underserved communities. These actions created a requirement that companies have a greater awareness of the needs of the communities in which they already operated and that they develop and adopt formal assessment methods to measure and get feedback from the community on new developments. This approach has started to give communities a voice and has required companies to engage in a meaningful way beyond superficial annual open houses or intermittent sponsorships of local events. Some companies are better than others at true community engagement where three levels of engagement—transactional, transitional, and transformational—have been identified.[17] Conservation efforts can support community engagement across all three levels.

Examples of transactional community engagement efforts can be found where a local business sponsors uniforms for sports teams, where they staff booths or tables at street fairs, or where they provide grants for community partners and materials for community development projects. Transactional community engagement is arm's-length and one-way only. Nature-based transactional community engagement efforts could include a company hosting Earth Day fairs, employees supporting community beautification activities, and donations of money or materials toward a school or community garden.

Transitional community engagement is a one-off engagement that meets both a community need and a corporate one but may not lead to long-term collaboration or relationships. Such efforts can, however, be beneficial if they are thoughtfully organized and connected to certain business drivers such as securing SLO, permit acquisition, or even government relations. Nexus, a joint venture between Spectra Energy and DTE, that is building a natural gas pipeline in eastern Michigan, uses transitional community engagement to build better community ties prior to and during construction. Working with Washtenaw county in eastern Michigan, Nexus brought day campers and Nexus employees together to plant pollinator-friendly plants in a local park in Ypsilanti. This effort was to support Nexus's eventual development in the community and, while it was a one-off engagement, it was participatory and engaged government, corporate, and community in action.

Transformational community engagement efforts are those where community decision-making leads the way, where alliances with partners are long-lasting and meaningful, and where the company is a collaborator. A truly transformational community engagement program was designed by CRH Americas as a collaboration project between the building materials company headquartered in

Atlanta, Georgia, and a local health care facility, the Marcus Autism Center. CRH Americas had a specific business need. It was seeking an opportunity for the employees at its corporate headquarters to participate in an existing corporate environmental stewardship commitment that saw its operations implement high-quality ecological stewardship programs in locations like quarries that had large tracts of lands available to use for conservation. CRH Americas corporate head office is located in a leased office building with no access to nature. As CRH was seeking lands for nature-based action by corporate employees, the Marcus Autism Center was seeking a good use for thirteen acres of mature hardwood forest that was underutilized and that also, coincidentally, served as a natural corridor between a suburban neighborhood and a nearby elementary school. Working together, CRH Americas "adopted" the site and developed it as a resource for the center, for its clients and staff, and for the community. As CRH developed access to the woodland, it mapped routes to connect the community but that would minimize environmental disturbance. It developed trails that would be accessible to all, regardless of physical ability. CRH and its employees built wildlife-viewing platforms, an outdoor learning space, benches, and an amphitheater to encourage use of the trails and increase appreciation of the surrounding nature.

Since its completion, the trails and nature area have played host to numerous CRH Americas workdays and to other area companies seeking environmental projects for their employees. Local conservation partners such as the Atlanta Audubon Society and Trees for Atlanta monitor the biodiversity, while families from the neighborhoods and the Autism Center enjoy the trails and quality time in nature.

For Cemex employees in the Dominican Republic, a transformational engagement with community was needed to help protect the endangered rhinoceros iguana, the largest endemic vertebrate in the area and a species considered vulnerable by IUCN. Working within Cemex's existing corporate biodiversity strategy and from a site-based biodiversity action plan developed with conservation partners Birdlife International and Grupo Jaragua, a local NGO, the team started a community engagement project that takes a holistic approach to protecting the iguana, starting with addressing the conditions that lead to poaching—poverty and food insecurity. The operation creates financial incentives through its community-based nursery that supplies plants for restoration at the quarry and also provides income to community members, including former poachers, through the sale of plants. The program educates community members about the issue and its implications, transforming the community and its attitudes to local biodiversity.

CORPORATE CITIZENSHIP DRIVER 4: FRAMING CORPORATE INVESTMENT IN EDUCATION

Many companies have corporate goals or intentions around education across a broad spectrum of efforts from philanthropic support for education innovation, relationships with colleges and universities to create pipelines that feed future workforce needs, to local education investments engaging community members of all ages in activities that increase knowledge and workplace preparedness. According to a 2013 Nielsen report, *Corporate Support for Education Is a Winning Proposition*, companies support educational initiatives for a variety of reasons, such as altruism, talent pipeline development, and brand reputation. More than 68 percent of people who responded to the global survey said that they would be more likely to buy products from a company that supports education initiatives, with 85 percent in Latin America most eager to do so, aligning with their strong sentiment around the importance of education. While North Americans and Europeans showed the most skepticism in their support for companies that support education, half still reported a willingness to do so.

In 2018, the retailer Target touted its $1 billion investment in education with $487 million in donated classroom resources, $208 million in books, $118 million in grants and scholarships, $98 million in education programs, and $88 million awarded for arts in school and its anti-hunger programs. While arm's-length philanthropy is the most common way that companies support education, going beyond monetary contributions and leveraging a company's natural and human capital creates a way to bring employees and students together for better and different educational experiences.

In addition to traditional approaches to support education, corporations can leverage their lands to meet corporate education goals as effective learning environments for both environmental education and STEM-focused programs. Corporate lands can provide access to communities that lack publicly protected lands with appropriate nature and interpretive centers or communities that lack budgets for travel to such places. Many companies that historically located their operations in poorer neighborhoods now provide extracurricular learning facilities that bring benefits to the community. In developing countries, corporate spaces can provide a focal point and a resource for community education efforts. Corporate lands can provide educational opportunities for learners of all ages, from preschool pupils to graduate students. For the younger age levels, corporate lands are safe places to explore nature and learn about the operations. For older students with higher levels of educational attainment, corporate lands—due to controlled access and reliable usage patterns—are unique situations for research on habitat restoration, ecological remediation, and impacts of nature-based engineering solutions. Corporate lands can be used for workforce training in ecological skills such as forest and grassland management and restoration techniques that are not restricted to the site.

Corporations that need STEM-educated employees make investments in STEM—science, technology, engineering, and mathematics—at all levels to increase STEM literacy and encourage students to pursue STEM careers. While STEM jobs are traditionally represented by white coats, laboratories, and tech start-ups, there are many more opportunities in the extractive, utility, and manufacturing sectors. These traditional sectors have a much smaller pipeline from schools and universities, as students choose careers elsewhere for a variety of reasons. The oil company Chevron has a highly visible STEM program in the United States investing for STEM education across the ages, providing support for classroom projects and the teachers who are advancing them and investing in workforce development by funding polytechnic schools in developing economies and giving scholarships to talented students.

Chapter 7 explores the many ways that companies can leverage their lands to meet educational goals that meet the needs of corporate or the community. Education is a strong intersection point between employee and community engagement with an overlay of SLO. The possibilities for conservation-focused education on corporate lands is limitless.

CORPORATE CITIZENSHIP DRIVER 5: SRI FUNDS AND ACTIVIST SHAREHOLDERS

Laurence Fink, the chairman and CEO of Blackrock, one of the largest investment firms in the world, wrote an annual letter to CEOs in January 2018. His letter made headlines by exhorting companies to serve a social purpose, to meet the needs of society currently unmet by government, and to adopt a sense of purpose in order to reach full potential.

In the second decade of the twenty-first century, shareholders voices have become increasingly important for social and environmental initiatives. The report from the Investor Responsibility Research Center Institute (cited on page 26) showed that shareholder-sponsored proposals on social and environmental topics increased from 30 percent of all introduced topics in 2005 to 40 percent in 2011, and the success rate of these proposals had almost doubled from fewer than 10 percent being approved in 2005 to more than 20 percent being approved in 2011.

Among the topics introduced by shareholders are proposals around climate change, sustainability and, to a lesser extent, biodiversity. Shareholder proposals tend to mirror current events with increases seen in proposals around energy extraction, paralleling the growth of hydraulic fracturing, or fracking. In 2004 and 2005, shareholders filed at least twenty-five shareholder proposals targeting corporate action on climate change, three times the number of filings in 2000 and 2001. Socially responsible funds and pension plans are the originators of most of the successful proposals, with faith-based groups, labor organizations, and individual shareholders also filing proposals (though with less success due to their smaller size).

Shareholder proposals around biodiversity are not common. A study by the Sustainable Finance Lab found that while half of all investors interviewed take impacts on natural capital into consideration, they focus on climate-related issues most and on bio-diversity issues only on an ad hoc and situational basis.[18] This trend may not continue, as the biodiversity crisis and climate change merge into a global ecological crisis message and more corporate reporting frameworks ask for biodiversity disclosures from member compa-nies. Strategic and integrated corporate conservation initiatives can be used to address shareholder proposals on biodiversity by showing that the company has taken a deliberate approach to understanding and addressing its impact on biodiversity. Efforts that go well be-yond compliance with existing regulations can strengthen responses to such shareholder proposals.

Shareholder proposals have also sought to impact supply-chain transparency and management. This new area of corporate respon-sibility can also be addressed by integrating ecological stewardship action into expectations for suppliers and vendors.

CORPORATE CITIZENSHIP DRIVER 6: SUPPLY CHAINS AND THE CIRCULAR ECONOMY

How sustainable is any company if the materials it sources from its supply chain are not? This question has driven the emergence of green and verifiable supply-chain initiatives to help industries make better purchasing choices by understanding the source of the materi-als and the impacts of their extraction and creation. Within circular-economy thinking, companies are concerned about the end-of-life treatment of the products they produce and send into the waste stream. The circular economy is one that is designed to minimize waste and maximize resources in order to reduce the impact of in-dustry on the planet. Recovering and reusing metals from electronics waste, reducing packaging that would normally end up in landfills, or encouraging companies to accept responsibility for the end-of-life disposal of their products are all concepts of a circular economy.

Addressing waste and reuse across a supply chain is a key compo-nent of circular economy thinking. The auto industry in the United States has created a supply-chain initiative, the Suppliers Partner-ship for the Environment, that brings together companies that supply the industry with materials from rubber to fabric and plastics and components. Convening different suppliers in this way, the industry sends a message that it is not just looking for the best price, but it is also looking for the supplier who can best mirror the sustainability values of the manufacturer. An interesting and easily unifying opportunity for supply-chain initiatives is for members of the effort to implement natural-resources projects on their lands regardless of what they are producing to show that large tracts of land are not necessary for biodiversity action and that such action need not be confined to either end of the value chain.

The Suppliers Partnership for the Environment promotes the research and skill-sharing that would be typically expected in a supply-chain initiative for such an industry sector—materials management, safe battery disposal, and energy conservation. It has also convened a working group to collectively achieve positive impacts on biodiversity, thus uniting its members around an issue that can connect further to employees and community members.

In Conclusion

These drivers are critical to understand, from both the corporate perspective and that of an NGO. For companies, they are a suite of options where nature can be leveraged to meet a business challenge or opportunity. They also provide companies with a frame for ongoing efforts and a way to talk about their conservation work that consolidates site-specific projects into a business-centered narrative.

Nonprofit partners can use the drivers to better understand business priorities and perspectives, which will create clarity around needs and yield projects that are better tailored to the desires of the company and will receive more resources for implementation and monitoring.

These drivers will differ across businesses. Large multinational companies will have resources and reason to address many of the drivers, while small and mid-sized enterprises may be interested only in those that are most mission-critical.

If readers takes nothing else from this book, they should accept the indisputable fact that companies will not engage in strategic, integrated, and sustained biodiversity action without a business reason to do so. Knowing this fact is a prerequisite to developing a productive *working* relationship with the private sector. A smart approach from a conservation NGO or other partner seeking to work with a company on a specific site of interest, or across the entire corporate footprint, is to identify possible business needs and craft a compelling story of how conservation can address it. Once it is identified, the business need will inform the conservation strategy and define the actions. The following chapters in this book will explore how to build a conservation strategy that connects to business needs and how, in a world with infinite distractions and competing priorities, to use business needs as a tool to center and prioritize conservation to benefit nature, community, and employees.

Not every company will start engagement with NGO partners already knowing that a business need can be fulfilled with conservation. Most will begin by engaging partners in conservation action and then realize that it meets a business need. Some will stumble across existing conservation actions and partnerships and connect them to a business need. Smart corporate leaders can connect the dots and develop strategies to replicate existing efforts to increase benefit to company, community, and nature.

03 SCALE AND PERSPECTIVE

—

Understanding the systemic complexity helps form a realistic view of one's role in it.

Knowing that companies can leverage high-quality biodiversity efforts to meet a business challenge is an important starting point for a conversation about corporate conservation. Understanding that many other factors will influence the effort is essential to sustaining such engagements in the private sector.

The biggest challenges to sustainable, corporate-wide conservation are scale and perspective. Conservation action—moving earth, planting trees, seeding meadows, or managing gardens—takes place at the human scale (sometimes assisted by machines.) Conservation planning is done at a regional or landscape scale. But corporate strategy is shaped at a national or global scale and cascaded to regions and operations. Stepping back to gain perspective on the various influencers at different scales is necessary for success.

Perspective requires awareness of the many plans, approaches, frameworks, and initiatives that can be adopted by the corporate office or at the site level, at any time. These frameworks and initiatives are designed to improve corporate behavior, establish corporate citizenship targets, and provide best-practice guidance to operators, partners and consumers. Efforts to integrate natural-resources projects into the frameworks that corporate leaders care about will strengthen the argument for adoption. Designing the strategic corporate conservation plan to fit reporting and disclosure needs will further shore up support for such initiatives. This chapter will explore the frameworks and initiatives that could be introduced at any stage in corporate conservation planning. It shows how to connect the dots between site-based conservation and the many initiatives that exist at all levels in a company.

The Salamander and the Sustainable Development Goals

A story about a construction materials company and an endangered salamander illustrate how the dots can be connected. In Ontario, Canada, the Jefferson salamander is a species of concern. Over the last thirty years, about 90 percent of the species' population has been lost to forestry and urban development. The salamander was listed as endangered in Ontario in 2011. Six years later, a curious sub-population of these salamanders was listed separately. This population contains no males because the female salamanders reproduce asexually through kleptogenesis ("stealing" male sperm to either activate cell division in the eggs or egg development without using the male DNA). These all-female populations live in the same geographical area as other Jefferson salamander populations, as the females still need access to male sperm donors. Today, the government oversees a recovery plan that seeks to restore habitat and expand the population of these fascinating creatures.[1]

In Milton, Ontario, Dufferin Aggregates owns and operates an award-winning limestone quarry that has a role in the salamander recovery plan. Dufferin Aggregates is owned by a subsidiary of CRH plc., a multinational building materials company headquartered in Ireland. CRH currently links its corporate citizenship efforts to two global initiatives: the United Nations Sustainable Development Goals (SDGs) and the Global Reporting Initiative (GRI). Contributions to these initiatives help CRH enhance its value through international recognitions on the FTSE4Good, Dow Jones Sustainability Index, and the Vigeo Eiris Eurozone 120 index, among others. CRH must satisfy reporting and disclosure needs (see in chapter 2, "Business Driver—Citizenship 1") and shareholder needs (see in chapter 2, "Business Driver—Citizenship 5").

At the quarry in Milton, progressive rehabilitation (the practice of restoring the land as the extraction progresses) across the site has placed 1,000 acres of land in conservation, with a third of the quarry now restored for wetlands, meadows, and wooded areas. At the quarry site, a water-management system of pumps and wells protects water quality and quantity both on the site itself and for off-site dependent features such as creeks and the breeding grounds of the listed Jefferson salamander, which needs vernal ponds or intermittent wetlands in order to lay egg masses in predator-free waters. Before the water-management system was installed, a single pond in the complex had good conditions for successful salamander breeding just once during an eight-year period. Since the system was installed in 2009, the pond has provided suitable habitat for salamanders every year, regardless of weather and seasonal variations.

The water-management project at the Milton quarry contributes to an effort by the Ontario Ministry of Natural Resources and Forestry, in partnership with Environment Climate Change Canada, to recover the local populations of Jefferson salamander. It also contributes to CRH's corporate citizenship efforts on the SDGs and for GRI. CRH plc was recently listed as a top performer in Vigeo-Eiris's ranking of business and biodiversity for 2018.[2] A salamander can impact a corporation's value.

By aligning its conservation efforts with initiatives such as the Ontario Ministry of Natural Resources and Forestry's Jefferson Salamander Recovery plan and others, Dufferin Aggregates ensures that its quarry restoration efforts have meaningful biodiversity outcomes at the site. By aligning the same efforts with global corporate initiatives like the SDGs and GRI, CRH can realize value beyond the site. If a company can report its ecological stewardship efforts through existing frameworks or initiatives, the efforts provide co-benefits to the company and increase the chances of continued buy-in and continued resources allocated to the conservation effort.

Exploring and understanding where the larger-framework initiatives that are undertaken across the corporate landscape dovetail with conservation-related opportunities can help secure support for implementation. It doesn't matter whether the conversation starts at the corporate level, in the office of a chief sustainability officer, or at the site level, in the office of an environmental, health, and safety manager, time taken to seek connections with the appropriate corporate plans and frameworks that the company currently reports into will be time well spent.

There are many such initiatives, each one connected to others in a web of plans, actions, and reports. No single initiative dominates across industry sectors. It could be argued, in fact, that too many corporate initiatives exist and that, together, they create the appearance of movement but result in little forward motion. These initiatives are generally met with resignation or cynicism at the site level, but corporate executives use their respective company's involvement with such efforts as currency for regulators and investors. Site-level enthusiasm can be created if (a) a corporation commits resources to the project, and (b) ownership for the efforts are ceded to the personnel at the local level. Corporate leadership should give the direction, provide the money, and then step out of the way.

A Summary of Efforts

Table 3-1 lists a selection of the most common initiatives that conservation partners may encounter when working with industry. Sustainability and corporate citizenship professionals working to implement such initiatives may also find it useful to understand that their needs can be met by local conservation action.

The varied efforts include global initiatives that are centered on biodiversity such as the UN Convention on Biological Diversity or on finance and development such as the World Bank's Equatorial Lending Principles. Companies may participate in one or more of these initiatives according to the needs of leadership and their level of engagement on global issues.

Industry sectors, trade associations, and others convene their members to develop and engage with sector-specific initiatives to drive better management on environmental, health, and safety. IPIECA, the oil and gas industry association, the Mining Association of Canada, and the Suppliers Partnership for the Environment are all examples of industry sectors advancing environmental action.

NGO FRAMEWORKS OF ENGAGEMENT

The nongovernmental organization (NGO) community also engages with the corporate sector in a number of different ways. For ex-

Table 3-1: A Selection of Corporate Frameworks and Initiatives with a Biodiversity Component

Select Global and Multilateral Initiatives	Owner	Details	Comments
	World Bank & International Finance Corporation	The Equator Principles	**Performance Standard 6:** protecting and conserving biodiversity, maintaining ecosystem services, and managing living natural resources adequately are fundamental to sustainable development.
	United Nations	Convention on Biological Diversity	**Strategic Goal A:** Address the underlying causes of biodiversity loss by mainstreaming biodiversity across government and society.
	United Nations	Global Compact	**Principle 7:** Businesses should support a precautionary approach to environmental challenges.
	United National Development Programme	Sustainable Development Goals	**SDG 14:** Life below Water **SDG 15:** Life on Land

Select NGO Conservation Products for Business	NGO	Product	Comments
	IUCN	I-Bat for Business	Framework for businesses to identify their impacts to biodiversity.
	Natural Capital Coalition	Natural Capital Protocol	A decision-making framework to identify direct and indirect impacts on the environment. It does not yet have a protocol for biodiversity.

Select NGO/ Corporate engagements	NGO	Company	Initiative
	Birdlife International	CEMEX	Created Biodiversity Action Plans for operations in sensitive areas.
	WWF	Rio Tinto	Explored company-wide net positive impact goal.
	The Nature Conservancy	Dow Chemical	Developed approaches to consider nature in development and operations.

Table 3-1: A Selection of Corporate Frameworks and Initiatives with a Biodiversity Component (*continued*)

Select Sectoral Initiatives	Owner	Initiative	Comments
	Global Cement and Concrete Association	Cement Sustainability Initiative	Members must implement sustainability projects across five pillars, including a pillar on environment and nature.
	International Council on Mining and Minerals	Mining with Principles	Members must commit to all 10 principles including **Principle 7:** Contribute to the conservation of biodiversity and integrated approaches to land-use planning.
	IPIECA	Biodiversity and Ecosystem Service issues management	Tools to help the industry meet global standards for biodiversity.
	Mining Association of Canada	Toward Sustainable Mining	Members adhere to guiding principles, including "Seeking to minimize the impact of our operations on the environment and biodiversity, through all stages of development, from exploration to closure."
	American Chemistry Council	The Science Behind Sustainability	A suite of principles to guide beyond compliance across nine topic areas, but no specific mention of biodiversity.
	American Auto Industry	The Suppliers Partnership for the Environment	Seeks to improve the sustainability of the automotive supply chain; includes biodiversity as a working group.

Select Reporting and Disclosure Initiatives	Owner	Standards	Comments
	Global Reporting Initiative	GRI Standards	**GRI 304 Biodiversity:** Protecting biological diversity is important for ensuring the survival of plant and animal species, genetic diversity, and natural ecosystems.
	Dow Jones Sustainability Index	Assessment against Criteria	Biodiversity introduced for certain industry sectors in 2018.
	International Organization for Standardization	ISO 140000	A site-based environmental management standard to enhance and assure environmental performance.

ample, the Nature Conservancy (TNC) had a multiyear engagement with the Dow Chemical Company to advance a methodology for considering nature in corporate decision-making. CEMEX, a global construction materials company, partners with Birdlife International to set a standard for biodiversity excellence in areas of high natural value. The International Union for the Conservation of Nature has participated in many project-specific engagements with companies to help minimize the impacts of extraction on ecosystems around the world. In each of these cases, the partnerships advanced the ability of the private sector and the NGO world to work together and learn from each other.

While NGO/corporate partnerships represent a sound solution to some of the planet's most intractable problems, it remains true that historically bad relationships, organizational cultural differences, misperceptions, an imbalance in resources, and even the different "languages" used by the two sectors can make such partnerships challenging. In *Nature's Fortune*, former TNC CEO Mark Tercek relates how, when the scientists at Dow sat down with the scientists from the Nature Conservancy, they found themselves talking past each other. The different drivers, expectations, and even jargons needed to be acknowledged to make the partnership work. Many NGOs have litmus tests for the companies they work with, based on a set of internal criteria. Others require behavioral pledges around climate or development that may make it difficult for companies to engage if they or their financial stakeholders cannot make the pledge. Every NGO that has worked with business has faced criticism for doing so but has, in the end, advanced the ability of the two communities to work together more effectively.

Frameworks and guidelines can be complex and difficult to explain, leaving both parties vulnerable to criticism and negative campaigns against their collaborations. An NGO that collaborates with a corporation on environmental action will likely be criticized more than an NGO that receives a contribution from the same company, or from a foundation associated with that company. Working with a company is considered by some to be an endorsement of that company's actions, whereas profiting from their philanthropy is not. Some conservation groups do not allow themselves to take corporate money in order to protect their ability to advocate for and against corporate action and to avoid any semblance of conflict of interest. It's tricky when an NGO engages with a company. When the Sierra Club partnered with Clorox to endorse a planet-friendly version of the popular chlorine-based household cleaner, local chapters protested, officers quit, and the long-term chairman of the group, Carl Pope, eventually stood down following the discontent caused by the move. The Environmental Defense Fund (EDF) was criticized for working with McDonald's, the World Wildlife Fund (WWF) for working with Coca Cola, and Greenpeace for working with Unilever. Close relationships between international NGOs and the corporate world caused author Naomi Klein to coin the term "Big Green" in her criticisms of the actions of TNC, EDF, WWF, Sierra Club, and others to address climate change effectively by implicitly supporting the existing global business model and merely tweaking the edges for climate action.

And yet positive outcomes from the partnerships between the conservation community and the corporate world are indisputable. Following its partnership with WWF, Walmart is now the largest retailer of organic cotton in the world. Conservation International has brought Starbucks on a journey toward sustainably sourced coffee that is not only environmentally friendly but economically viable for coffee farmers. EDF and McDonald's worked to eliminate the company's use of polystyrene clamshell containers.

Critics claim that such actions legitimize business as usual and enable unsustainable business practices. Proponents claim that this is one way to make change within "the system" and that these partnerships move the entire system to better behavior. McDonald's shift from polystyrene paved the way for others to follow. Local and state bans on polystyrene food containers have proliferated, and the last big holdout, Dunkin' Donuts, pledged to finally eliminate its iconic Styrofoam cup by 2020. When big companies show that environmental change is not an economic disaster, smaller companies and consumers follow.

ECOLABELS AND CERTIFICATIONS

Ecolabels and certifications have proven to be an effective market-based approach that conservation groups and corporations have developed to advance better action on the planet. Ecolabels, standards, and certifications arose from a search in the late twentieth century for new ways to mobilize the private sector to more environmentally friendly practices. Today, many conservation practitioners working with corporate partners will eventually come into contact with this world of labels and certifications, called voluntary sustainability standards (VSS). Some consumer-focused ecolabels, such as Fairtrade and the Forestry Stewardship Council (FSC) certification, came from partnerships with conservation NGOs such as WWF, while others such as the Sustainability Forestry Initiative, arose from industry groups.

In her book *After Greenwashing*, Frances Bowen highlights the tensions that arise when the public seeks information about how green a company is while mistrusting the company as the source of information. The rise of the VSS addresses that tension and provides companies with third-party verifications that allow them to communicate their environmental and social performance to consumers and others. In 2018, the Ecolabel Index tracked 463 labeling or certification initiatives providing this service to the private sector and consumers.

VSSs are found across all industry sectors. They are a market-based approach to promoting sustainable practices using customer demand to drive change in production processes.[3] Many standards are focused on specific commodities and seek to improve corporate environmental, social, and governance practices around the exploitation of a given commodity. These standards, such as Shade Grown Coffee, which is overseen by the Rainforest Alliance and FairTrade certifications, apply to multiple products and focus on the welfare of producers and growers, while others focus on the sustainability of the commodity, such as the Marine Stewardship Council's (MSC) labels for wild fish or those produced from sustainable fisheries. These certification programs have helped drive better behavior to benefit planet and people, especially in the southern hemisphere, where companies from the United States and Europe operating in the region are now being held to higher global standards than those set by local governments.

Whether a standard or certification is "greenwashing" or a credible standard can be assessed through the transparent nature of the standard. If a consumer can easily access information about the standard, its cost, what it assesses, and who oversees it, then they can make a determination of its veracity. If no such information is easily available, the standard is not credible.

When designing a project or discussing collaboration, thinking about whether an opportunity exists to use an existing ecolabel or certification can help build credibility with consumers.

Lands Management and Process Improvement

Frameworks for better corporate action, whether through partnerships with NGOs or through adherence to VSSs, usually fall into two approaches: enhanced land management or process improvement. Enhanced lands management drives a company to look at its lands and consider development and reclamation efforts through a framework such as the mitigation hierarchy and to make commitments for reduced impacts through no net loss / net positive impact (NNL/NPI) goals. Process improvements inspired by supply-chain initiatives or circular-economy thinking drives a company to consider its overall footprint and explore where process changes and materials innovations can save water and energy and reduce waste to have positive impacts on the planet. NGO partners working on strategic corporate conservation plans will intersect with the mitigation hierarchy, NNL/NPI, supply chain, and circular economy at some stage, so it's good to know about their challenges and possibilities.

The Mitigation Hierarchy

The mitigation hierarchy is a tool that guides land managers to consider the impacts of their actions on biodiversity. The steps in the mitigation hierarchy are avoidance, minimization, restoration/reclamation, and offset. Avoidance, as the first and most important step, simply means that the development will have no impact on biodiversity. If avoidance is achieved, then the other steps in the hierarchy are not needed. Avoidance can result in the development not happening at all or being fundamentally changed in both siting and overall footprint. In reality, though, this rarely occurs. The most common complaint about the mitigation hierarchy is that assessments of most development projects ignore avoidance for a number of reasons, including political pressures, lack of capacity to assess impact, and absence of local regulations.[4] Avoidance assessments fail because of lack of agreement in what constitutes avoidance.[5] Too often, the assessment moves straight to the offset option. The fact that offset is an option in the mitigation hierarchy is controversial. Accepting an offset means accepting a guaranteed negative impact on biodiversity in one location for no guaranteed gain in another. Further criticism of offsets is that many offset programs are loosely governed and do not provide adequate monitoring to prove that there has been a net positive impact on biodiversity.[6] Governance of offsets is fragmented across countries and regions with no unified approach.

The concepts of no net loss and net positive impact arose from the mitigation hierarchy. Starting with the first adoption of these goals in 2001, NNL/NPI (as the concepts are commonly known) have now been adopted by more than thirty large global corporations. But the future of NNL/NPI as a viable goal is uncertain. The recently ended Business and Biodiversity Offset Program (BBOP) defined NNL/NPI as "No net loss is a target for a development project in which the impacts on biodiversity caused by the project are balanced or outweighed by measures taken to avoid and minimize the project's impacts, to undertake on-site rehabilitation/restoration, and finally to offset the residual impacts, so that no overall biodiversity loss results. Where the gain exceeds the loss, the term 'net gain' [or net positive impact] may be used instead of 'no net loss.'"

In 2018, mining giant Rio Tinto acknowledged that its 2004 NPI goal was unachievable across all operations. Rio Tinto had applied the goal across all its sites, regardless of location or age. In 2019, it recognized that it was not possible to achieve it. Some locations had operated long before the goal was in place and could never reach an NPI for their past impacts. Some of the challenges of NNL/NPI are defining the scope of biodiversity and impact, measuring the outcomes, and assessing the outcomes in a realistic timeframe.[7] While the target itself is a laudable one, there is in all of these efforts a heavy dependence on offsets (purchasing actions and land off-site that contribute to the goal), which is criticized as giving a company credit for someone else's good behavior.

Nature Valuation

While companies and international conventions have been focused on industry-specific initiatives to identify and ameliorate impacts on biodiversity, the academic conservation world has focused enormous resources on framing the issue in the languages of the private sector, finance, and accounting to create a system for valuing nature in a monetary sense.

It is impossible to make your way through a conservation conference today without coming across economists and their nature-valuation arguments. Dominant in conservation discussions for about a decade now, ecosystem-services economics and its offshoot, natural capital valuation, are deployed to present the "business value" of nature to policy makers and others. A controversial approach, eco-economics has been promoted for a decade as the best solution to engage the business community in the preservation of nature.

In 1997, a seminal paper by Robert Costanza et al., "The Value of the World's Ecosystem Services and Natural Capital," posited that the services provided by nature to humanity across the planet could be valued at $33 trillion, while the gross national product total for the entire world was $18 trillion.[8] Costanza's paper was written to illustrate the value that the earth's processes contribute to commercial markets. This paper started a conversation about what the contribution of natural resources to manufactured goods really was and whether this contribution was accounted for properly.

Since then, the study of the value of ecosystem services has exploded and evolved. Today the planet's natural systems are generally categorized into four main services: provisioning, regulating, culture, and habitat. *Provisioning services* represent the goods and materials that we extract from the earth as commodities. These have a clear monetary value in a capitalist society but are usually undervalued with respect to connections to other parts of the natural world. *Regulating services* are the ability of the earth to adjust the climate, absorb and manage stormwater, clean the air through oxygen cycles, and replenish the aquifers through the hydrologic cycle. *Cultural Services* are the most anthropocentric of these services, covering recreation and tourism as well as aesthetic and spiritual value. *Habitat services* were not included in early definitions of ecosystem service but are recognized today in most European models; they serve the survival of all species—for example, oak trees, which provide habitat for a large number of caterpillar species that in turn provide essential food to birds. Mangrove swamps with nutrient-rich waters and plentiful hiding spaces provide nursery services for many marine species. Tropical rain forests host much of the world's natural abundance, especially the species uniquely adapted to live there.

The natural capital movement, focused primarily on valuing tradeoffs in both provisioning and habitat services, emerged from ecosystem-service valuation efforts. The Economics of Ecosystems and Biodiversity (TEEB) is a global initiative whose focus is to "mainstream the values of biodiversity and ecosystem services into decision-making at all levels," and the Natural Capital Coalition, an outgrowth of TEEB that advances valuation best practices to the corporate world, are the two leading programs in the valuation community. It should be noted that none of these efforts have been successful in creating a valuation protocol for biodiversity. Recently the efforts have evolved to include nonmonetary valuation following pressure from indigenous people whose value systems are not the same as those of Western-educated conservationists and economists. The main valuation promoted for use in *biodiversity* tradeoffs is the contingent valuation method, which was developed for things that are not sold. The contingent valuation method explores willingness to pay to maintain or willingness to accept payment for compensation of loss. There are many critics of this approach, in indigenous communities and elsewhere, for whom the idea of placing a value on an intrinsic aspect of life is anathema.

While proponents of valuation schemes can be very persuasive, there is no universal agreement that placing nature in the hands of economists is a good thing. George Monbiot, a columnist and environmental activist, has written extensively on the subject and calls natural capital valuation schemes morally wrong, saying, "The natural capital agenda reinforces the notion that nature has no value unless you can extract cash from it."[9] These criticisms have encouraged proponents of natural capital to soften their language and ensure their audiences that they are not seeking to monetize nature.

The Intergovernmental Panel on Biodiversity and Ecosystems Services (IPBES) controversially declined to use the terms from the valuation community in its assessments and focused instead on what it calls "nature's contribution to people" in an effort to reframe the discussion away from economic value focused on environmental damage and toward policies that embrace the multiple values of nature's contribution.[10]

In any case, valuation efforts are not moving the needle. Research has concluded that economic valuation estimates provide a very incomplete perspective on the unknown value of biodiversity changes.[11] The Global Environment Facility, the UN's finance mechanism for environmental projects, has found that "Valuation is not leading to the development of policy reforms needed to mitigate the drivers of biodiversity loss and encourage sustainable development through the better management of biodiversity and natural capital, nor is it triggering changes in the use and scale of public and private finance flows on the scale necessary to address threats."[12]

For many in the corporate world, the valuation systems is an academic exercise with little practical use in development, restoration, or operations. Jim Rushworth from the Lafarge Group expressed what many in industry think when he told me that until there is one standard, one protocol, and a way to differentiate between the impact that the operation is actually causing to biodiversity and impacts to the environment caused by actions off-site, valuation schemes will never be broadly adopted by industry. Other corporate leaders have also expressed concern about the issue of attribution of impact, saying that ecosystem valuation schemes cannot differentiate between what happens off the site—where specific species may be negatively impacted from existing human or environmental concerns, or where air and water that is flowing onto the site may already be impacted—from what happens on-site due to operations. In addition, many biologists recognize that there is an enormous gap in knowledge about the role of specific species in ecosystem functionality, which, as Jessica Dempsey states in *Enterprising Nature*, her bluntly written assessment of nature valuation efforts, is an issue because of the difficulty in describing to a chief financial officer the specific risks a firm will face from a change in land use or biodiversity.

The core philosophy of nature valuation is simple. It is that we are not paying the true price for what we use and what we impact. Corporate conservationists and their NGO partners can use this core philosophy to frame strategic conservation plans and actions around impacts of operations on nature.

Whether through the mitigation hierarchy, NNL/NPI, or natural capital accounting, large global companies continue to partner with NGOs to develop workable approaches to calculating, minimizing, or eliminating the impacts of their operations on nature. As this work continues, many more companies are exploring beyond their own operations' impacts and into their supply chains to identify and address negative impacts on society and the environment.

Value-Chain Initiatives

The value chain (or supply chain) is the network of people, processes, and materials that contribute to the manufacture and distribution of a product. Supply-chain and circular-economy initiatives look more deeply into a product, whether a car, a cell phone, or a shampoo bottle, and consider how its components can be redesigned for lower environmental impact, recycled for a second purpose, or removed entirely from the chain. From extraction site to landfill, the supply chain impacts nature, and efforts within many of these initiatives seek to identify these impacts and to minimize them. Most value-chain initiatives are in their infancy, with working conditions and human rights as a primary focus. Once important social concerns are addressed in a systematic and transparent manner, biodiversity will become a more prominent supply-chain issue for companies with direct impacts. Companies further along the supply chain still need some persuasion.

According to Prue Addison, a former NERC Fellow at the University of Oxford who has spent a number of years looking at business and biodiversity, the further down the supply chain a company is, the less it views its impact on biodiversity as material.[13] It has to be recognized that every company, regardless of the product or service it sells, has an impact on biodiversity. An auto manufacturing company may have a relatively small footprint of assembly plants and test tracks, but its entire business model is based on habitat fragmentation, since its products are not possible without the roads to support them. A tech company may be contained in clean laboratories, offices, and server farms, but server farms take power from electric utilities, take space that could be habitat, and utilize devices made from extracted materials such as oil and components made from rare earth metals. Today, new electric vehicles contain four times as much copper as traditional cars. There is no commercial enterprise that does not impact biodiversity in its broadest sense, whether by habitat destruction or fragmentation, diversion of resources such as water, creation of new hazards such as highly reflective buildings that cause bird strikes, or non-source pollution caused by storm-water runoff from impervious surfaces.

In the United States, the Suppliers Partnership for the Environment, the auto industry's supply-chain initiative, opted to include biodiversity from the beginning. Encouraged by auto companies Toyota USA, General Motors, and Fiat Chrysler, the Suppliers Partnership recognized that nature could unite members along the supply chain quickly and through positive action. An inspiration for this decision was driven (pun intended) by the work of John Bradburn, former global manager of waste reduction at General Motors.

John Bradburn was considered something of a MacGyver at General Motors. He has the ability to see the potential in things that other people wanted to throw away, and he has a superpower for extracting second and third lives from materials that would normally have found their way into a landfill. John's innovative approach to materials reuse is one of the reasons that General Motors has progressed rapidly toward global sustainability, with 142 landfill-free facilities out of a goal of 150. GM's business drivers for biodiversity action were many, but in this case it is Citizenship, Driver 6 (see chapter 2.)

One of John's first material innovations to benefit biodiversity was to reuse surplus packing material for cavity-nesting ducks, especially the scaly-sided merganser, an endangered species of duck in China. The composite material that protects the batteries that power the Chevrolet Volt, GMs plug-in hybrid, during shipping, cannot easily be recycled. The battery case has an A-frame shape that is perfect for deployment as an artificial nesting structure. John designed the "battery-box birdhouses" to be easily installed by attaching the case to a wooden structure, creating a hole in the cover to mimic the traditional tree cavity and, in the case of the scaly-sided merganser, a second hole for quick escape from tigers seeking easy food

in the nests. Over 700 of these boxes have been placed in GM facilities across North America, and many were shipped to China
and installed by conservation partners Wetlands International and
the World Wildlife Fund for scaly-sided merganser restoration. The
boxes have been successful, with documented proof of use. GM has
reached into the community to engage school and youth groups to
assemble the boxes prior to their deployment around the world.

In further materials innovation and as an experiment in habitat creation, GM created artificial stalactites in artificial caves to provide habitat for bats using leftover adhesive from the manufacture
of Corvettes. The leftover glue is coated with surplus textured coating that is part of the car's anti-chip paint. The glue and coating
have been installed as artificial stalactites in man-made caves to provide bats with roosting surfaces. John also used the Volt battery cases
to create maternity bat-roost structures, aka bat boxes, and instead
of installing wood for the chambers, he used another unrecyclable
product, circuit trays. He treated these with paint and sand to provide gritty surface for bats to get traction and installed them as internal structures for the bat boxes made from the aforementioned

Figure 3-1: GM's John Bradburn works with young NASCAR fans to
build bat boxes from battery cases, diverting waste from landfills while
creating biodiversity value. (Used with permission of General Motors.)

Volt battery covers. Again GM reached into the community with the Chevrolet Racing team, assembling a pit crew of fifty young NASCAR fans at Pocono Raceway in Pennsylvania to build fifteen bat boxes that are installed around the property. These activities, led by the vision of John Bradburn, were initially driven by GM's net-zero waste aspiration, but they also connect the dots between GM's biodiversity enhancement work and its community engagement efforts.

John's work on the value chain is diverting materials from land-fills. Similar efforts by the Suppliers Partnership and others are advancing effective and environmental action around nature in all directions along the chain, with the companies at the beginning of the value chain, the mining and quarrying companies, taking the most initiative. Very few companies or industry sectors that exist down-stream on the value chain have intentions for biodiversity. They do not yet consider it a material risk.[14] To complicate matters, many suppliers and vendors in the supply chain do not have the same footprints as the extractive companies, although many will have legacy remediation sites as well as surplus and undeveloped real estate, but all have the potential to mainstream biodiversity as a nonregulatory, nonmaterial, positive key performance indicator (KPI) for sustainability.

By encouraging best practices across supply chains and adopting the tenets of environmentally friendly supply-chain management through product traceability, transparency, management, and commitments, all industries can drive change and make supportable claims about their products and, in the words of Frances Bowen in *After Greenwashing*, connect sustainability symbolism to substance.

Reporting

Another corporate tool that turns sustainability symbolism into substance is in aggregated global reporting such as the Global Reporting Initiative (GRI) and the Dow Jones Sustainability Initiative (DJSI). The public benchmarking that comes from these efforts causes companies to raise their games across a range of environment, social, and governance concerns.

In *The Big Pivot*, Andrew Winston cites radical transparency as one of the big-pivot drivers for improved corporate responsibility. Reporting initiatives are key to this. In recent decades, the number of companies publishing their own corporate social responsibility (CSR) reports has grown to 85 percent of S&P 500 companies in 2017, a substantial increase from 20 percent of such companies in 2011.[15] Today there are calls in Europe and the United Kingdom to mandate enhanced and integrated financial reporting to be done alongside ESG issues in order to provide a clearer picture of corporate risk and sustainability. There are also calls for a standard format for CSR reporting, as there has been much discussion about the use and misuse of nonfinancial reporting by companies to enhance their reputations without actually disclosing their material and immaterial impacts and risks.[16] Corporate citizenship reports publish goals adopted by the company and report on progress made toward achieving those goals as well as other endeavors of corporate citizenship. The best reports are audited by external verification firms. This fact is usually listed in the small print beyond the infographics and heartwarming stories. Readers of CSR reports can mistrust the facts and the photos or they may misunderstand the nuanced way the information is presented. Third-party verification is important for providing the reader with confidence in the information. A report that is externally verified should highlight the fact, not hide it in the small print.

The Global Reporting Initiative (GRI) seeks to bring unity and comparability to corporate reporting by establishing a set of global standards to drive global best practice in sustainability and CSR reporting. GRI Standard 304 addresses biodiversity across four specific topic areas: operations near protected lands and areas of high biodiversity; significant impacts on biodiversity by activities; habitats protected or restored; and rare and imperiled species and their habitats present on the company's lands. With a focus on materiality and risk, GRI echoes the predominant treatment of biodiversity in corporate disclosures. The Dow Jones Sustainability Initiative (DJSI) is a similar reporting framework for companies that have recently adopted biodiversity reporting standards, but only for companies with a direct and material impact on biodiversity. The focus on rare and imperiled species and key biodiversity areas is understandable, but it facilitates a decoupling from nature and misses an opportunity to mainstream biodiversity goals across entire operations and to promote ways to live and produce in harmony with nature. This decoupling feeds the misguided narrative that you cannot have both healthy profits and a healthy planet.

If a company is not operating in a key biodiversity area, or if its lands do not contain rare or imperiled species, it may feel "off the hook" when it comes to biodiversity. If a reporting initiative promotes holistic lands management regardless of biodiversity "value," it could start making a difference in how a company's lands are viewed and boosting the value of actions to enhance them.

Most companies will contribute to more than one reporting effort. General Motors, for example, reports to the Carbon Disclosure Project (CDP), the GRI, the UN Global Compact, the UN Sustainability Development Goals, the Sustainability Accounting Standards Board, and the Climate-Related Financial Disclosure framework. Today, many corporate sustainability professionals agree that "reporting fatigue" and overreach by some of the reporting frameworks will likely impact this world of corporate initiatives in the future, with some companies withdrawing from the most onerous but least valuable efforts.

Regardless of whether the company adopts one or more of these initiatives or frameworks, it is sensible to design a link between conservation implementation—the project on the ground at the site—and the corporate conservation strategic plan with whatever initiative and sustainability reporting the company does. A conservation effort that fits into the data or the narrative of a sustainability report will have greater value than an effort that does not.

The recovery project for the Jefferson salamander at the Dufferin Aggregates quarry connects on-the-ground conservation to CRH's global goals and CSR reporting. John Bradburn's innovative materials reuse connects materials management and biodiversity conservation efforts to General Motors' global goals for landfill-free facilities and increased biodiversity action at manufacturing sites. By joining the dots from conservation to corporate reporting, the value of the nature-based action is maintained and amplified.

Also, efforts at both GM and CRH tie to their respective corporate commitments toward the Sustainable Development Goals. GM's commitment to Goal 12—*Responsible Production and Consumption*, Goal 15—*Life on Land*, and Goal 9—*Industry, Innovation and Infrastructure*, are all encapsulated in John Bradburn's efforts.

Sustainable Development Goals

The United Nation's Sustainable Development Goals, or SDGs, represent the best opportunity to link corporate goals and reporting to biodiversity.

The SDGs were developed by the UN as a follow-up to the Millennial Development Goals. They seek to create a world with greater equity. The SDGs have been adopted by the business community with twenty-four of the forty-nine Fortune 100 companies addressing biodiversity in their corporate reporting, doing so within the framework of the SDGs.[17] The SDGs are beautifully branded; the color wheel of goals is easily recognizable. Thanks to an action campaign, they are in the public domain on billboards and mass transit, and in public places like airports. Marketing aside, the reasons the SDGs have greater uptake in the business world is their accessibility, the timing of their launch at a moment when the corporate sector began flexing its muscles in the absence of effective national governments, and the fact that business can readily see the interconnectedness between different goals. A concerted effort to engage the private sector in the SDGs facilitated their adoption. A 2015 study by PwC found that 92 percent of businesses are aware of the SDGs, with 71 percent planning to integrate them into strategy.[18] In contrast, very few businesses engage with the Convention on Biological Diversity (CBD) the UN-driven approach to halt biodiversity loss. Only six of the top 100 Fortune 500 companies referred to CBD goals in their reporting. The proliferation of the SDGs into corporate reporting has spawned a new term, "rainbow-washing," to describe a company's adoption of the SDGs for style rather than substance.

As more corporations pivot toward reporting around the Sustainable Development Goals, the interconnected nature of biodiversity is an advantage for corporate conservation. Prue Addison

Table 3-2: Translating the International Biodiversity Goals into Corporate Biodiversity Goals, with Example Business Actions*

	International Biodiversity Goal	Relevant Biodiversity Targets & SDGs	Corporate Biodiversity Goal	Example Business Actions
A	Address the underlying causes of biodiversity loss by mainstreaming biodiversity across government and society	Aichi Targets 1, 2, 3, 4 SDGs 1, 2, 4, 8, 9, 11, 12, 13, 14, 15, 17	Embed biodiversity into decision making	• Raise awareness about biodiversity internally, e.g., among employees • Biodiversity embedded in corporate strategy • Adopt and implement voluntary certification schemes and industry standards
B	Reduce the direct pressures on biodiversity and promote sustainable use	Aichi Targets 5, 6, 7, 8, 9, 10 SDGs 1, 2, 3, 6, 7, 8, 9, 10, 11, 12, 13, 14, 15	Reduce impacts and promote sustainable use in operations and/or supply chain	• Reduce or eliminate impacts on species and habitats directly affected by operations and/or supply chain • Adopt measures to ensure sustainable use of natural resources • Prevent the introduction or spread of invasive species
C	Improve the status of biodiversity by safeguarding ecosystems, species, and genetic diversity	Aichi Targets 11, 12, 13 SDGs 2, 3, 6, 9, 11, 12, 14, 15	Improve the status of biodiversity	• Establish private protected areas, or support establishment or management of public protected areas • Implement ecosystem restoration actions • Invest in solutions that work with nature, such as natural infrastructure
D	Enhance the benefits to all from biodiversity and ecosystem services	Aichi Targets 14, 15, 16 SDGs 1, 3, 5, 6, 7, 8, 9, 10, 11, 13, 14, 15	Enhance the benefits society draws from biodiversity	• Account for the needs of indigenous groups, women, the poor, marginalised and vulnerable groups, and individuals in business actions • Ensure access to, and benefit sharing from, natural resources while operating within sustainable limits • Adhere to or incorporate international, regional, and/or national rules that relate to biodiversity
E	Enhance implementation through participatory planning, knowledge management, and capacity building	Aichi Targets 17, 18, 19, 20 SDGs 2, 3, 4, 5, 7, 9, 10, 12, 13, 14, 16, 17	Stakeholder engagement, support, and knowledge sharing	• Engage in multi-stakeholder dialogue to manage impacts on biodiversity • Incorporate traditional knowledge into strategic planning for sustainable management of biodiversity • Share biodiversity monitoring data to assist decision making and adaptive management

* Adapted from: Thomas Smith et al., "Mainstreaming Biodiversity Targets for the Private Sector: Main Report & Case Studies," Joint Nature Conservation Committee, Interdisciplinary Centre for Conservation Science, University of Oxford, n.d. Final Report available from: http://jncc.defra.gov.uk/page-7678. (Used with permission.)

and her colleagues mapped crossovers between the CBD's strategic goals that are specific to biodiversity and the SDGs, and found that there every single one of the seventeen SDGs contains a potential for crossover with one or more of five biodiversity strategic policy goals. The co-benefits for environment, society, and business are obvious.[19]

An NGO or corporate planner seeking to develop a strategic approach to conservation will find the corporate biodiversity goals listed in the table above to be very valuable in conversations that seek to link corporate reporting to corporate action around conservation, especially if the SDGs are part of the company's citizenship efforts.

To be fluent in the world of corporate frameworks and initiatives is to understand that infinite links exist and that the value of bio-diversity action can be deployed broadly. Helping a site connect its efforts to a corporate framework, or connecting the dots from head office to an operation, strengthens the argument for biodiversity, garners support for a corporate conservation plan, and makes the ecological stewardship or restoration action more meaningful to all. Mainstreaming biodiversity into operations results from under-standing these connections.

04 THE PROCESS

—

Plans are of little importance, but planning is essential.

—WINSTON CHURCHILL

Successful corporate conservation approaches connect a business driver to conservation action. There are many ways to do this, but the most efficient way is by developing a strategic plan for conservation. The planning process is as valuable as the product because it signals commitment to ecological stewardship. The plan creates a structured approach for decision-making to help efficiently and effectively identify conservation opportunities across a company's landholdings. It also provides a method for matching resource availability and need to conservation action that has a strategic objective. By developing a conservation plan, a company and its nongovernmental organization (NGO) partner draw a blueprint for action that is resilient to inevitable corporate disruptions and budgetary cycles.

In a perfect world, a business need would be identified, a plan would be developed, action would happen, and everyone would be satisfied. But there is no perfect world, so this chapter and the one that follows provide guidance and options for maintaining forward momentum in ways that make sense to a corporate landowner in the real world—acknowledging the difficult work of adapting to shifting priorities, limited budgets, staff turnover, and more.

Unlike conservation planning, strategic planning for conservation on corporate lands does not start with the conservation projects, habitats, ecosystems, or species to be targeted. Those will be evaluated at a later step in the planning process. Instead, assessment of need and opportunity will drive project choice later in the planning effort. It is best to move with an open mind through the process and let the strategy determine the action.

Strategic Planning

The process of developing a corporate conservation plan borrows heavily from traditional strategic planning, which has been a cornerstone of organizations since the early twentieth century, but a conservation focus includes some important distinctive elements as well.

Strategic planning is a deliberative approach toward identifying and addressing business opportunities and challenges. Strategic plans differ from operational plans, development plans, and business plans by focusing on a long-term vision for the success of the organization as a whole.

At its most basic, a strategic plan is a blueprint for an organization to coalesce around simple, consistent, and long-term goals that have been informed by an analysis of the internal and external business landscape. A strategic plan appraises and understands available resources and describes a path toward implementation. Effective strategic plans also contain metrics linked to the goals. Strategic conservation plans have these elements, but the landscape they analyze is different. They focus on local opportunities and conservation needs rather than competition or global trends. The resources to be appraised relate to lands and community more than budgets or materials. The goals and metrics may be softer and less predictable, subject to whims of the natural world like weather and migratory patterns. However, the reasons for designing such a plan are the same: to get buy-in, establish a goal, determine resources, and report outcomes.

Three factors important to the success of any strategic planning effort are process, communication, and measurement. For any plan to be accepted and implemented, significant and supported involvement of the right people in the process is essential.[1] There must be strong communication along the lines of responsibility and reporting.[2] Finally, meaningful and integrated measurements of progress must be established as part of the planning process and made explicit in the final plan.[3]

Strategic corporate conservation plans have a lot in common with organizational strategic plans. They support decision-making, helping a company choose, design, and implement conservation projects that meet their business needs and bring ecological value. They are informed by the business landscape more than the ecological landscape. In strategic corporate conservation plans, the design of the conservation project happens last.

Strategic corporate conservation plans have very little in common with traditional conservation plans. The main difference between traditional conservation planning and corporate conservation planning is the focus on the plan. In traditional conservation planning, restoration or management of a species, habitat, or ecosystem is the focus. But the business need is the focus of a strategic corporate conservation plan that could end up focusing on multiple projects, species, or habitats. Placing business at the center of a corporate conservation plan links efforts to business drivers and enables business to adopt conservation goals and integrate appropriate conservation practices across different operations. By borrowing the language and approaches of business, a path is created to engage more businesses in meaningful and integrated environmental stewardship activities.

Starting a Corporate Conservation Planning Effort

A business leader, site manager, or employee in a company has many responsibilities and concerns: productivity, profitability, health, safety, and corporate governance. Biodiversity is not usually foremost among these concerns unless the employee is that rare and lucky person whose job title and position description includes biodiversity or natural resources.

What, then, is the impetus for a company to embark on a strategic planning exercise for conservation? Compliance is the objective for many companies. But what drives a manager responsible for compliance with environment, health, and safety (EHS) regulations to develop and embrace a plan that seeks to go beyond compliance for conservation and stewardship?

It is not common for corporate leaders to consider natural-resources stewardship as a strategic matter or even recognize it as a tool for addressing business challenges or opportunities. (If it was common, this book would not be needed.) Companies that come to adopt strategic approaches to conservation usually have prior success leveraging existing ad hoc or opportunistic stewardship activities to meet a business challenge. If a company has a history of solving problems using conservation at a site level, then leadership will be more likely to embrace conservation as a possible solution. If a company embraces a beyond-compliance ethos, it is also likely to look at environmental stewardship as an option for illustrating this commitment. If a company benchmarks against others in its sector, it will begin to see the value of natural-resources programs in other companies and embrace the need for its own plan or strategy.

Leading companies that have reached a higher level of compliance with existing regulations may turn to biodiversity programs as a way to differentiate themselves within their sector. Sue Kelsey was General Motors' global biodiversity program manager. Sue, one of those lucky corporate employees with biodiversity in her job title, was responsible for bringing GM's biodiversity goal into manufacturing facilities across the world. Asked why GM, of all companies, would adopt a biodiversity goal, Sue has explained that the company had already reached compliance with many regulatory and some voluntary programs, and that it was seeking to show leadership beyond air, water, and waste to really look at the environment surrounding GM operations. In the early 2000s, a number of GM facilities were engaged in conservation action on their lands. The efforts were disorganized and not bringing value to corporate sustainability efforts. There was little growth in the adoption of conservation action with, on average, one new conservation program started per year.

This changed in 2012, when the company formalized its commitment to conservation on its lands and communicated a sustainability goal that all GM manufacturing facilities around the world would implement conservation programs by 2020. GM leveraged existing efforts and counted them in the new sustainability goal as a way to show existing leadership in the "beyond-compliance" aspect of its environmental management.

In the corporate environment, timing is also key. Following the success of the Woodlawn project at Bridgestone (discussed in chapter 2), Tim Bent waited for the right leadership and successful completion of a number of other ecological remediation projects before he broached the idea of making these efforts strategic and moving them into operations. He knew he would have greater success when the right planets were aligned.

The following are other common situations that can lead a company to view conservation as a strategic opportunity and start a planning process to formalize it.

1. When environmental stewardship programs are happening on corporate lands in an opportunistic, employee-driven manner, they can be leveraged wisely by management to benefit the corporation. In this situation, leadership is aware of the efforts and is more likely to formalize the approaches within a strategic framework in order to capture maximum value. Good leaders understand that, in this scenario, ownership of the projects must remain with employees as the projects are folded into a corporate plan.

2. While it is becoming less common, companies can still experience events like spills, leaks, or other accidents that impact both reputation and social license to operate. If the event affects biodiversity, the company will be compelled by regulators, stakeholders, and shareholders to mitigate the event and present a plan for avoiding it in the future. Smart leaders recognize the benefit of embedding the response within a strategic framework in order to better illustrate intent, communicate through metrics, and secure support after the crisis has abated.

3. Another common scenario is that a company already has conservation programs on its lands that realize high local value but receive little corporate support or attention. A business event like a merger, divestiture, or restructuring places pressure on the company to address social license to operate (SLO), boost employee morale, enhance corporate reputation, or strengthen relationships with agencies or stakeholders throughout the upheaval. This emerging business need and existing conservation programs create the right environment for a strategic corporate conservation plan.

Starting at the Right Scale

While timing is important for plan development, the scale at which planning happens is also essential for success. Large companies will scale most of their planning efforts around a subsidiary, business, or territory, depending on the company structure or the business driver. While traditional conservation planning is scaled to a watershed, ecoregion, or specific species, business-centered conservation plans will organize around its own operations. The business reason for the conservation plan will determine the scale.

Because every company is different, it is impossible to define a single best scale for plan development. The right scale is the one that allows the effort to move easily from planning to implementation without having to pass through too many managerial obstacles. A plan originating in the corporate office of a global or even national organization will be significantly changed and weakened by its passage through the corporate hierarchy, where managers add or remove emphasis, messages, or resources according their own needs and predilections. The ideal situation is for corporate leadership to agree that a conservation plan is needed, indicate the scale at which it will be developed, provide the resources to make it happen, make statements in support of it, and step out of the way. When General Motors, building on efforts that started in 2000, announced its global goal for biodiversity in 2012, the announcement for the goal came from the corporate public policy office. The plan to implement was developed closer to the operational level.

The Elements of a Strategic Corporate Conservation Plan

The elements of the plan outlined in the rest of this chapter are an amalgam of experiences with different companies' efforts to build sustainable beyond-compliance approaches to environmental stewardship and corporate citizenship. The elements will inform the process, and no one process will work for every company. Different elements will be useful in a variety of circumstances depending on company size, culture, business driver, scale, and the availability of time and resources.

Further, equal importance should be given to both the process and the product. With any organizational innovation or development, there are many forces arrayed against success. Inertia is one of the most powerful forces against and is often cited as a reason for failure.[4] The strategic planning process must be designed throughout to overcome corporate inertia and address other common challenges to success: lack of clarity, lack of communication, and absence of champions.

The business need is the reason the company is developing a strategic conservation plan. It remains the touchstone of the planning process throughout. If the business need is not made explicit and is not referred to throughout the process, the resulting plan will be a sprawling wish list of actions that will not achieve the hoped-for result. An unfocused, sprawling strategic conservation plan will be ineffective, as corporate value will not be realized with an incoherent success story or metrics that may have local meaning but no global relevance.

Table 4-1 lists the elements of a strategic corporate conservation planning process. These are not steps that need to be taken sequentially; rather, they are elements, some or all of which can be used to create a strong plan. Explanations of each element follows.

Table 4-1: The Elements of a Corporate Conservation Strategic Planning Process

The Element	*The Reason*
The Planning Team	Ensure that the right people are part of the conversation for content and political reasons.
The Survey	Can be used to both collect information and frame the message.
The Assessment	Assess the external political, social, and environment aspects as well as internal operations.
The Ultimate Stakeholder	Narrow the plan to meet the business need and satisfy the ultimate stakeholder.
The Success Story	Who tells the success story, when do they tell it, and what is the story?
The Guiding Principles	An essential element to drive structured decision-making at implementation.
Risk Assessment	What could go wrong and how bad could it be?
Socialization	Start and maintain a conversation about conservation planning to encourage ownership and acceptance.
Metric Development	Develop metrics for the plan that can be easily cascaded to the site and integrated into larger frameworks.

THE PLANNING TEAM

Deciding who should be on the planning team is one of the most important decisions of the process. The makeup of the team will affect success even if the participants are not themselves the ones who will be implementing the plan. When considering who should be on a planning team, it is important to consider all aspects of the organization and all employee categories where possible. There are many places within a corporate organization where responsibilities and goals intersect but where priorities and budgets compete. Clarity around areas of intersection and competition is essential for success.

Different corporations have different organizational structures or use different names for similar functions. Table 4-2 below lists some of the functions and the reasons for their inclusion in the Planning Team.

Table 4-2: The Planning Team

Function	Responsibility	Intersection with a Corporate Conservation Strategy
Facilities management and real estate	Nonoperating lands.	Management of landscape crews and consultants. Holding the budget for landscape maintenance.
Environmental, health and safety (EHS)	Operating lands like quarries, rights of way, or test tracks.	Compliance with regulations and permit requirements and anything that impacts safe operations.
Government affairs	Relationships with elected officials and regulating agencies.	Knowledge of existing relationships and pending legislation or regulations.
Human resources	Employee engagement.	Can connect existing employee engagement efforts and metrics to the strategy.
Community relations	Local or regional community engagement efforts.	Knowledge of community concerns and needs.
Corporate citizenship/ sustainability	Reporting and disclosure into corporate frameworks. Management of corporate citizenship or sustainability goals.	Ensures the plan contributes to corporate citizenship goals and that metrics will meet corporate reporting needs.

Including all of these functions on the planning team can ensure that the final plan amplifies corporate ambitions, adheres to operational restrictions, and leverages existing resources. Other functions or teams that may be included depending on the business need and the scope of the plan, including legal, capital investment, and site remediation.

Beyond function, it is also valuable to think about specific employees and consider which employees are essential to contribute leadership, knowledge, and social capital to the effort. As with any new corporate initiative, employees will react in different ways, given their levels of loyalty, stress, and cynicism.[5] Some employees will be cheerleaders for the initiative, highly engaged in making it a success and bringing others on board as needed. Most employees will be neutral, and as engaged as directed by the leaders and cheerleaders. A small number of employees will actively work against the initiative, for a variety of reasons.

Resistance to change is innate in people and organizations, regardless of the size and scope of the effort and the organization. Accepting this fact is very important, as attempts to minimize or ignore resistance will lead to failure of the effort. The ability to overcome the resistance depends on the culture of the organization as well as an individual's disposition to resist.[6]

When considering the functions and employees to engage in the planning exercise, leadership should ask:

1. Whose buy-in is necessary for leadership, resources, and implementation?
2. Who from leadership can act as a sincere messenger?
3. Who can act as a bridge between leadership and operations and communicate effectively in both directions?
4. Who will cheerlead this effort?
5. Whose resistance will derail the effort?
6. Who has a network through which the effort can be socialized?

Once these considerations have been made, the ideal mix of individuals from a diverse set of functions can start to create a plan that meets the business need; integrates with operations, compliance, and other corporate initiatives; and includes reporting and metrics.

THE SURVEY

A survey can gather both informational and attitudinal responses, providing information that is essential to the process, and can be deployed at various stages during the process. It can benchmark attitudes at the beginning of the process and be used during implementation to measure changes. It can also frame the process to manage expectations. The survey can be restricted to team members only, but will be more useful to planning if it is deployed as a communications and buy-in tool and sent to a wider audience.

The survey can gather intelligence for the assessment element of the planning process and can uncover the distance in responses between corporate functions. A survey seeking information on stakeholders, the political landscape, or other qualitative issues will garner different responses from the community affairs and EHS functions but then provide, in an inclusive planning process, an opportunity for the entire team to consider all the responses. The survey can also measure attitudes and knowledge against the current situation or existing industry benchmarks. The survey can bring previously unknown but existing conservation projects into the light and expose potential obstacles to implementation.

The survey can be used as a filter for other elements of the process, especially the assessment, ultimate stakeholder identification, and development of the guiding principles.

THE ASSESSMENT

In traditional strategic planning, a tool called a SWOT analysis (of strengths, weaknesses, opportunities, and threats) is used to assess the internal and external circumstances of an organization. Strengths and weaknesses are identified as those internal to the organization, while opportunities and threats are external forces. Another commonly used tool called the environmental scan focuses entirely on external factors across political, economic, social, and technological (PEST) considerations. For corporate conservation strategic plans, a hybrid between the SWOT analysis and the environmental scan is most effective. The planning team will focus mainly on reviewing external political, environmental, and social considerations as opportunities or threats and then assess the internal landscape by considering operations and their potential to contribute to the effort.

The weight on each of the four factors—political, environmental, social, and operational—will be different depending on the business need. If the business need driving the development of a conservation strategy is SLO and community engagement, then external issues will be more important, while internal operational concerns will have greater weight for no net loss / net positive impact (NNL/NPI) goals or license and permit renewals.

The four factors relate to the sixteen business needs as follows:

- **Political:** secure social license to operate; improve government relations; inform reporting and disclosures; and provide a sustainability goal and performance metric.
- **Environmental**: mitigate biodiversity impacts; inform better remediation remedies; address climate change; implement nature-based solutions; and improve lands management and realize cost savings.
- **Social:** secure social license to operate; increase employee engagement; create meaningful community engagement; frame corporate investment in education; position for talent acquisition; and satisfy SRI and shareholders.
- **Operational:** mitigate biodiversity impacts; permit acquisition and renewal; increase employee engagement; implement nature-based solutions; and drive action along supply chain / circular economy.

The assessment looks at existing situations as well as future ones across all four factors. The objective of the assessment is to create a shared understanding of opportunities and obstacles to conservation implementation.

Political Opportunities and Threats

Political issues may be potent or trivial, depending on the business need. Either way, they need to be assessed if only to be ruled out.

Starting at the same scale of the planning effort—local, regional, etc.—political assessments should look at the pending legislation and regulations that may impact the effort. A legislative effort to mandate pollinator plantings in rights of way, require native seed mixes, implement a rain tax, or list a particular species as endangered may all impact the conservation plan. The people involved in the politics are also a factor. It is important to know about an elected official with a personal concern for a specific waterway or community.

To carry out an assessment of the political landscape, the following questions can be considered:

Is politics a factor? Within the target region, what are the political conditions that will enable or challenge the implementation of environmental stewardship projects? What is the relationship between the company and its operations with elected and appointed officials? Can political alliances be made using environmental stewardship projects? Do political nemeses exist? Who could threaten the effort?

Environmental Opportunities and Threats

Because the conservation plan will be implemented at a local scale, it is important that the final plan is specific to the respective conservation contexts, and builds on existing conservation plans or priorities. A company can increase the value of its stewardship effort by aligning its efforts with existing conservation plans, whether local watershed-restoration plans, statewide Wildlife Action Plans, or other priority plans developed by conservation partners or government agencies. Aligning with local conservation plans can also improve stakeholder relations by framing the effort within a conservation priority that enjoys deep support from the community. (Chapter 6 of this book examines conservation alignments in more detail.)

To assess the environmental landscape, the following questions should be considered:

What are the existing environmental conditions in the target region with respect to stewardship opportunities? What local or regional conservation plans exist? Which plans have a high level of support? What is the pattern of land ownership and how will it impact environmental stewardship projects off-site? What does environmental governance look like in the target region? Are there certain government agencies or commissions that must be engaged for any activities both on- and off-site?

Social Opportunities and Threats

External social considerations, like political considerations, may be important or not. The social aspect presents some of the best opportunities to grow external support for a corporate conservation strategic plan. But community and stakeholders can also erect obstacles by voicing resistance to efforts to manage lands differently, whether corporate-wide or at a single site. Buy-in from vocal, engaged, and enabling stakeholders is critical for outward-facing initiatives. Community engagement can amplify the efforts, bring resources to the projects, and inspire long-term involvement.

To carry out an assessment of the social landscape, the following questions can be considered:

Who are the stakeholders? Do internal stakeholders have an impact/interest in this effort? Is the number of stakeholders manageable, or does there need to be prioritization? What are the general concerns of the external stakeholders? Have stakeholders expressed specific concerns? Can they be connected to environmental stewardship? Can any stakeholders help or hinder this effort?

Operational Opportunities and Threats

There are many ways that existing and future operations impact both the environment and the community. In traditional strategic planning, operations are simply the tools for implementation. In strategic corporate conservation planning, operations are a key part of the plan because the corporate lands under consideration for conservation action are generally at the operation's location. A good conservation plan will look at existing operations and consider planned future operations. Existing operations represent the logical place to start with any natural-resources stewardship projects, as (a) efforts may already be occurring at the site, and (b) there are fewer hurdles to implementation of a company's own strategy on company land. Understanding how conservation can mitigate the impacts of planned operations is very important if risk reduction around successful permit acquisition is the business driver.

To carry out an assessment of the operational landscape, the following questions should be considered:

Where are the operations in the target region? What footprints do they have? What neighborhoods are impacted directly or indirectly by operations? How do the operations currently impact the natural environment, both on-site and across the fence line? What future development of existing or new operations is planned? How many of these future plans are public? How important is it that these operations have a positive relationship with neighborhoods?

Much of the external assessment can be done through a desktop exercise collating data owned by the company or in the public domain with the more objective information collected through a survey. The company will know its future development plans and existing operations and infrastructure. Certain departments or units will have mapped their stakeholders and points of political interest. If an NGO partner is helping a company develop such an assessment, they will be expected to sign a nondisclosure agreement, as information about site location and future development plans is sensitive and will not be readily shared.

Once the assessment has been completed, it can be presented to the planning team in the form of a report or a slide deck. The assessment report tees up the process to move on to identifying the ultimate stakeholder and refining the guiding principles.

The Ultimate Stakeholder

A stakeholder is "any group or individual who can affect or is affected by the achievement of the organization's objectives."[7] In business management, stakeholders emerged as a concern in the mid-1980s. Throughout the late twentieth century and into the twenty-first, as corporate citizenship efforts evolved into the mainstream, stakeholder considerations have become integrated into corporate social responsibility, sustainability, and shared value-creation initiatives. Today stakeholder involvement is a necessary part of doing business, and good stakeholder management can increase shareholder value.[8]

Most large companies maintain lists of stakeholders, and many convene representative stakeholders on advisory committees across a variety of functions and locations. Government regulators such as state and federal departments, oversight bodies such as public utility boards, and local community members are all considered key stakeholders. The corporate function within the company will focus on national or regional advocacy groups, elected politicians, and high-profile community institutions. Local operations will maintain lists of local stakeholders who are especially engaged with the site and are important for SLO and community engagement efforts. As anyone who works in an organization knows, internal stakeholders also need to be managed, whether they are an individual's direct-line supervisor, a vice president, or other senior figure in the sustainability or government affairs office—even the CEO and board of directors. Understanding who is an internal stakeholder for a corporate conservation planning effort takes knowledge of both the business driver and the internal political landscape of the company.

For many businesses, the stakeholder landscape is very large, containing many groups and individuals that impact or are impacted by the company. Keeping focused on the business need helps narrow the stakeholder field to those who intersect with the business need and conservation action. In a traditional conservation plan, the ultimate stakeholder is the species, habitat, or ecosystem that will be restored, recovered, or managed. In a corporate conservation plan, the ultimate stakeholder will be defined differently. For a corporate conservation plan developed to address SLO stakeholders from the community, local and regional government agencies, possibly including elected officials, will have to be considered. A corporate conservation plan developed to contribute to a sustainability goal or metric will instead consider internal stakeholders from the sustainability office and any sustainability governance committees, as well as any executive committees overseeing sustainability and, possibly, financial managers in socially responsible investment firms. The survey can identify stakeholders by asking respondents to list their top three stakeholders. The assessment starts to narrow the field. If a large number of stakeholders remain following the landscape assessment, a final exercise should be used to identify the ultimate stakeholders, those who are impacted by or can impact conservation plans and actions. The objective is to narrow the number of stakeholders to one or two ultimate stakeholders around whom the plan will be developed.

THE ULTIMATE STAKEHOLDER EXERCISE

The ultimate stakeholder is the group or individual the planning team would like to see changed by the effort. The ultimate stakeholder can be a specific individual such as the mayor, a group such as a specific NGO partner or a school, or a government agency such as a licensing body or rate commission. The ultimate stakeholder can also be a "bucket" of stakeholders defined by mission, geography, or other shared characteristics such as a collection of diverse community advocates focused on youth employment or environmental justice. The ultimate stakeholder must be identified, because a conservation plan designed for multiple stakeholders may not address the specific business need or drive meaningful change on the ground. Too many stakeholders will also result in a diluted effort and confusing success stories.

In preparation for the exercise, the list of stakeholders obtained through the survey or through the assessment is organized into buckets of similar types of stakeholders. Typical buckets for any corporation's stakeholders will be as follows:

- *Elected officials at a variety of scales.* Local officials will be mostly engaged with issues on a site-specific scale, while state-wide and national elected officials will be concerned with larger, less local concerns.
- *Government agencies charged with promulgating and implementing rules and regulations.* These agencies will be concerned with site-specific and company-wide permits and licenses and might also be concerned with any proposed off-site conservation efforts being considered for publicly owned lands. Government agencies may also have conservation plans or priorities that can be used to provide alignments for corporate conservation.
- *Commissions and boards or other appointed bodies charged with public interest decision-making such as public utility boards, or planning and zoning commissions.* These may be collapsed into

the same bucket as government agencies, but there may be a specific agency with a specific interest in the company or one of its operations.

- *Communities containing the neighbors of existing or future operations.* They may or may not be organized into formal community or neighborhood groups. Their relationship with the company and its operations will vary according to the history of the company and its past, current, and future impacts on the community.

- *Nongovernmental organizations (NGOs) and other formal groups that may be activist or may be focused on conservation or education.* For a company, its NGO relations will span a wide spectrum, from sports teams and museums to environmental-justice advocates and hands-on conservation groups. This group of stakeholders must be critically assessed, as it will initially contain too many NGOs to be meaningful.

- *Internal stakeholders ranging from line managers, the CEO, and others whom the planning team members are concerned about.* Depending on the business driver, an internal stakeholder can be the ultimate stakeholder, but care must be taken not to allow an internal stakeholder to be the ultimate stakeholder for externally focused business needs like SLO or community engagement.

A large corporation will have multiple groups in each bucket, but a small or mid-sized operation may be so local that only one representative of each stakeholder type can be identified.

The first action is to eliminate stakeholders whose relationships with the company are through arm's-length philanthropy or witout a direct connection to conservation, such as a foodbank or local sports team. Internal stakeholders should be assessed critically. There may be a strong sense from team members that the CEO or a supervisor is the ultimate stakeholder, and energetic discussion may be needed in order to give team members a level of comfort in eliminating such stakeholders.

Once the buckets containing noncritical internal stakeholders and external stakeholders with little or no connection to environmental stewardship are eliminated, the remaining stakeholder list must be narrowed further. If the planning team is big enough, create breakout groups charged with considering a list of questions that will help rate the importance of the stakeholder or group of stakeholders to a project's success. The breakout groups rate each stakeholder on a relative scale of importance. Having a team large enough to contain breakout groups is valuable, as it will minimize a single individual's dominance over the conversation and allow for further discussion and refinement once the groups get back together.

The following questions guide the breakout groups as they consider the relative importance of the stakeholder group or particular stakeholder to the conservation initiative. Other questions may be added to assess specific contexts or to probe certain preferred outcomes. If there are, for example, five stakeholders or stakeholder buckets under consideration, the team can rate each one on a scale of 1 to 5—with 1 being the least important to the question and 5 being the most important. The stakeholder with the highest score is considered the ultimate stakeholder for this conservation initiative.

1. Whose support is most critical to the success of this initiative?
2. Whose opposition would derail this initiative?
3. Who possesses the resources to support this initiative?
4. Whose expertise is most important to the success of the project?
5. Whose involvement has the potential to bring the highest visibility to this initiative?
6. Who has the authority to make decisions that could impact the project?
7. Whose mind would you most like to change?

These questions must be framed by the business need, whether in the explicit wording of the questions or as a reminder to the planning team about what the business need is. Once the discussion has reached its conclusion, the breakout groups present and discuss their conclusions. The numerical score for each bucket under consideration provides clarity for the discussion. Some adjustment to final scores may be made if intelligence from one breakout group is given to the entire team. The discussion allows the team as a whole to reach agreement and, in so doing, strengthen support for the conclusions.

Given the interconnected nature of local stakeholders, it is most likely that more than one stakeholder or stakeholder group are considered key to the initiative. The ultimate stakeholder is the group or individual the group would like to see changed by the effort. Secondary stakeholders are those that have the power to support or derail the effort. By identifying the ultimate stakeholder, the group establishes the limits and the possibilities of the effort.

The ultimate stakeholder should be now be checked against the business need. Is there a match? If the business driver for adopting environmental stewardship programs was to use corporate lands for science, technology, engineering, and mathematics (STEM) and environmental education, and the ultimate stakeholder is identified as a the mayor of a local community, a mismatch has occurred. The ultimate stakeholder must align with the business driver. So a better match in this case would be an ultimate stakeholder of local educators engaged with raising STEM proficiency. A business driver to secure social license to operate would be pertinent to a mayor or other local official engaged with the operation. Once the ultimate stakeholder has been identified and is acknowledged to be in agreement with the business driver, the success story element can be tackled.

The Success Story

Most corporate strategic planning efforts include the articulation of a vision—a coherent and powerful statement of what a business should aim to become.[9] The visioning exercise, which is usually completed in the early stages of the strategic planning process, establishes the preferred end state and condition for the business and provides a compass bearing for the entire plan.

With corporate conservation strategic planning, the articulation of a preferred end state is best done through the concept of the success story. By framing the preferred end state as a success story, the planning team avoids confusion and possible conflict with corporate or other business-related visions. In addition, articulating the success story links to the development of metrics and a communication plan which will be essential to the success of the effort.

The vision discussion should include identifying who the story-teller is as much as what the story should be. The success story and storyteller must relate to the ultimate stakeholder and business driver. The storyteller must have credibility with the ultimate stakeholder. If the ultimate stakeholder is the local community and the business need is improved relations between the community and the company, the story should not be told by an academic with a research paper at a scholarly conference. It will be a more powerful story if it is told by a storyteller the community respects, such as a local community group or a trusted politician or journalist, and told through a channel that the community has access to, such as a local newspaper, a government meeting, or a ribbon-cutting event. The success-story exercise brings the elements together.

THE SUCCESS STORY EXERCISE

To get the planning team thinking about the success story, the facilitator of the meeting will present a series of statements. These statements should be written in advance and each associated with a specific storyteller. The pre-written statements should be as specific as possible, with names of real people, events, publications, and media channels. The team members move into breakout groups to prioritize the statements, rewriting and refining as the discussion advances.

Here are some examples of success-story statements:

What: "The company has surprised many of us and has shown itself to be a model corporate environmental steward since its merger in 2017."
Who: local politician
Where: at a council meeting

What: "The company's award for their environment management at their operations is an example to the entire industry."
Who: head of trade association
Where: at an annual meeting

What: "The company's contribution to our capital campaign to build our youth training program made all the difference, and

now we are seeing the results in the education programs we can offer."
Who: NGO executive
Where: in the NGO's annual report

What: "Our research shows that the company's approach to community engagement and environmental and STEM education had a measurable impact on perceptions about the company in the local community."
Who: a researcher
Where: an academic conference

Team members discuss how the statements will serve the ultimate stakeholder. For example, if the ultimate stakeholder is the mayor, then a statement at a trade association meeting will not speak to the mayor, but a statement from a community advocacy group will. If the ultimate stakeholder is the company's competitors, a statement or award from the trade association will be more powerful than a community advocacy group.

In the exercise, the planning team members prioritize the statements for pertinence, with those most pertinent to the success story having the highest priority. The planning team is also asked to suggest a timeline for the statements. In a corporate conservation effort, timing of success is critical. Early wins must be identified and communicated as part of the storytelling. The suggested statements can be ranked according to when they will occur on a near-, medium-, or long-term timeline.

During the exercise, the planning team can take the statements and the makers of the statements apart and can assign different spokespeople, different media, different locations, and different points on the timeline. The team can create their own statements and storytellers.

The result from these discussions may be as follows, where some aspects are changed to make them work better for the team members.

What: "The company has surprised many of us and has shown itself to be a model corporate citizen since its merger in 2017."

Who: ~~local politician~~ *journalist who covers local issues*
Where: ~~at a council meeting~~ *on a local radio show that has a substantial audience in the community*
When: *by end of 2019 and before the next rate-adjustment hearing*

Just like the business need and the ultimate stakeholder, the success story becomes a touchstone as the guiding principles for decisions on projects are determined.

The Guiding Principles

Once the ultimate stakeholder and the success story have been agreed upon, a set of guiding principles should be adopted to structure decision-making for environmental-stewardship projects. The guiding principles take all the elements—the survey, the assessment, the ultimate stakeholder, and the success story—into consideration in order to help determine the favorability and feasibility of certain project types.

The guiding principles are created from a series of decisions developed according to the direct and indirect footprint of the company, its customer and stakeholder catchment areas, the business driver, the ultimate stakeholder, and the success story.

The Decisions

1. On whose lands should the stewardship projects be implemented? The options under consideration can be the lands owned by the company, neighboring businesses, the community, or the government.

   This question looks at feasibility and visibility. The company will have more control over environmental stewardship efforts on its own lands. It will be able to direct its own resources, develop its own timeline, and encounter less bureaucracy than similar efforts on publicly owned lands. While easier to implement, an environmental stewardship project on company lands may lack visibility and community access compared to a project implemented on public lands with open access.

2. Should environmental stewardship projects be distributed
    equally across the entire footprint of the company? Should
    every operation be compelled to implement a project? Should
    every adjacent community be engaged?

    The suitability for all corporate locations to engage in
    stewardship activities differs according to the footprint of the
    site, the operational restrictions, existing natural resources,
    and the size and proximity of the community. The needs and
    opportunities in host communities will also be different. A cor-
    porate headquarters may be located in an anonymous office
    tower in an urban setting with no community engagement or
    conservation potential at all, while a manufacturing facility
    or mine will likely be well known in its community and have
    a large footprint on which to carry out conservation action.
    The decision to include all areas or instead to pick those
    with the most need or opportunity will relate to the ultimate
    stakeholder and the success story.

3. At what stage are others—employees or community mem-
    bers—engaged? Should they be engaged in the planning pro-
    cess or for implementation only? What about maintenance
    and monitoring? Will the projects require different stake-
    holder engagement at different points in time? Will the projects
    require external consultants at any stage?

    The early involvement of others may be essential to pro-
    ject success, or it may be an obstacle to initial progress. The
    location of project implementation will help answer this ques-
    tion, as implementation on company lands may curtail or re-
    strict access. If the company wants to fully engage community
    members, they must make their involvement meaningful
    beyond the transmission of information.

4. If students are engaged, what grade and what type of engage-
    ment is appropriate? What educational alignments should be
    sought? What are the other considerations for student en-
    gagement?

    Leveraging corporate lands and environmental stewardship
    programs for education purposes is one of the sixteen business
    drivers for corporate conservation. If the initiative is being
    driven by education, then the involvement of students is a

Figure 4-1: Planting a pollinator garden at FCA headquarters in Auburn Hills, Michigan. Engaging employees or community members is a decision to be made during the planning phase. (Used with FCA permission.)

given. If the initiative is being driven by another business reason, the involvement of students becomes a question to consider for the guiding principles. Regardless of whether education is central or peripheral, a number of questions must be answered for the guiding principles.

The grade level for participation can be addressed based on the type of stewardship project that is being considered, the potential for alignments with official curricula, and the ease with which students can travel to the projects. If education will be a component of the effort, student involvement should be consistent across projects to allow education to be reported under a single metric and success story. The timing of student engagement is important in order to align with academic schedules or engage with summer camps. Transportation needs are always a challenge and must be considered and, if possible, funded. Aligning with a state's standard curriculum, federal educational guidelines, a company's own internal STEM programming, or other education policies and initiatives will strengthen the outcomes.

Other considerations will relate to company operations. Companies with security restrictions or those that have remote locations will be unlikely to welcome students easily. Companies engaged with site remediation may be unable to welcome students in the early years of the cleanup but may open their doors to students participating in monitoring activities following the project. (Education opportunities are fully explored in chapter 7 of this book.)

5. What local or regional conservation plans should be aligned with the initiative?

   Today almost every inch of the natural and built world is governed by an environmental plan of some sort, whether a hyper-local sub-watershed plan or a national environmental priorities plan. These plans are owned by different entities: governments, NGOs, and others. By aligning stewardship efforts with an existing plan, a company contributes to the plan's objectives, secures the goodwill of the plan's owners, and also saves time and effort by not developing its own environmental objectives. If a specific environmental plan has the support of the ultimate stakeholder, the company may view that plan as a priority. (For more on the aligning with existing environmental plans, see chapter 6.)

These questions will provide the planning team with a set of guiding principles that it can use to determine where, how, and what projects will contribute most to a compelling success story for the ultimate stakeholder and for meeting the business need. The guiding principles can be a statement like *The best stewardship projects are those that are done on company lands, include all landholdings except for dealerships, align with State Wildlife Action Plans in all the states where we operate, offer the opportunity for high-quality education programs for third-grade students from nearby schools, and are designed and implemented by employees.* The guiding principles can also be a priority list or a decision tree that does not exclude any option but clearly shows which options are preferred. Such a decision tree can also guide resource allocation for implementation by assigning more resources to those projects that will best satisfy the business need.

Risk Assessment

As the corporate conservation planning effort moves toward implementation, an assessment of risk will be carried out. This assessment can be formal and extensive or merely an acknowledgment of possible areas of caution for the future.

For many companies, risk assessment of new or ongoing endeavors is routine. For the purpose of conservation planning, risk assessment is essential for two reasons. First, it allows participants to understand the risks of and to specific conservation stewardship objectives. Second, risk assessment is essential if the participants are to plan and discuss how and whether to mitigate or avoid the risk. The planning team should be able to identify a wide range of risks and understand the probability of a given risk occurring and the severity of its impact on the effort under way.

In a discussion about risk, a three-by-three matrix is a good visualization tool that focuses discussion in the northeast section of the matrix. The northeast section lists the risks that have the highest probability of occurring and whose impact will be the most severe.

To carry out a risk assessment, the team generates a list of risk statements and places them on the matrix. The goal of the exercise is to create a full picture of possible risks, identify the risks that need careful consideration. A secondary outcome will be to identify risks that may seem important but that, once placed on the matrix, have a low probability of occurring and a low impact on the effort.

Planning teams are never short of risk statements. In an exercise with an energy company in 2017, over 100 risk statements were developed in under five minutes. The following risks may be discussed:

- A utility company faces a likely significant storm event and the impact could be material on non-core business initiatives like the stewardship plan if resources are diverted to maintain systems or rebuild following a storm.
- When the business need is focused on government relations, an election is a risk. It is certain to happen and its impact will be unknowable. An election is more likely to be immaterial

Table 4-3: A Risk Assessment Matrix

Severity of Impact →

	Immaterial	Material	Major
Certain			
Likely			
Remote			

Probability ↑

for natural-resources stewardship efforts a local operation, as regulatory change in this arena is slow.

- For a company seeking to connect its stewardship efforts to education in the local school district, the resources of the district, including its ability to bus students and provide staff off-site, is a risk with a high probability of occurrence. The impact could be material if no students can participate in the planned program.
- Ongoing resources to support the implementation of the conservation plan are identified as a risk area for any company whose budgets ebb and flow according to revenue and profitability and whose spending priorities focus on essentials first. This risk is especially acute at operations with low profit margins.

Figure 4-2 : An insect hotel is an example of a low-risk project that can be done at all corporate sites, regardless of size. It can also connect to community engagement and education efforts. (Photo by author.)

Some risks like school resources can be mitigated, others like weather events cannot be mitigated but can be anticipated and planned for. Completing the risk assessment allows the team to understand the aspects of the conservation plan that present the most risk and to plan accordingly. It also allows the team to have ready answers for the 'What if?' questions they will face as the plan moves toward implementation.

A risk of any planning effort in any organization is the distance between the planners, the decision makers, and the implementers. Socialization is a very important element of corporate conservation strategic planning due to the voluntary nature of the activities under consideration and the absence of a bottom-line driver.

Socialization

In businesses around the world, office shelves are laden with reports and strategic plans, the result of efforts that were launched with fanfare and energy but then faltered in the face of corporate inertia. While the terms *disruption* and *agile* tend to be used to describe business culture in articles filled with laudatory profiles of "change agents" and "innovators," the reality at most companies is that inertia is the most powerful force. Many innovations are easily derailed by inertia or the many other organizational forces that array against change. Weak alignment between employees and management, a corporate culture that frowns on risk of failure, lack of accountability, and failure to communicate are all factors that create resistance to change.[10] When developing the corporate conservation strategy, the planning team should consider all the internal forces that can stop the plan from moving toward implementation.

Communication is critical to change whether incremental or transformational. Clear and frequent communications will reduce the chances of the strategic conservation plan failing to launch. Socialization as a communication tactic is essential for continued forward motion.

When considering a socialization plan, it is important to consider the audience for such a plan. Is socialization necessary? It is an element in the process but may not be required. If socialization is required, though, does it go up the chain to the corporate team, out along the management layer, or deep into operations? A smart socialization plan will recognize the importance of all avenues as possible disablers of progress. All employees, whether in leadership or operations, juggle many priorities and initiatives and can easily lose sight of initiatives they are not fully engaged with. Socialization helps to maintain awareness of the effort across the company. In addition, the resources needed for implementation can be secured through socialization by increasing the understanding of planning and acknowledging budgeting cycles. Socialization decreases the time between plan adoption and implementation, which increases the chances for sustainable conservation.

The elements of a good socialization plan that can be developed by the planning team are as follows:

- A one-page document outlining the effort, which contains a short summary of the business driver behind the plan, the time line, and a short description of the process and the hoped-for product. This document should be designed to allow those who may be involved in the implementation but not the planning to understand what efforts are under way and why they are happening.

- A regular agenda item at recurring meetings at all appropriate levels of the company. The planning leaders report on the effort as part of their regular check-ins with managers, but all those involved in the effort should be encouraged to report at their respective team meetings.
- Conversations with colleagues should be encouraged to allow for informal socialization that will set a tone of broad ownership when the plan is communicated, and to set an expectation of involvement. One of the obstacles toward plan implementation, regardless of the subject, is a sense that it is "owned" by others. By talking about the plan and using the language of inclusion, the barrier of perceived ownership can be removed or reduced.

Every meeting of the planning team should include an update about socialization in which team members share experiences and agree on next steps. Socialization should be the responsibility of all the members of the planning team.

Metric Development

Biodiversity metrics are the holy grail of the conservation community—much discussed and sought after but never actually found. A strategic corporate conservation plan might contain biodiversity metrics, but it is more likely to contain metrics that are easier to gather and provide value to the company's reporting and disclosure efforts. (The difficulty of biodiversity metrics and some workable alternatives are discussed in greater detail in chapter 6.)

During the conservation planning phase, the metrics and indicators must be agreed upon. Useful indicators could be acres restored or planted to achieve a specified outcome, employee hours contributed to the effort, school groups engaging with the project, and the number of community members active in management or monitoring. Biodiversity-focused metrics can be developed to record success rates of plantings, presence of target species, use of habitat, etc. To be useful to the business need, the metrics must flow easily through the plan to the ultimate stakeholder and integrate seamlessly with the success story.

The guiding principles will dictate the metrics. For most conservation activities, acres restored or managed are an obvious starting point, but in an urban setting areas may not be the best metric, as acreage will never be significant, but impacts may be seen in other aspects such as reconnecting ecological communities, engaging human communities, providing resources to underserved communities, or developing educational pipelines for local schools and other education efforts.

Since environmental stewardship or conservation work is not a core business activity, the metrics chosen must be accessible and affordable. Data must be simple to collect and not require expensive, expert, and technical approaches. Highly technical metrics may be appealing to conservation practitioners but will have little business value in the long run, as their collection will wane once initial excitement in the project fades and the cost of the collection adds risk to the project. Metrics must be able to withstand changes in team members and resources. To be useful, metrics must also be deployable for a number of other reporting purposes.

The Strategic Corporate Conservation Plan

At the end of the planning effort, the team should know

- *The Business Driver*—what business challenge or opportunity is being addressed with natural-resources efforts.
- *The Ultimate Stakeholder*—who has the environmental stewardship strategy been developed for.
- *The Success Story*—the vision for the plan, the changes that the environmental-stewardship plan will make for the company and the community.
- *The Guiding Principles*—a hierarchy of decision-making that will guide project choice and implementation designed to contribute to the success story.
- *The Risks*—the threats to successful implementation of the environmental-stewardship plan.

- *The Metrics*—accessible and affordable metrics that will inform the success story and be useful for a variety of reporting efforts.

A Note on Conservation Projects and Implementation

This planning process is designed to embrace all possible conservation efforts to meet a corporate objective. It creates a structured decision process to allow conservation projects from small DIY pollinator gardens to multimillion-dollar site-reclamation efforts to contribute to corporate business needs and be supported as such. Discussion on specific projects will be taken at the site after the plan is adopted following the guiding principles.

At some stage during the planning exercise, the tactically inclined will want to promote their pet project and discuss what implementation will look like. As existing efforts are shared and the business rationale is clarified, inspiration will strike and a flood of project ideas will flow. Discussion of specific projects will start to bubble up into the conversation, and while this discussion is important and will help to anchor the planning in reality, specific projects should not dominate the planning process. It is important that the final strategy drives the project choice.

When the discussion begins to move toward implementation, the planning team can begin to "park" a separate list of sample projects that may or may not fit the guiding principles. At the appropriate time the sample project list can be assessed against the principles. The parked sample project list will be the starting point for moving the plan toward implementation. At the operational level where implementation will occur, a different planning team can repeat some of the elements of this process in order to assess sample projects against the business need and the guiding principles and to ground-truth the result against the realities, especially the risk assessment related to that location. (Site considerations are discussed in more detail in chapter 5.)

A Note on Terminology

The words we use are very important. Recently, an international conservation group was developing an approach to biodiversity metrics that would engage business in better managing its risk and impacts. The group considered calling it a BMP—short for "biodiversity management protocol." However, the business world and indeed the conservation community have long used the term *BMP* in a significantly different manner to describe a best-management practice. By advancing the same name for a completely different effort, the conservation group could have created an unnecessary obstacle to adoption.

Companies, like all organizations, have their own internal jargon. Understanding this jargon and how it is used is important. The term *environment* may be used specifically for air and water, so *natural environment* may be needed in the conservation context. *Stewardship* may be confined to waste-management efforts, in which case it cannot be deployed for conservation without clarification. Risk assessments in some companies may use the terms *probability* and *impact*, but they may also use *likelihood* and *consequences*. Companies adopt specific terms like *SHE* for safety, health, and the environment or *HSE* for health, safety, and the environment. They may call remediation sites *legacy sites* or *liability sites*. They may use the term *operations* for a subset of activities or use it as a catch-all for non-corporate-headquarters locations.

It is important to avoid confusion of terminology. Doing so will reduce the time needed to explain meaning and context. Wherever possible, learn the terminology used by different companies as a way to minimize confusion. Removing confusing nomenclature and ensuring that usage is in line with the language of operations can be a very important outcome of socialization and an indication of respect for the corporate culture.

Understanding the difference between traditional conservation planning and corporate conservation planning means understanding new jargon, appreciating business planning, and framing the plan around the business, not the biodiversity outcomes. The next chapter will delve more deeply into the corporate psyche and how implementing conservation on a corporate site differs from activities on lands whose primary purpose is for natural-resources management.

05 OBSTACLES AND HOW TO OVERCOME THEM

—

A car is thirty thousand parts you're putting together.

—MARY BARRA, CEO GENERAL MOTORS

In 2016, I spoke at the Ontario Biodiversity Summit about working with the private sector on natural-resources projects on corporate lands. At the beginning of my presentation, I said that I was not going to talk about how to get money from a corporation but instead how to move a company toward strategic and integrated implementation of natural-resources stewardship programs. I spoke for forty-five minutes about understanding a company's need, acknowledging operational restrictions, working with operational cycles, and not treating the company as a private bank. I wrapped up my presentation and invited questions from the floor. The very first questioner asked, "If you want to get money from a corporation, where should you start?"

We need a paradigm shift—we are habituated to think about a corporation as having infinite financial resources. It's not surprising to think this way. Conservation nongovernmental organizations (NGOs) are in a constant struggle for funding so the idea of "working" with a company can quickly morph into the idea of receiving unrestricted funding. But this approach to the NGO–corporate relationship is one of the biggest hurdles to engaging companies in a meaningful and long-term relationship.

While this traditional NGO view of business creates unnecessary barriers to action because of unrealistic expectations, the structures and dynamics of the corporate world itself are enough to delay, derail, or diminish implementation of a carefully developed strategic conservation plan. Internal politics, inertia, disruption, operational differences, and restrictions are all factors that will impede implementation. Careful planning and communication from both parties can overcome some of these factors, mitigate others, and in the cases of the most serious corporate disruptions such as mergers, create a safe holding place until forward motion is once again possible. This chapter will outline the common challenges and obstacles and show how structure, planning, and creative approaches can overcome them.

The Common Challenges

One of the first challenges to working with the corporate world emerges far from the site of conservation implementation. Driven by market forces and global business trends, the corporate world is in a constant state of change.

CORPORATE DISRUPTION

A casual reader of business and management literature can easily come to believe that companies are exemplars of efficiency rolling forward smoothly on wheels oiled by management methodologies and processes such as Kaizen, Lean, and Six Sigma. The reality is a lot messier. Management trends wax and wane, and leaders seem— to employees and middle management, at least—to change directions continually. The corporate world is in a constant state of flux. Mergers, acquisitions, spin-offs, divestitures, and bankruptcies are the norm, and for a variety of reasons. Twenty-eighteen was a record-breaking year for corporate consolidations.[1] Industries constantly downsize or retool in reaction to markets, tariffs, and trade wars. Oil, energy, and other kinds of companies start, stop, and continue their transformations toward a carbon-neutral economy. In addition, *innovation* and *disruption* remain buzzwords that constantly drive some companies to seek to accelerate the already fast pace of corporate change.

For those working at the intersection of business and nature, it is a given that corporate change will happen and that this will be a barrier to either the completion or implementation of the strategic corporate conservation plan. At best, the process will be delayed. In the worst cases it will be derailed completely. Knowing that change will happen is important in order to acknowledge and plan for it right from the beginning. The effects of any change on the conservation plan can be mitigated by setting up a relationship that allows an NGO partner to remain a thoughtful and supportive presence throughout the disruption. Whether the disruption is occurring at the corporate level due to a merger, acquisition, or divestiture, or at the operations level because of weather events, accidents, or workforce changes, displays of understanding and offers of support will be remembered, and gentle persistence will pay off.

For both corporate-level and operational disruption, it is important to recognize the scope of the disruption. Some issues, such as an acquisition, may impact the entire company, while others, such as a weather event or accident, may only impact operations at a single location. Some disruptions may last a number of years, such as a merger that must be approved by multiple jurisdictions, or they may last a number of months, such as a budget-planning cycle when all expenditure is put on hold. The outcome of corporate disruption will differ too. With mergers and divestitures, an operation may be required to integrate into a new company with a new structure and culture. Staff changes, including lay-offs, will occur during any such disruption and for a time following. Resources will remain limited during and following any disruptive period while budgets for nonessential expenditures are cut or frozen.

When building materials companies Lafarge and Holcim announced their merger in early 2014, all nonessential operations were put on hold. At the time, both companies were developing biodiversity frameworks for no net loss / net positive impact. Each company had taken a different route in developing these frameworks. Lafarge—with Jim Rushworth, the former VP of environment and public affairs, helming the effort—was looking at developing simple site-based tools to screen sites for biodiversity sensitivity, easily measure biodiversity value, and report back gains or losses of biodiversity value across the life cycle of the site. The Lafarge approach was to provide their worksites with such tools that were sensitive to the context of specific sites (quarries, cement factories, ready-mix terminals, etc.). The entire program had taken years to develop, with the support of stakeholder input, internal communications strategies, and multilevel engagements across the company. The merger put a stop to the entire effort and as the two companies, now called LafargeHolcim, moved through the merger process—divesting locations and markets according to regulatory need, and reducing employee numbers according to budgetary need—biodiversity strategies were forgotten. The merger took over a year to complete, and the biodiversity efforts have yet to be resurrected, as new teams in the new company are slow to recognize the value.

Depending on the scale of the disruption, patience is the watchword. All employees will be focused on surviving the disruption, and distractions will not be welcome. On the other hand, any offer of help will be very welcome, whether it be to assume management of a specific project, strengthen an existing partnership, or hold off on earlier planned effort. For an NGO partner, periodic check-ins with the company or site as the disruption progresses should be brief and focused on the plan; these check-ins should not be sources of added stress.

When such disruptions derail conservation planning and implementation, existing and planned ecological and natural-resources projects can be positioned to be viable and affordable option for post-disruption activities. In fact, a recently merged company developing, adopting, or implementing a strategic conservation plan can sometimes unite formerly disparate operations under a shared conservation goal. For a specific operation, ecological approaches may mitigate damages from weather events or other disruptive site-specific incidents. Conservation action can address many post-disruption business needs.

While corporate disruption waxes and wanes, operational differences and regulatory restrictions at sites are a constant that a good partner will need to be aware of, to respect, and perhaps, with ingenuity, to overcome.

OPERATIONAL DIFFERENCES

The best strategic corporate conservation plans have local relevance and global value. The planning process ensures that the business driver, the ultimate stakeholder, the success story, and the guiding principles are aligned. Implementation must now align with operational needs. Across the corporate landscape, every operation is different. Corporate sites are located in different communities. They work within different regulatory environments. They have different resources in terms of land, employees, and budgets. They have different operating margins. All will have different reasons for participating in the corporate conservation plan—or not. Understanding operational differences and restrictions will enhance the plan's acceptance at the site level. The distance between corporate planning and operations can sometimes seem vast, and all too often frontline employees feel invisible. An employee whose job involves safety, maintenance, or other routine operations may seem like a perfect candidate to absorb additional responsibilities for conservation projects, but that person may already be overwhelmed with responsibilities. A smart approach is to illustrate knowledge of how any additional duties will impact employees.

When Jim Rushworth was rolling out the biodiversity plan to the Lafarge sites, he knew that the same approach and the same message would not work at an aggregates quarry where land is plentiful and margins are low, and a cement plant where land is scarce but margins are higher, or a ready-mix terminal where available land is almost nonexistent for conservation work. Jim remarked, "We had different approaches for each type [of operation], but the goals were still the same." Having an approach tailored to the specifics of the operation is necessary if the same goals are to be met.

It's also very important when working with any corporate operation to acknowledge that ecological stewardship projects will never be a priority. Regardless of whether it's a manufacturing facility with landscaped lawns, a utility right-of-way across protected public lands, a nuclear power plant with large acreage of forested buffer lands, an open landfill, an actively operated quarry or mine, or a closed remediation site, none of these locations will prioritize conservation. Each location has a primary operational objective, and for conservation projects to be implemented successfully, it is critical that these operational objectives be understood and honored. Operational objectives may place limits on the types of activities that can be implemented due to regulations, restricted access, or constraints on land management.

REGULATORY CONSTRAINTS

Different industrial operations will have different regulations governing what can and cannot be done on-site. Understanding these restrictions is a key to success. Seeking to go against site-based regulations will delay and eventually derail implementation.

Regulations for revegetating closed landfills generally prohibit planting trees and shrubs and other deep-rooted species due to a fear that roots could weaken the cap, causing soil erosion and leaching. Recent research has shown that this fear is not well founded.[2] But, given that regulating agencies are slow to change, these regulations will likely stand for some time. Woody vegetation on utility rights-of-way is likewise prohibited, as a fire-prevention measure to protect overhead lines or buried pipes. Restoration or ecological management projects on such lands will more than likely focus on grasslands or meadows. Likewise, any remediation site with pump-and-treat systems to clean groundwater, or capped areas to protect against leaching, will have restrictions on the ecological activities allowed.

In another example, vegetation management at an automotive test track or proving ground may not be regulated by a government agency, but ecological enhancement projects that create habitat for large animals will not be allowed, as they would place test drivers at unnecessary risk. Natural-resources management projects on these lands can focus on habitat and species that present a low or no risk to operations.

Efforts to control deer or other overabundant species through hunting may be impossible on the many corporate sites where weapons are strictly prohibited. Projects that require citizen-science operations or monitoring using cameras will be unwelcome at research and development facilities, or inside the fence at nuclear facilities. Food- and beverage-processing sites may prohibit projects that encourage bees.

However, it may be very worthwhile for ecological or strategic reasons to push the boundaries of regulations. In the case of Woodlawn, the site that Bridgestone worked to remediate, the effort to change the record of decision from a traditional cap-and-treat remedy to a less intrusive ecological approach took many years of meetings with the Environmental Protection Agency (EPA) and stakeholders. It took the determination of the partners to keep the conversation moving toward the right decision—one that is now considered a success for both the company and the community. There are many reasons why a site may not want to challenge or change the regulations governing lands management. They may not have the resources to engage with the regulating entities on a site-by-site basis. They may feel that a challenge, even if for a conservation reason, will be bad PR, or they may not have the appetite for an engagement with a regulator that could last a long time. When regulated activity is expected to stand, it is wise to start where the site is. This will hasten implementation and will increase chances of success and long-term support.

But there are a number of compelling reasons to push the boundaries of regulations. In the case of Bridgestone and Woodlawn, the reason was simple: there was an opportunity to return the site to the community as an asset, which would not have happened under the original proposed remedy. Other reasons may be determined by location, if, for example, the site overlaps with habitat of rare or imperiled species, or if local conservation action is being undertaken toward a specific objective that might be met more easily with the inclusion of the site in the overall project. In all of these cases, patience will be required to address regulatory restrictions.

RESOURCE PROS AND CONS

The availability of resources is another aspect of working on a corporate location that will impact action for the project. This can be both a constraint and an enabler for action.

The great thing about mines, quarries, and landfills is that heavy machinery is already on-site and can be deployed to move earth as needed to implement conservation projects. The same cannot be said for a corporate campus, server farm, or distribution facility. Utility rights-of-way will have a vegetation-management budget and a schedule for maintenance, while a manufacturing plant may only have a landscaping budget paying for seasonal plantings every quarter. Knowing about resources and budgets is very important for site-based efforts.

Starting conservation programs with the tools and equipment that are easily available will increase the chances that first and future projects will be successful and increase the likelihood that a business case can be made for larger efforts requiring larger budgets. During a visit to Ford Motor Company, I was told a story about Henry Ford that was supposed to illustrate Ford's early adherence to sustainability principles (or his thriftiness): he was rumored to have directed his suppliers to build packing crates to his specifications so that the boards in the crates could be reused as floorboards in the Model T. It's a lovely story but, according to a Ford Motor Company historian, there is no documented proof that it is true.[3] But today, at General Motors' Warren Tech Center, the company has indeed repurposed packing crates into mobile gardens that are planted with native species and then mounted on wheels so that they can be moved around the site as needed to create barriers for traffic or to cordon off areas for employee or community use. This implementation was a smart use of existing materials for a highly visible and popular nature-focused purpose. At GM headquarters in the Renaissance Center in downtown Detroit, the same packing cases are also used as mobile planters to create a barrier to protect the rooftop garden that supplies restaurants in the center with local produce.

Reusing existing materials and tapping into existing resources will get a project started more easily than having to budget for or requisition new resources. Existing resources may be a determining point of where to start first.

Moving to Implementation

Which operation gets to go first? Which site can easily implement a corporate conservation strategic plan? How are sites chosen and how are later sites included in the effort? Where a company starts and how it onboards a site, location, or operation is a determinant of success. When a strategic conservation plan is introduced, two different responses will emanate from the sites. If a strong, structured communication effort is undertaken, one that ties the message to operations and provides incentives for implementation, a big positive response will result. Many locations will become excited to start and implement projects. But with a weak communication effort that starts with a corporate dictate that ignores existing conditions and ongoing efforts, there will be a collective shrug as operations react to yet another pronouncement from head office. While, in the strong-communications scenario, the first response may be great, the risk of "fast fade" is nevertheless high, as other responsibilities take priority. And in the weak-communications scenario where a corporate dictate is met with indifference or hostility, further effort will be needed to rebrand the plan and relaunch the initiative.

In the case of the enthusiastic response, care must be taken to back up the communication with resources, or else momentum will be lost and locations where conservation work is done will soon run out of steam. Projects started with great enthusiasm will falter if not fully supported. The apathetic response will, without intervention, lead to no action taken on the ground, and the conservation strategy becomes yet another shelved plan. A middle ground exists. The middle ground is found in a more structured way to capture the excitement of a well-communicated conservation goal or overcome the inertia at operations that are underwhelmed by the plan. It includes a pathway to sustainable onboarding of new projects in the launch communications.

CRH Americas is a large building materials company that supports conservation efforts across a wide variety of its quarries and other locations (such as the Marcus Autism center profiled in chapter 2). CRH has been very successful at creating an onboarding process that measures the readiness of a site to engage in conservation activities. No location can enroll in the formal program unless the conservation activity has been in place for at least two years, has clear conservation and education objectives, and has secured support from a member of the executive team. In this way, CRH sees little delinquency in its conservation projects. It creates clear communications around each new project and adds the effort to its corporate conservation scorecard. Requiring executive interest and support adds an extra lever for maintaining longevity, as no site wants to disappoint the boss.

A corporate conservation strategy will only be as good as what happens at each site. By taking the time to gather an understanding

Figure 5-1: The nature trail at the Marcus Autism Center in Atlanta, Georgia. (Used with the permission of CRH Americas.)

of the site with its operational restrictions and opportunities, as well as a recognition of the possible conservation *and community context*, employees will have better buy-in and the corporate plan will have ownership at the local level. For conservation practitioners more used to working on protected lands, a mental pivot needs to be made, and sometimes expectations should be lowered at the beginning. Investing the time to make a strong partnership is worth it, though. Partnerships such as that of CEMEX, the construction materials company, and Birdlife International, which helped mainstream biodiversity considerations into quarry locations in Important Bird Areas (IBAs) across South and Central America, create conservation transformation that has regional meaning as well as corporate value.

GETTING STARTED AT THE SITE

Sue Kelsey understood the distance between a conservation strategy developed at the corporate headquarters and implementation at a specific facility. She saw the missteps and false starts at the beginning of General Motors' engagement with biodiversity and was responsible for building a bridge between lofty corporate plans and practical local implementation. She did this through the development of an onboarding process for sites and by providing tool kits that contained elements common to most locations as well as specific information that acknowledged the unique cultural, ecological, and industrial aspects of each place.

There are many approaches for the onboarding process, but the ones that work best start with a team and a leader and include processes for action that may include budget codes for timesheet reporting, purchase orders for materials, and details on deliverables and reporting requirements. Good processes start where the site is and then build from there, recognizing the value of existing work and rolling it into the conservation program.

Effective processes differ across companies, but they will all follow an approach similar to the one outlined below:

- Create a structure:
  - Appoint a strong leader.
  - Convene a team.
  - Create consistent support materials.
- Start where you are:
  - Acknowledge operational restrictions.
  - Understand resource constraints.
  - Leverage existing activities.
- Maintain Momentum:
  - Communicate internally.
  - Create competition.
  - Celebrate success.

Create a Structure

When Jim Rushworth assumed responsibility over the biodiversity program at Lafarge, he had a lot of operational experience in the industry but little familiarity with biodiversity. He approached the development of Lafarge's biodiversity program as an engineer, breaking the program into its component parts and addressing each part separately. Sue Kelsey took the same approach at General Motors, imposing structure on a sprawling global program to better manage, maintain, and measure it. Tim Bent at Bridgestone quickly developed a format to secure middle-management support by convening the presidents of the operating divisions into an executive environmental committee, allowing the upper-tier management to see the benefits of conservation action. These successful conservation program were rolled out and implemented in a highly structured way, due in part to the leadership of the individuals and in part to the need for structure in a very large company.

It's important to note that not every successful conservation program needs to start as a highly structured process. Many, especially in smaller operations, start as ad hoc implementation that may be wrapped into a structured process once the value of the program to meet a business need is recognized. A small company with one or a few locations may decide that a more organic approach works fine in the absence of dedicated resources. A company with a culture of local ownership may also choose to advance a more organic approach.

Appoint a Team with a Leader Who Has Resources and Interest

Regardless of how structured the process is, it remains important to appoint someone on-site who has resources and social capital, and who can enable or lead the project. Most operations have EHS managers, community relations managers, and PR people, as well as an overall plant manager responsible for the day-to-day running of the plant. One of these individuals will be a good person to appoint as leader of the team. The leader should reflect the strategic conservation plan's objective. If the objective is outward-facing, the community-outreach staffer would be an obvious choice, whereas if it is focused on improving environmental outcomes at the plant and on its lands, the EHS manager will be the most effective leader. Jim Rushworth considers these people, whom he calls "champions," essential for success. Recalling his early days of developing and rolling out the initiative, Jim says, "One of the key things that I did learn from a very early stage and very quickly, is the importance of having a champion or somebody ideally on every site who has a passion for biodiversity or nature." By encouraging the champions to share success stories with each other, Jim was able to grow the programs at the sites and jump-start implementation using a regional champion who brought excitement and inspiration to the effort.

Engage as Many People as Possible

Time and again, great conservation programs have stalled because the person who was the champion was the only person involved. When only one person is involved, retirement or reassignment will cause the conservation program to falter and fail. Unfortunately, it is a very common occurrence in corporate conservation projects that passionate individuals dedicate hours to specific conservation projects but no time obtaining buy-in from others to secure the future of the program.

Successful programs, the ones that achieve their goals and contribute to corporate conservation plans, the ones that grow year after year and last for a long time, are overseen by a team. These teams—wildlife teams, restoration teams, green teams, garden teams—can be effective in large landscapes and at smaller sites. They all perform the same function providing a framework for action. The members see their role as facilitating implementation toward the corporate success story while engaging a broad range of employees and the local community. In contrast, conservation efforts led by individuals tend to be exclusive, reflecting that individual's personal preferences while disregarding the larger corporate need or relevance to a larger community.

It makes sense to populate the team, if possible, with individuals who were also on the strategic planning team. By keeping a connection to the planning team, the connection to the business need, success story, and ultimate stakeholder will remain strong. Effective internal communications plans should seek to strengthen that connection if it is not possible to populate the implementation team with individuals from the planning team.

As global biodiversity program manager at General Motors, Sue Kelsey traveled the world implementing biodiversity programs at GM manufacturing facilities from Detroit to South Africa and Brazil. Just as each country across the world has its own culture, each corporate location has its own ethos and its own set of challenges and opportunities. But despite these differences, Sue identified a common theme across every facility: people wanted to get engaged, but they needed a nudge or positive encouragement to do so.

At every location she visited, Sue would talk to the plant manager and others and learn who on-site was interested in nature, education, or community outreach. She would ask who reported wildlife sightings, who stayed outdoors a lot, and who had connections into the community for education initiatives. Because Sue had the power of "corporate" behind her (as well as her formidable personality), she could appoint these individuals as members of the wildlife team and give them responsibility for certain aspects of the program. She knew they would take such responsibilities seriously, thanks to the individual interest she had expressed in them and what they had already shown through their actions. As Sue says, "You need to invite people in to participate and to let them bring in their excitement about a particular aspect."

Not everyone has the power to appoint a team, but Sue's understanding that there are always individuals on-site who have an interest in nature or biodiversity was key to her being able to develop multifaceted and sustainable teams. Her willingness to identify and draft people onto the teams allowed GM to build a strong foundation for its conservation programs. Sue's successful approach to team building started with identifying where passion for conservation already existed and then build on this passion by assigning specific responsibilities to team members, whether for species monitoring or program design. Her understanding that people really want to be involved and only needed to be asked, encouraged, or pushed led to the creation of many strong teams at GM locations across the world.

Develop Support Materials

Whether working with multinationals like GM or with local and regional businesses, a structured process and consistent approach will enhance the chances of success by removing guesswork and increasing transparency for the entire effort.

Companies love tool kits and guidance documents. They are a way to enforce consistent approaches across a range of locations and operations. When working with a company across different locations in different countries and on different landholdings, a guidance-type document will streamline the onboarding process and create consistency while also recognizing the unique situation at each site. A consistent approach will make it easier to connect each project into the larger corporate success story in a way that realizes the value of the effort and provides encouragement to continue the effort and improve it with better management or a larger conservation footprint.

A good outline for a biodiversity guidance document is as follows:

- A statement about the importance of taking action for biodiversity and the role that a corporate landholding can play. This introduction can also state the corporate conservation strategy and provide guidance for metrics and monitoring in order to ensure that the project can be reported on in such a way that it will satisfy corporate reporting needs. The introduction will be the same in every document provided to every site.

- Site-specific information follows, helping the site understand its conservation context. Many site managers may not know that their location is under an important flyway or is proximate to critical habitat for migrating species. The conservation context can also highlight regional environmental issues such as stormwater control or invasive-species management. The guidance will highlight the environmental concerns that conservation programs at the site can address or conservation objectives that the site can contribute to.

- Existing conservation policies and plans will complete the conservation context by highlighting the pertinent conservation plans that exist for the region. In the United States, most locations can refer to their state's Wildlife Action Plan in order to understand priority species, habitats, and conservation actions for the location. In Europe, the Natura 2000 program can align a site's efforts with local priorities. All locations exist in watersheds that are managed under watershed plans or even sub-watershed plans. These may be focused purely on water quality, but the best ones encompass biodiversity. A plethora of plans will be available for most sites and the guidance can show which plans are most useful.

- Opportunities for conservation projects at the site should be highlighted. Start by acknowledging the efforts already underway on-site and then describe opportunities for expansion or addition to existing efforts. This section should illustrate how existing efforts align the corporate goals with external conservation plans and priorities. It will show how any recommendations for new activities will build on (and not replace) existing activities. The section should illustrate an understanding of the operational constraints of the site. The opportunities should also reflect any interests already collected from the wildlife team, since it's essential that the team feels heard and that corporate actions are not being forced upon them.
- Any good guidance document will recognize resource constraints and include a section on partnerships. Many site managers and wildlife team members may not know what external resources are available to them to support their efforts and many may be loathe to connect with groups that, they may feel, have a negative disposition toward the site. It is very important that resources are listed so that the team members have confidence that they are doing the right thing and that they are securing the right resources from supportive community partners to help them design and implement a sustainable project. Community partners can include local and regional NGOs, local educational establishments, interested residents living near the site, youth groups, and, in locations where the company has a long history, retirees from the company.

The guidance document can be developed without a site visit, as much of the localized information can be found via a desk exercise with the help of tools as simple as Google Earth and as sophisticated as Landscope by NatureServe. But as Jim Rushworth says, "There is no alternative to setting foot on the site and seeing firsthand what the possibilities are. When you're on-site—in a quarry, for example—it's really the people from the local communities or it's the people in local nature organizations who understand what is important for that area and what are the important habitats." A site may also have a different profile from that of the surrounding landscape. An industrial location might have more "green space" than the surrounding community if it's in an urban or suburban landscape. It might have more ecological structures if it's a quarry or a mine, and it might have large areas of undisturbed natural lands if it's a nuclear power plant or other secure facility. Nothing beats a visit to the site with the experts from the operation and the partners who know the local situation best and can drive good project choices.

START WHERE YOU ARE

Working on lands set aside for conservation, such as public parks, wilderness, and natural areas or on privately held lands with conservation easements, is relatively straightforward. The key purpose of such land's designation is ecological, and fewer barriers exist to conservation action. On corporate lands, ecological outcomes are not front of mind for managers who must remain in compliance with regulations, ensure a safe work place for employees and contractors, and stay within budget for all aspects of the operation. Ecological management and environmental stewardship are usually seen as an added burden. That is why it's very important to make sure that conservation opportunities don't compete with or create added burden to existing operational restrictions, which will always receive priority.

In Freeport, Texas, Dow's chemical plant makes plastics at a facility that covers 5,000 acres on the coast of the Gulf of Mexico. Among the pipes and condensers, the oil storage and the power plants, sits a protected area for ground-nesting shorebirds, including black skimmers, least terns, and gull-billed terns. This four-acre nesting area was once an employee parking lot that became disused during staff reductions. Its substrate of crushed oyster shell and limestone attracted the nesting shorebirds that have used the site since the 1970s. A wildlife team on-site works to keep this area protected from feral cats and other predators. The team monitors the birds' reproductive success. Ground-nesting shorebirds face difficulties throughout their ranges, but the colony in the parking lot thrives. In 2013, over 600 nests were counted, with more than 800 young birds successfully fledging. The Texas Colonial Water Bird Survey, conducted by the US Fish and Wildlife Service and the Texas Parks and Wildlife Department, has said that the colony is one of the most successful shorebird nesting colonies on the Texas coast, showing that a four-acre parking lot on corporate lands in a chemical plant can, through simple management and a small financial investment, provide valuable habitat for at-risk species.

Investigate Current Activities

There is always something happening at a site in terms of lands management, whether reclamation of a mine or quarry or landscaping of lawns and flower gardens. To minimize disruptions to operations, it is smart to start where the work is actually occurring. In many operations, existing activities, both regulatory in nature and not, can be tweaked to contribute to voluntary conservation programs that help to meet a corporate goal. It is also smart to acknowledge the impromptu conservation action that is likely being undertaken in a forgotten corner or underused portion of the site. This acknowledgment will avoid disenfranchising employees who are already engaged in natural-resources efforts and will secure these employees' support for the effort.

The following section outlines some of the most common scenarios for existing efforts that can, with minor adjustments, contribute value to the conservation strategy, including post-extraction reclamation requirements, ongoing landscaping efforts, or regulated vegetation-management programs.

Interim or dynamic reclamation: Many extractive operations, such as mines and quarries, and development projects, such as pipelines and landfills, will be required to implement interim or dynamic reclamation to stabilize disturbed surfaces, minimize fugitive dust, revegetate land, provide erosion control, and address visual concerns of neighbors.

Interim reclamation efforts can easily contribute to corporate conservation plans if the company is going beyond compliance by designing to maximize the ecological function of the reclamation through simple steps like using native seed mixes in a stabilization effort that will also provide for a biodiversity outcomes; implementing reforestation projects with larger and more diverse species of trees; or managing intermittent wetlands or scree slopes that are caused by operational disturbances and can be valuable as nontraditional habitats. In addition, maintenance of interim restoration efforts with delayed mowing or other ecological best management practices (BMPs) can also provide for better biodiversity outcomes.

Manufacturing locations, landfills, and power plants all maintain buffer lands that provide relief to the community from sound or sight disturbance. These lands can be managed according to regulations or beyond compliance to provide ecological benefit. Buffer lands can be managed as pollinator habitat by reducing mowing and overseeding with native seed mixes; a buffer can become a visually pleasant and ecologically productive location while saving the site landscape-maintenance costs.

Landscaping: It is easy to redesign formal landscape into ecologically productive places that maintain the "formal" aesthetic but also, through sensitive and intelligent design, add the right plants and structures to provide benefit to biodiversity. Changes to maintenance routines can also affect ecological health and bring about better outcomes for nature. Delayed mowing, for example, provides more time for ground-nesting birds to successfully fledge offspring and for butterflies and other insects to complete their life cycles.

In many corporate locations with "light industrial" or non-extractive operations or in corporate locations with business units such as marketing, human resources, legal, and research and development, there is a strong preference for the "pastoral capitalism" aesthetic of grand buildings of commerce set into settings designed to mimic university campuses.[4] These landscapes are managed to minimize mess and maximize symmetry but could, through engagement with the facilities managers and the maintenance crew, be transformed to become much more valuable for biodiversity. They can be managed as stepping-stone habitats—ecologically intact habitats that allow species to move in otherwise fragmented suburban landscapes.[5] These habitats will become increasingly important under changing climate conditions as species' ranges shift with increasing temperature and species are forced to move with them. They can also contribute to corridor-creation efforts that allow movement of nonavian species. By connecting to conservation efforts across the fenceline, a corporate campus can become less of a barrier to movement and more of an enabler. They can also provide safe places for rehabilitated wildlife to return into the wild.

Newly built office spaces are increasingly being designed with the outdoors in mind; one example is ExxonMobil's campus in Spring, Texas, where native-species landscaping and other design elements enhance the employee experience. At ExxonMobil's campus, working outdoors is promoted. Campus-wide wifi and conveniently situated furniture make it possible for employees to leave their indoor working areas and convene to meet or work outside. Other opportunities for enhanced employee engagement include walking trails through nature areas and the chance to monitor or just observe pollinator gardens or wetland areas where species can be easily seen. Older campuses, like those built in the 1950s, are perfect places for returning nature to the suburbs and providing opportunities for biodiversity to increase, and community and employees to benefit. Many have mature trees that can be the foundation for a rewilding effort—creating a meadow and planting more trees to increase the functionality of the habitat for a variety of species.

Interesting species are already using corporate campuses. Along Route 1 in West Windsor, New Jersey, a corporate campus from the 1950s sits back from the highway with an expanse of well-maintained lawn running from the office building's picture windows to one of the most congested traffic arteries in the state. A number of mature trees dot the lawn, providing visual interest and a buffer against noise from Route 1. For a number of years in the late 2000s, one of the trees hosted a pair of bald eagles that established a nest, laid eggs, and hatched young beside a six-lane road that carries upward of 100,000 cars every day. The presence of Canada geese and an artificial wetland provided the eagles with good hunting grounds, and the absence of people using the landscaped area for recreation kept the nest protected from human disturbance. It was a curious location for a species that was, at the time, federally protected. The drivers who passed every day were mostly oblivious to the fascinating nature unfolding on their daily commute. The grounds maintenance team were the first to notice the nest, and the employees soon got involved with monitoring the activity at the nest as part of New Jersey's statewide eagle-monitoring network. This lucky occurrence can become a starting point for thinking about nature on such a campus and then working to increase its capacity for species from eagles to bees.

Although it may seem counterintuitive at first, there are many ways for a business located in a highly maintained landscape to contribute to a corporate conservation goal—and a corporate conservation goal just might be the best driver for changes to improve the ecological health of landscaping on a corporate campus. If operations are expected to contribute to the corporate conservation goal, shouldn't the corporate head office too? On many corporate campuses, undeveloped areas previously set aside for future development are being placed into conservation projects, former landscaped areas are being converted to pollinator gardens, and meadows and surplus parking lots are being reused or repurposed into green infrastructure.

In Monroeville, outside Pittsburgh, Pennsylvania, PPG, a paints and specialty materials company, manages 122 out of 185 of its campus acres for nature, featuring two nature trails, butterfly gardens, and wildlife structures for cavity-nesting birds and other species. PPG also has a facility in San Juan del Rio in Mexico, which is lo-

OTHER CORPORATE CAMPUS ACTIVITIES

*O*ther *conservation-focused* activities on corporate campuses include installation of nesting structures for birds or other species across the property; replacement of traditional annuals and other nonfunctional landscaping design elements with natives and perennials that bring more conservation value; reforestation to create groves of trees to fill in the space between the traditional solo sentinel trees; regrading ornamental water features to provide better ecological outcomes; vegetating stormwater basins; flooding stormwater basins to create wetlands; designing for outdoor health by incorporating walking paths that provide nature interpretation; reducing mowing frequency so meadows can thrive for a season and allow grassland birds to nest successfully; allowing prescribed burns on prairies and meadows; and planting nectar sources and larval host plants for butterflies.

cated along the monarch butterfly's migratory route and which itself manages a butterfly meadow. PPG has created a programmatic connection between the two campus locations using the monarch. It invites students in Monroeville and San Juan del Rio to visit the locations and make observations about the butterflies using the site. The data from the United States is compared to the data in Mexico, and educators in both countries develop lessons to help the students interpret the findings.

Vegetation management: Utility rights-of-way for electricity transmission, pipelines, landfill operations, and other commercial sites operate under mandatory vegetation-management regulations. Existing plans to meet the regulatory requirements can be augmented to encourage better biodiversity outcomes. The vegetation-management industry has been moving toward practices that can provide benefit to biodiversity within the regulatory framework. The old management approach to vegetation on rights-of-way entailed broadcast herbicide application and indiscriminate mowing. Today, the best practice requires that applications of herbicide be more focused and mowing be done in accordance with ecological needs and opportunities. This evolution across the industry is driven by increased awareness in both the industry and its community members of the opportunities for rights-of-way to be productive habitats for pollinators and other species without sacrificing safety and reliability.

Community members can also be one of the biggest challenges to transitioning to an ecologically friendly approach to vegetation management on rights-of-ways and other lands. It can be a challenge to educate the public that these formerly neatly mowed lands are now better managed even though they may now appear unruly and wild. In Maryland, Baltimore Gas and Electric (BGE) began to institute integrated vegetation management on some of its rights-of-way across its transmission system. The change from neatly trimmed vegetation to a vibrant grassland concerned many neighbors whose properties abutted the rights-of-way. BGE engaged with the concerned residents and, through printed materials and posted signs, explained the biodiversity benefit of the new regime and the reason for the more natural look. Signs along the rights of way illustrate the importance of native species as habitat. By engaging with community members, BGE acquired champions for this new approach. In addition, BGE purchased the National Wildlife Federation's certified habitat designation, a consumer-facing statement of habitat management that helped further inform the community. Rights-of-way management is a compliance-focused aspect of the business, but it can be redesigned to contribute to a corporate conservation strategy as a "beyond compliance" activity.

Maximizing operational outcomes: Among the most exciting types of operations from a conservation-opportunity point of view are quarries and mining pits, lands where the inescapable consequences of extraction create real opportunities to develop and manage ecosystems that may be rare or absent due to locally dominant land uses such as agriculture or residential. With geology as destiny, a mine site can have ecological influences on flora and fauna in two basic ways: first, in the direct influence of the rock type itself and the role that it plays in soil formation, and second, in the development of structures that influence the distribution of plants and animals at a range of scales.[6]

Certain rock types and the soils they influence may be home to specially adapted plants like gypsophiles, "chalk-loving" plants that grow on exposed gypsum or gypsum-rich soils, or xerophilous species that love dry, arid places and thrive in limestone. Earliest succession barrens and later succession scrub habitats have declined all around the world due to intensification of agriculture, but these habitats are commonly found in quarries, where they provide sanctuary for the species that depend on them.[7]

These location can also provide physical structure that is absent elsewhere. Quarries and mine sites may have cliffs, bare lands, scree slopes, and intermittent wetlands, which are all ecological textures likely absent in surrounding heavily managed and agricultural landscapes. These structures allow pioneer species to take hold on a temporary or permanent basis.

When mine and quarry operators understand the opportunity to use their sites for biodiversity, they can start to develop small projects across the quarry. Natural-resources management work can take place on quarries in two ways: through dynamic management during operations and post-operation reclamation that values the successional habitat that emerges, and designs reclamation efforts to keep it.

Jim Rushworth tells the story of a quarry in Spain where the original reclamation plan called for the site of excavation to be filled in and the land regraded to a flat grade for future agricultural uses. Over the thirty-year life of the the Yepes-Ciruelos Quarry in Toledo, Spain, novel ecosystems had established in the quarry site, featuring rare plants that included two protected endemic plants; and the quarry also acted as an important corridor for species, connecting two areas of high biodiversity value off-site. Jim and the team at the quarry invited students and a professor from the University of Castilla–La Mancha to examine the site for biodiversity. The quarry staff convened a community stakeholder group to discuss nature-based post-extraction uses. The combination of the academic research, the location between two Natura 2000 sites, and the engagement of community persuaded the regulating authority to allow for a more natural reclamation effort that would increase connectivity, enhance existing wetlands, and allow for the new plant and animal communities to remain. The company saved significant yet undisclosed sums of money and the conservation value of the site wasn't compromised by a one-size-fits-all regulatory approach to dealing with expired extraction sites. As Jim pointed out, the support of the academics and community was critical to make all this work. "We were able to convince the authorities that this approach had conservation value and was not just a cost-cutting exercise."

During operations, small habitats such as scree slopes, intermittent wetlands, and pioneer grasslands can be created. Of course, operations also damage habitats. Well-planned quarry operations know in advance where disturbance is going to occur, so protected areas can be created where blasting or heavy truck traffic will not disturb species using the habitats. Many areas remain inactive for years and some will be inactive permanently, depending on the plan for the quarry. Future planned disturbance can be mitigated by moving the habitats during non-growing or non-breeding seasons, although this too results in impact.

In the province of Quintana Roo in Mexico, Vulcan Materials operates the Calica quarry. Across 5,000-plus acres, 12 million tons

Figure 5-2: Vulcan Materials Calica Quarry in Playa Del Carmen, Mexico. (Photo by author.)

of limestone is being quarried annually to supply building materials to the Gulf Coast of the United States. Operations at the quarry are regulated by the Mexican government with strong dynamic restoration regulations that include a requirement to protect and recover endangered plant species. As the quarry pit is excavated, the topsoil is saved to be used as seed banks in areas undergoing restoration. Trees that are removed from the site during excavation are immediately reused in restoration areas, where branches are planted into the recovered topsoil and, in this tropical climate, quickly take root and grow to contribute to the restoration of the surrounding rain forests. As the operations shift across the quarry site, a line of reforestation follows it, filling in mining pits with a mix of rainforest plants. Remarkably, these reforested areas have been found to host similar species abundance to the undisturbed surrounding lands. Along the Yucatan peninsula from Cancún to Playa del Carmen, the dominant land use is resort development. At the quarry, the ecological management on this landscape results in a higher biodiversity outcome than the manicured, managed golf-course landscapes of the all-inclusive resorts.

There is growing interest in how quarries can contribute their unique habitats within heavily managed landscapes like agricultural lands. Using dynamic restoration, leaning in to ecological reclamation, and including research on-site can all have substantial benefits for conservation outcomes and the corporation's business needs, whether strategically included in their conservation plans or not.

MAINTAINING MOMENTUM

Once implementation is under way, maintaining momentum becomes important, as competition for time, interest, and resources persists. Communications, competition, and recognition are all ways to overcome the challenges of maintaining voluntary conservation programs in corporate locations.

Create an Internal Communications Strategy

At the sprawling Woodcreek campus in the energy corridor of Houston, Shell Oil has been managing both development of the site and nature conservation programs for many years. The campus, which was first developed in the late 1970s, has undergone a lot of building and development over the years and today contains office buildings and parking structures with natural landscaping throughout. The campus has been actively managing nature-based programs since the early 2000s and has faced many challenges to its momentum as development took lands formerly under conservation, staff retired and moved on, and leadership and its vision of ecological stewardship changed and evolved.

To counter these forces, the social investment team at Shell charged with employee engagement and corporate citizenship efforts developed a number of internal communications tools that kept the team moving forward but also kept the rest of the 5,000-plus employees on-site informed and engaged. The team hosts bird walks at the campus on such a regular schedule that they have become institutionalized and well known among employees. The bird walks welcome everyone, and one of the team's experts is always on hand to point out interesting birds and other species seen along the way. The sightings from the bird walks have been captured on a list on

Figure 5-3: The monarch-themed reminder notice from the Social Investment Team at Shell USA. (Photo by author.)

Woodcreek's intranet, open to all employees to add their sightings to the list whether they attend the walks or not. Species as diverse as the gulf fritillary butterfly, the chihuahan hooknose snake, and the yellow-rumped and the black-throated green warblers have been identified and listed in the weekly published "Woodcreek Sightings and Nature Notes."

In addition, Shell's Social Investment Team has created materials on-site to remind the employees that the campus has nature-based projects, especially those created on behalf of the monarch butterfly. Across the campus, employees must use electronic keycards to gain access to buildings. For a time, a message reminding employees to remember their keycard was placed beside every access location. To highlight Shell's conservation efforts at the campus and elsewhere, the reminder message was branded with a photo of a monarch and a message encouraging people to check out Shell's monarch station located on campus: "Smart monarchs are migrating. Smarter ones take their badges." In addition, the sign provides a link to a Shell website highlighting the company's conservation efforts at Wood-creek Campus and beyond. This integrated communication strategy is seen by every employee at the site and serves to connect on-site work at Woodcreek with work being done across Shell's footprint, including an artificial reef installation in the Gulf and other conservation efforts where Shell has operations.

Another smart technique is to engage the corporate communications professionals in storytelling. Wildlife stories are a popular and accessible antidote to dry communiques on health, safety, and production targets. Corporate communication professionals jump at the opportunity to write something other than quarterly business reports and to add color to the technical data required for standard corporate sustainability or corporate social responsibility reporting. In addition, corporate communications around site-based conservation efforts can result in valuable local press coverage.

Use Competition

The corporate world is an inherently competitive place, with individual business units competing to be most profitable, different operations competing to be the safest and healthiest, and companies competing against their peers to be leaders in their respective fields. Use this inherent trait to advance and maintain conservation momentum.

Freeport-McMoRan, the mining giant, supports conservation programs across its entire portfolio of sites. An annual photography competition gives recognition and provides incentives for the sites to maintain high-quality conservation programs. Every year, a call is sent to locations around the world that engage in ecological stewardship programs, asking for sites to submit the best photographs of nature on-site. The submissions are judged and the twelve best images are professionally framed and hung for one year in the head office in Phoenix. At the end of the year, the framed images are sent back to the site and auctioned off, with the proceeds going to a local charity. Competition is fierce for this effort and winners are very proud of their achievements—both the recognition from corporate but also the ability to give back to their communities through the auction.

The Heidelberg Cement Group is one of the world's largest building materials companies, with quarries and cement plants in 3,000 locations in 60 countries. In 2012, it presented its first global corporate award for biodiversity called the Quarry Life Award. The aim of the program is to highlight the ecosystems that evolve in quarries and to promote the use of quarries for ecological research. This, in turn, connects the quarries to communities and educational establishments, forging new partnerships. While there are many outcomes from this conservation competition, one highlight is the increase in the number of quarries opening their locations to biodiversity restoration and recovery programs. The projects are very diverse and show the multiple uses of quarries for biodiversity and education. In North America, the three projects that competed in the 2018 Quarry Life program illustrate the different types of efforts possible at quarry sites.

At the New Windsor quarry in Maryland, a group of students from nearby McDaniel College proposed to pilot a framework for using partnerships with educational institutions to monitor corporate restoration efforts. The project sought to assess the success of the restoration of a wetland and stream called Haines Branch, which Heidelberg Cement restored as part of a quarry expansion. The program brought students from conservation biology, ecology, and animal physiology together for a cross-disciplinary approach that would (a) provide the company with detailed reports on the effectiveness of their restoration efforts, and (b) provide the students with a dynamic outdoor laboratory. The overall approach of a university partnering with a company for co-benefits is a concept worth replicating, especially in the area of post-restoration monitoring, which is typically under-resourced once compliance has been met.

In Alberta, Canada, the Cadomin Quarry near Jasper National Park was the location of two quite different entries into the Quarry Life program. One team with a research project called "Ruling the Roost—Developing Thermally Optimal Roosts to Enhance Microbat Population Biodiversity," found the quarry to be an optimal site for the research because of the availability of land and its location close to a known bat hibernaculum to test a technologically superior bat box. Such a bat box could potentially increase success of bat maternity colonies and contribute to population resilience in the face of white-nose syndrome (WNS), a North American scourge of bat populations that was rapidly approaching Alberta from its initial emergence on the East Coast of the United States.

The students from Northern Alberta Institute of Technology (NAIT) formed a cross-disciplinary team from biological sciences, alternative energy technologies, nanotechnology, mechanical engineering, and technology management and designed a number of different bat boxes. They were interested in ensuring optimum thermoregulation for the maternity roosts, which could increase the chances of survival by helping bats preserve more body fat during spring and summer and enter their hibernaculum in fall at peak health and weight. This would give the bats a better chance of resisting WNS, which is a cave-dwelling winter disease. The team tested three different box designs in an environmental chamber to determine which box would maintain a constant temperature under fluctuating conditions. Their research found that a box designed with phase-change material, a new type of insulation, recorded the least internal temperature fluctuation. The box is now being field-tested at the quarry in a series of different locations and at different heights and exposures.

The second project at Cadomin saw a group of local high school students from Hinton, the town closest to the quarry, and researchers from fRI Research, a wildlife biology research group, examine whether and how grizzly bears use the quarry and how they coexist with the quarry operation. The team installed a number of wildlife cameras to track visits, barbed-wire fencing as a hair trap, and blood-soaked woodpiles as lures.

The project achieved more than data collection. It provided local high school students with hands-on experience using the latest non-invasive sampling techniques and engaged quarry workers in sampling and learning to understand the usage patterns on the site. The staff took the presence of grizzly bears very seriously from a safety point of view, but they were also very proud to be working among them. The study determined that generations of bears were using the quarry, passing through it on a regular basis.

This competition has allowed hundreds of quarries across the Heidelberg footprint to work with partners on biodiversity projects that restore habitats, connect communities, and provide education and research opportunities. By opening their sites to outside groups, Heidelberg Cement is encouraging better management of their lands for natural resources and helping the industry as a whole by developing new approaches and techniques for ecological stewardship.

Celebrate Success

If the goal of a company's strategic conservation plan is to have active conservation programs at every site, it must continuously communicate progress toward that goal as a way of showing that forward motion is happening, and encourage action where progress may be lagging. For multinational companies, it's a constant challenge to communicate to the farthest reaches of the corporate empire. A scorecard or continuous reporting mechanism helps to keep employees in remote locations feel involved and inspire others to take action to be included in the story.

Celebrating the success of efforts through internal or external awards programs provides companies and their employees with platforms for communicating progress. Many trade associations promote environmental excellence through awards programs, and outstanding conservation projects can contribute to an awards application even if the focus is on operations, emissions, or waste management. (The importance of recognition is discussed further in the next chapter.)

Working on company lands is different from working on public or protected lands. There are many challenges that come from culture, leadership, operational restrictions, and corporate disruption.

There are also many opportunities that arise from the fact that these lands exist and that there are always employees and others willing to work on them toward a conservation or community benefit. As Sue Kelsey says, "People are anxious to do the right thing, and when you give them the information to do it, they'll work miracles." When you understand the context they are working in, those miracles become easier to realize.

06 MONITORING, METRICS, AND RECOGNITION

If you don't know where you are going,
any road can take you there.

—LEWIS CARROLL, *ALICE IN WONDERLAND*

To be supported, corporate conservation must have value both locally and globally. A corporate conservation program must be able to show value to the company and its stakeholders. It should also have demonstrable habitat or ecosystem value. A locally relevant conservation action should be able to be recognized as an example of globally significant corporate citizenship. An individual site-based effort like a grassland restoration project that also acts as an outdoor classroom for a local school will be seen as "more valuable" if it contributes toward a strategic corporate conservation objective. But how is value calculated? How can those with a stake in the success of the effort know that they are on the right road? Calculating value is a challenge across the entire conservation community, where the subject of biodiversity metrics and indicators bedevils conservation practitioners and academics alike. This challenge is also at the core of mainstreaming conservation into the private sector, which is needed in order to fully engage business in the global biodiversity goals of the Convention of Biological Diversity (CBD).

In an ideal world, a company develops a corporate conservation strategic plan that meets a business need with an ultimate stakeholder and an associated success story. The plan will be cascaded to a region or a business unit and onward to a site, the physical location where actual implementation will occur. Following implementation, the site will report back "up" to corporate through the region or business unit with information that the head office can then integrate into the larger corporate message. Thus, the conservation action's value at the site can have value in a larger sense.

A successful journey from site-level implementation to corporate-level storytelling starts with monitoring that can easily be translated into data and the stories that are necessary for reporting and credible recognition. From an ecological perspective as well as a business perspective (to show return on investment), monitoring efforts should also contribute to adaptive management of the project. If a site is going to invest resources in monitoring efforts, the results should do more than tell the story. They should also inform future management, as effective monitoring will show what efforts have borne success, what efforts have been more challenging, and what efforts have failed, and why.

This chapter seeks to set a simple course for the monitoring of conservation efforts on corporate lands, and also to highlight the importance of the flow of monitoring to reporting and to recognition. In classic ecological conservation activities, monitoring data is meant to be used to assess outcomes and address areas in need of improvement. In the corporate sphere, monitoring is the foundation from which all value is realized, from conservation outcomes to corporate reports.

Monitoring

This statement from a group of scientists in Australia sums up the state of biodiversity monitoring today: ". . . while everyone thinks biodiversity monitoring is a good idea, this has not translated into a culture of sound biodiversity monitoring, or widespread use of monitoring data."[1] The scientists looking at their own community of practice identified four barriers to more effective monitoring: poorly articulated objectives, poorly understood need for monitoring, lack of institutional support, and lack of appropriate standards.

These four barriers impact corporate conservation monitoring efforts just as much, if not more than traditional government or nongovernmental organization (NGO) efforts. If implementing a conservation project is a challenge in the corporate workplace, monitoring the program over the long term is even harder. Project implementation will always receive more support and resources than monitoring success and evaluating outcomes—even though monitoring is the only way to generate the information that will prove the value to secure further resources and support.

Two main factors make effective monitoring difficult for projects on corporate lands: the effort needed to maintain a sustained monitoring endeavor over years, and the need to obtain precise-enough monitoring data to show changes across space and time.[2] Additionally, the corporate need to tell the conservation story may not be satisfied quickly or easily with traditional monitoring. Changes may be difficult to illustrate especially as the time elapsing between a specific conservation action and a corresponding reaction is uncertain and could take years. Unusual weather conditions, which are increasingly frequent, can impact growing seasons. Ecosystem restoration projects may not attract targeted species in the early years following implementation. A pollinator meadow may require many growing seasons to become established and productive. Artificial nesting structures may remain unused year after year until residents appear and create nests.

In addition, long-term monitoring programs on corporate lands must be defended during annual budget cycles. The expenses of a monitoring program will always be in question and highlighted in any cost-cutting exercises driven by the budgetary needs of the site or corporate mandates during the inevitable downturns, reorganizations, mergers, and other disruptive activities that impact the private sector at all times.

The need for immediate results and the challenge of accessing funds should be factored into the design of any monitoring protocols for corporate lands. Operational considerations should also be factored in. To increase the likelihood of success, a corporate conservation monitoring program should be designed in a way that can either be easily integrated into existing work, such as site inspections or grounds maintenance, or outsourced to a community partner or consultant. While the four dimensions that characterize most monitoring design are sample size, biological coverage,[3] spatial coverage, and temporal coverage, monitoring on corporate lands must also prioritize rapid results, low-cost approaches, and operational sensitivity. These additional requirements for successfully monitoring conservation success on corporate lands suggest that designing an effective monitoring program should be carefully integrated into the strategic plan from the beginning, not as an afterthought.

Monitoring should also align with the business need. If the business need is to secure social license to operate or make a contribution toward global goals such as the SDGs, monitoring should collect information relevant to the goal such as the number of community members attending a conservation action as a contributing metric toward securing social license to operate. It should also keep in mind the success story that the company wants to tell as well as the ultimate stakeholder. A strong monitoring program should reflect the site-based effort but have meaning to the corporate conservation objective or success story. It should speak to the ultimate stakeholder with clear and concise data but have a detailed foundation that can contribute to a larger national or international effort. It should be immune to the disruptive cycles of the corporate world. It should, in fact, be a monitoring unicorn, satisfying various and complex needs but using uncomplicated methods integrated into operations and doing so on a shoestring budget. Of course, it will be very difficult to design a monitoring program to meet all these needs, but simple approaches will increase the chances of success.

At the US headquarters of Fiat Chrysler America (FCA) in Auburn Hills, Michigan, there is a test track known as Evaluation Road. Test tracks are always restricted areas in order to protect trade secrets when new vehicles and concepts are being road-tested. In the case of Evaluation Road, the site is protected from public view by trees and fencing and from public access by security gates.

The property is wooded, with extensive wetlands across the site. The wetlands are managed with infrastructure designed to minimize runoff from the road surfaces that could cause silt buildup or erosion, or otherwise impact water quality. Water quality is important, as the property is home to one of the largest great blue heron rookeries (nesting colonies) in the region.

FCA partners with the Oakland Audubon Society to monitor the colony. The group visits the site every year to count nests and document nest success. The wildlife team of FCA employees also monitor the colony through photo documentation that captures changes in the rookery over time. Nesting colonies are very susceptible to human disturbance, so the highly restricted nature of the test track, while an impediment to easy monitoring, provides the herons with ideal conditions for a successful nesting season.

The efforts at FCA are an example of the challenges and opportunities of a conservation program on corporate lands. The challenges are lack of open access to the site and lack of expertise among the staff. The opportunity is the existence of a large rookery in an otherwise heavily managed landscape. The challenges are overcome and the opportunity is realized by securing a conservation partner from the community and planning and providing access around operations. With a credible conservation partner, FCA also gains the ability to tell the story of the rookery, while (as anyone who spends time with passionate birders knows) its employees gain knowledge about the species and increased enthusiasm for the project.

MONITORING OPTIONS FOR CORPORATE LANDS

Monitoring can be done by employees, by citizen-science volunteers from the community, by partner NGOs, by agency staff, or by consultants. A number of considerations specific to operations and the business need will determine which monitoring approaches to adopt.

The accessibility and location of the operation and the number of employees on-site are important considerations. Remote locations such as mines or large linear properties such as utility rights-of-way may not be able to deploy many employees or secure long-term partners or community members for monitoring support. For these sites, consultants are likely to be hired to collect relevant data. Locations with controlled access, such as surplus properties, closed operations, or remediation sites, may also have no permanent staff, so employees in other locations will likely have to coordinate access for the purposes of monitoring. Some locations, such as corporate campus settings, will be wide open to community members to come on-site, while others, such as nuclear facilities, will be heavily restricted, with the use of photography equipment prohibited site-wide. The majority of corporate operations will have some restrictions, but most will allow access.

For any corporate conservation program, the team at the site should first determine what it wants to monitor. That this

Figure 6-1: A right-of-way managed for pollinator habitat can be difficult to monitor due to its size and location. (Used with permission from Baltimore Gas and Electric.)

determination needs to be made at all may seem simplistic to conservation professionals, but many corporate efforts do not involve professionals. For any project, the team can monitor the success of new plantings, the presence/absence of certain species, or other aspects of the project. The team should adopt or adapt existing protocols or design site-specific approaches over which it can exercise control so that it gets the information it needs in the time frame in which it is needed.

Existing monitoring protocols are easiest to adopt and adapt, and many come with the added benefit of contributing data to a larger effort, which can increase engagement. Some of the better-known monitoring programs are friendlier to non-wildlife professional data collectors, while some are specifically designed for citizen scientists. Mass participation projects, such as eBird, Trektellen, and Birdtrack, which all focus on avian species, or the broader iNaturalist platform, which records plants and animals, are very attractive to corporate conservation teams. iNaturalist is one of the largest citizen-science projects today, with 1.5 million participants who have contributed over 21 million observations. These programs provide feedback and community, which can be added incentives for enthusiastic partici-

Figure 6-2: Apps like iNaturalist encourage amateur naturalists and wildlife photographers to submit images of their sightings for identification, like this barn owl at Waste Management's Guadalupe Recycling and Disposal Facility. (Used with permission of Waste Management.)

pants. Existing monitoring options exist along an ease-of-use spectrum. Simple observational protocols designed in large part for citizen scientists also include the Backyard Bird Count, the Summer Bat Count, the Calling Amphibian Monitoring Project, and others. They are available off the shelf and require only basic training.

Certain corporate conservation efforts will require more in-depth monitoring than others and may need to be carried out by consultants or, with additional training, by employees. For example, to have proven value, invasive-species-management programs must start with the establishment of a baseline against which the efforts are to be conducted. The extent of monitoring for invasive species will depend on the type of management and whether eradication or prevention is occurring. In the United States, training for invasive-species recognition and baseline monitoring may be available from local offices of the Natural Resources Conservation Service, an office of the USDA. For ecological remediation programs, extensive testing will be done to assure regulators that chosen remedies such as phytoremediation are having the desired effect and are moving the site toward a determination that no further action is needed. This type of monitoring will be done by consultants using test wells. If a company is engaged in a reforestation effort toward climate mitigation, tree measurement programs such as i-Tree or verification protocols from the American Carbon Registry will be used to prove captured carbon.

USING TECHNOLOGY

There are many technologies to help monitoring. For corporate conservation, image- and sound-monitoring programs are increasingly popular as the costs of the technologies continue to fall, making them more accessible. Technologies that operate from smartphones or other mobile devices are attractive to younger citizen scientists, whether employees or community members. Wildlife Acoustics bat-detection monitors have opened the world of bat identification to a larger corps of citizen scientists. Cameras are prohibited on some corporate lands, but camera traps are increasingly being deployed as cost-effective solutions on others. Corporate lands are great as secure locations for camera traps, since the technology is less likely to be stolen or tampered with. The motion- or heat-activated cameras give valuable insight into the use of the site by wildlife and balance the corporate need for privacy. Security cameras on corporate locations have even been used to capture images of larger species that trip the camera through motion or heat sensors.

At the other end of the cost and sophistication spectrum, unmanned aerial vehicles, more commonly known as drones, are being deployed to monitor large and inaccessible and/or lightly staffed locations such as linear infrastructure or inaccessible parts of a mine or quarry operation. Drones of all sizes are being deployed for lands-management uses, from mapping vegetation and populations to monitoring special areas for poaching or other disruptions. For remote corporate lands, drones can easily monitor conservation success, and when equipped with specialized sensors, can measure temperature and humidity, and, by applying thermal or laser vision, can produce sophisticated monitoring that can inform management of lands over a large scale.[4]

BUILDING RELATIONSHIPS

Monitoring programs are a great way to create long-term relationships with local conservation NGOs. Just as with FCA's heron rookery in Michigan, Vulcan Materials' Grandin Sand Plant in Putnam County, Florida, engages with a local Audubon chapter to monitor its bird species on-site. Vulcan Materials, one of the largest producers of sand and stone for the construction industry in the United States, has quarries and mines across the country. The Grandin Sand Plant reclaimed a former mine site as a natural area. As the fourteen-acre area became revegetated, wading birds and other species flocked to the wetlands on the site. The former sand mine is now the home to a multi-species rookery where twenty-two species of wading birds have been identified, including herons, ibis, and egrets. During peak season, 3,500 birds have been counted using the rookery, and sixty-three other species of birds have also been identified on-site. The employees at the plant know these facts because of their ongoing partnership with Santa Fe Audubon, one of forty-plus Audubon chapters in the state of Florida. Together they have erected seven blinds across the property and established transect points for monitoring. Every two weeks during nesting season, volunteers wearing camouflage monitor the nesting birds and track changes across the habitat.

Monitoring programs are also a good way to establish long-term relationships with education partners. In Burlington County, New Jersey, Ashland Inc., a specialty chemicals company, is actively managing seven acres of a former remediation site polluted from waste disposal during the 1950s, '60s, and '70s and cleaned up in the late 1990s. Located in a heavily developed part of the state, the company is managing the site for birds and bats. Ashland has a long-term partnership with Rutgers University, which offers a course called "Practical Experience in Ecology, Evolution, and Natural Resources." This course provides undergraduate students with hands-on experience of monitoring the habitat, especially the structures such as boxes for bats and cavity-nesting birds that they have installed there. Students visit the site twelve times over the course of a year and perform a variety of monitoring activities and maintenance of the boxes. Their data is then provided to NestWatch, a mass-participation citizen-science project from the Cornell Lab of Ornithology.

By using monitoring programs to secure long-term relationships with community, whether through citizen-science-focused groups such as NGOs or formal education offerings such as the relationship between Rutgers and Ashland, a company realizes co-benefits—obtaining important data to tell its story, benefitting from volunteer help and securing positive community relations.

Once monitoring approaches have been established, translating the data into useful metrics is the next challenge for a corporate conservation effort. The ease with which the collected data can be used, both inside and outside the company, will have a direct bearing on continued support for the collection of the data. If the data has no use beyond the single site where it is collected, the project will not get the support it needs for the long term. But, if the data can be translated for a company to report into the Global Reporting Initiative (GRI) or the Dow Jones Sustainability Index (DJSI) the monitoring effort will have corporate support.

Metrics: The Challenge

In 2016, at the annual Ceres meeting in Boston, I was talking about General Motors, its global goal to have conservation activities at all its manufacturing facilities, and its efforts to grow the number of GM facilities adopting conservation and related education programs. At the end of the presentation, the inevitable question came from a conservation NGO representative in the room. She asked, "What indicators and metrics do you use?"

Somewhat flippantly, I replied, "None. We chose to pursue action over measurement."

While the reality is a little more nuanced, the truth is that GM and other companies like it prefer to see action rather than wait for biodiversity metrics, the holy grail of conservation, to be agreed upon. My questioner approached me later, in private, expressing a similar desire to be able to sidestep the metrics question in her work and just get on with it.

We agreed that discussions about biodiversity metrics and indicators slow down implementation and sometimes cause projects to be derailed completely, making perfection an enemy of practice.

This exchange was not unique. Time and again, I've been asked in the public forum to defend not developing indicators and metrics for corporate conservation, but then, in private, I'm assured that metrics are overrated and overcomplicated. These Janus-like conversations worry me—the public voice calling loudly for metrics, the private voice whispering that maybe metrics are not all that important. But, if we are to frame natural-resources conservation efforts as having a business-value framework, we must be able to somehow show the value. If the private sector wants to be able to tell its story in a credible manner, it needs a credible way to do it. How do we then find a middle road between the often over-complex and expensive metrics and indicators that the conservation community continually discusses, and the reality of time and resources available for and dedicated to a corporate conservation effort?

METRICS AND INDICATORS: THE CURRENT LANDSCAPE

Across the community of practice, a variety of obstacles to effective metric development for biodiversity have been identified. The most obvious and seemingly insurmountable obstable is the complex nature of biodiversity itself.[5] In addition, different monitoring protocols or sampling systems give different results depending on when, where, and how the protocols are implemented. The Convention on Biodiversity (CBD), its Aichi targets, and associated indicators contains clear examples of this challenge.

The CBD, the global treaty for biodiversity protection, is structured around a strategic plan for 2020 which contains twenty targets, the Aichi targets, collected under five goals. These targets are associated with a list of suggested indicators from a variety of iniatives all around the world. How progress is measured against these indicators—or indeed against any biodiversity indicators or goals—is under constant debate. An indicator such as the International Union for the Conservation of Nature's Red List measures change in the number of threatened species since the last assessment, while the Wildlife Picture Index measures change in the presence or absence of birds and mammals at sixteen sites across the world. Both of these indices are used to measure progress against the CBD's Aichi Target 12. But they will give different measurements of progress against that target.

Because the targets and goals in the CBD's Strategic Plan are designed to influence national policy, it is important that good indicators exist to measure progress toward policy goals, but even here there are many weaknesses. In a review of the 193 signatory parties to the CBD, it was found that very few countries (36 percent) had adopted evidence-based indicators. These countries tended to be more developed, with stable institutions and a well-resourced civil society. The report also found that partnerships between government, NGOs, and academia produce the best indicators for national biodiversity plans.[6] The report found many reasons for the lack of national biodiversity targets, with a common reason coming from an online survey: "Lack of political will. Biodiversity is seen as a cost rather than an asset."

The indicators that are in use across the parties to the CBD are not aggregated, nor are they integrated with any other framework. There is no consistency in data collection and no consistency in data sharing.[7] At the global level where international bodies such as the United Nations Environmental Programme (UNEP) and the Intergovernmental Science-Policy Platform on Biodiversity and Ecosystem Services (IPBES), national environmental agencies, the NGO world, and academia operate, there are few metrics or indicators that everyone can agree on, and no consolidated approaches to sharing and reporting have yet been established. There are a number of efforts to establish consistency, such as the proposal for a biodiversity dashboard suggested by a group led by NatureServe in the United States, or essential biodiversity variables (EBV) suggested by a group of academics in response to the IPBES. But so far there is no global system for measuring biodiversity change. If the corporate world looks to the conservation community for metrics, it will not find a simple answer.

A recent industry-focused report, "Biodiversity Indicators for Extractive Companies," written by UNEP and the Proteus Partnership, illustrated the challenge of indicators for corporate conservation. The report examined existing frameworks for biodiversity and business.[8] Of the existing frameworks, they selected twenty-two of the indicators most appropriate to business and found only three that were useful to the corporate world without further refinement or additions. The three indicators were the Wildlife Picture Index, the Trends in Tree Cover, and the Local Biodiversity Intactness Index. Not a single indicator was identified as being easily adaptable to business. None of the frameworks met the needs of all the companies participating in the report.

The two main challenges to developing, using, and integrating biodiversity indicators in the corporate sector are (a) the drivers for indicator development, and (b) the difference and distance between site and corporate levels.

Just as in the government and NGO sectors, the impetus for indicator development varies both between and within companies. The UNEP indicators report examines the range of drivers from local regulations to international NGOs. It finds that local pressure is the most effective driver for indicator development. Local regulation was seen to be almost *ten times more effective* than pressure from an international NGO for the development of a biodiversity indicator. But, while local drivers are very effective at the site level, at the corporate level needs differ as investors or corporate stakeholders drive indicator development supported by existing frameworks such as the Dow Jones Sustainability Index (DJSI) or the GRI, which require companies to report on biodiversity. Companies that report into the DJSI will be driven to develop indicators to meet the needs of this framework, as will companies that contribute to other reporting frameworks such as the GRI, the CDP, Ecovadis, Together for Sustainability, or the myriad of other reporting frameworks that exist across the globe today providing CSR, sustainability, supply-chain management, and reporting platforms for business. Of these frameworks that seek biodiversity information, no two ask for it in the same way.

Many companies report into more than one of these frameworks and each asks the questions in different way. (These competing frameworks and the challenges they present to corporate conservation efforts were covered in chapter 3.) Corporate offices, not operations, decide which frameworks to adopt and report into. They chose a framework based on the need it will fulfill. To enhance or secure its reputation, a company will chose a consumer or investor-facing framework like DJSI or GRI. The Coca Cola Company, General Motors, and others highlight their participation in GRI to send a message about their commitment to corporate sustainability. For benchmarking purposes, a company will participate in a framework that includes enough peers or colleagues to make the benchmarking exercise more meaningful. The Global Cement and Concrete Association's sustainability framework provides a benchmark against which the leading cement companies can measure performance. It is only useful as a benchmark if enough companies participate. If a company is joining a framework to address supply-chain sustainability or environmental performance, the chosen platform must also contain vendors and customers.

The usefulness of any reporting framework for a specific business need is the driver. In addition to needing indicators for reporting into frameworks, corporate offices also need indicators to satisfy ad hoc information needs from executives, institutional lenders, and large shareholders. Middle management may need indicators to inform environmental management metrics, and the site-level personnel will seek indicators and a suite of metrics to meet the requirements of local regulations.

The differences in the needs of site, management, and corporate functions represent a serious obstacle to adopting a single biodiversity indicator. At the site, where good monitoring may be occurring, driven by both regulatory and nonregulatory biodiversity action, aggregation of data into one or two metrics for corporate use is likely not happening. It is difficult to achieve this common metric, as corporate level indicators must tell a more global story. If a site is engaged in a robust monitoring program of its outstanding ecological efforts and the data is not reported up the chain to the corporate reporting officers, its value will be locally relevant and will not be fully realized at the corporate level where the decision to provide ongoing support for such efforts resides.

To be successful is one thing. To be *seen* as successful is another. For any corporate conservation activity, a mechanism to collate and aggregate site-based success for corporate needs is a prerequisite to secure ongoing support. When developing a corporate conservation plan, corporate reporting needs and site-based actions around monitoring and metrics should dovetail where possible.

Beyond the main challenges of the different needs of site-level actors and corporate report writers, the UNEP report outlines a number of requirements for monitoring corporate efforts that can present a challenge, as follows:

- **Communicate impacts easily.** The indicator must allow for easy communication in corporate reports, press releases, and other vehicles and not require further explanation through footnotes or references.
- **Be cost-effective.** The indicator must not add a financial burden to a site where budgets are already tight, especially if the corporate office is not providing financial support for monitoring or reporting. The requirement for indicators to be cost-effective cannot be stressed enough. Monitoring costs are borne at the site level, where margins may be small and where budgets are tight. High-cost indicators required by corporate but not financially supported by corporate will be unwelcome at the site and will never receive full support.
- **Be accessible to specialists and nonspecialists.** Many sites will not have specialists on staff to collect data and construct indicators. If accessible indicators are created, nonspecialists can become involved in data collection and reporting, and the responsibility for data collection can be shared.
- **Align easily with standard or common monitoring efforts.** When monitoring efforts align easily with common standards, nonspecialists can be involved, training requirements are minimized, and the resulting data may be co-beneficial to a citizen-science observational program
- **Present a comprehensive picture of biodiversity values onsite with both the risk to biodiversity and the performance that benefits biodiversity.** A historic focus only on the negative impacts to biodiversity has been a demotivating factor for many sites. Allowing sites to report on positive biodiversity impacts can increase participation and support for the effort.

- **Present a comprehensive picture of the limits of the site's impact.** Biodiversity is not an isolated aspect of any site. It is linked to drivers and impacts across the ranges of the species in the ecosystem. It is dependent on soil and water as well as other factors that may or may not be on-site. Where does the impact of the site and its operations stop, and impacts beyond the control of the site begin? Indicators that report negative impacts beyond the site's control are not useful. Attribution is one of the most difficult aspects of biodiversity indicators.
- **Allow for differences across operations within a single company.** A mining operation will have different impacts and outcomes from those of a processing operation. Some companies may focus only on one type of operation, but to truly mainstream biodiversity and consolidate metrics, all operations from the beginning of the value chain through to the corporate headquarters should be included.
- **Be comparable across companies within and across industry sectors.** For companies feeding into industry-specific frameworks or global reporting initiatives, the biodiversity indicators from sites must map easily into the various frameworks to allow for comparison.
- **Allow for the full story to be told.** A biodiversity indicator in isolation from other factors does not allow a site or corporation to tell the whole story about its impacts and mitigation efforts. Incidents, weather, operational disruptions, and other aspects may contribute to the data that informs the indicator and should be included in the full story.

Pragmatic Solutions to the Metric Problem

The almost-universal difficulty of developing biodiversity metrics and indicators suggests an alternative route to measuring success, a route that focuses primary energy on implementation but adds two simple approaches for assessing the effort. The first assessment evaluates implementation versus intent through use of best management practices (BMP). The second assessment looks at the value of the conservation action within larger ecological and corporate frameworks. These assessments are a proxy for biodiversity indicators and metrics, but they allow the limited time and resources to focus on implementation, permitting action to proceed unencumbered by the impossible and time-consuming expectations of indicator development.

The first assessment marries intent with implementation that reviews specific conservation objectives against the subsequent action taken. This assessment uses best management practices as the yardstick against which action is measured. While the concept of the environmental BMP started in water-quality management, over the last half century BMPs have been developed and deployed for many aspects of environmental and conservation management. Across industry and government, BMPs are available for all types of environmental activities, safety procedures, and operational processes. In some cases, permit approvals and license renewals depend on strict adherence to BMPs. As an example, within the extractive industries, in shale gas extraction alone there exist 429 oil- and gas-development BMPs. Of these, 28 BMPs are designed for ecosystem health.[9] It is one of the many contradictions of the conservation community that the time and energy of one set of experts are spent developing BMPs, and then more time and energy of other experts is required to prove that they are effective.

The second way to assess the relative value of voluntary corporate conservation efforts is the degree to which the effort is aligned with with local conservation priorities.

From the outset, it's important that a conservation action be implemented specifically to meet a business need or objective and to contribute to a corporate citizenship initiative. Nesting a site-specific initiative into a corporate conservation plan or citizenship strategy will secure support over time. Aligning the conservation action with an existing *external* conservation plan will strengthen the outcomes.

Across the globe, conservation plans exist at multiple scales, and in more-affluent, developed nations there exist a multitude of such plans from local sub-watershed planning efforts to large landscape plans that cross state and even international boundaries. Aligning action with existing conservation priorities is essentially the foundation of the recently popular landscape-scale conservation approach that encourages coordinated action within a specific ecosystem or region to achieve jointly held conservation objectives.

Conservation plans can help anchor integrated corporate approaches to local or regional ecological stewardship goals. Companies that have operations across the country and across the world can benefit from aligning their actions with the appropriate plan, since determining a single conservation objective or action (e.g., prairie restoration on all properties) for multiple operations in places with different climates, conservation needs or opportunities will be impossible and will guarantee less than optimal outcomes. A species-specific conservation goal like restoring and managing beach habitat for the piping plover or grasslands for the boblink will exclude sites and operations with no beaches or grasslands. If a company adopts a species-recovery or -management program, it needs to be sure that all of its locations will be able to contribute to the goals of the program. Different operations and sites will have different potential to contribute to different conservation objectives. A company that adopts a conservation objective to restore prairies/grasslands will exclude facilities with smaller footprints, those in ecoregions that don't support grassland growth, or those locations that have an opportunity to support a locally rare population requiring habitat other than grasslands. By aligning with place-based conservation objectives, disparate approaches from diverse sites can contribute to larger efforts. Alignment with existing plans allows conservation action to be locally meaningful and reportable. Alignments can also provide the reporting frameworks, as existing conservation plans generally contain some ideas for metrics or indicators. A local paint-manufacturing plant owned by Sherwin Williams in the city of Baltimore was able to leverage its conservation action to contribute to the city's stormwater-management plan. The factory, located in the industrial edges of the city, reduced its impervious surfaces with rain gardens that were also designed to provide habitat for pollinators. The corporate office viewed the project's contribution to the city's stormwater-management goals as important, with the pollinator habitat viewed as adding extra value.

Aligning with a conservation plan can also save time and energy in determining appropriate action and deciding what conservation project will make a meaningful contribution to a larger landscape-scale effort. Partnership with a local NGO will help the site-based team better understand what plans exist and how to design conservation actions that align with them.

A great place to start in the United States is with the State Wildlife Action Plans (SWAPs). Each state and territory has such a plan, which is designed to keep common species common and avoid adding new species to threatened and endangered species lists. The focus on unlisted species makes the State Wildlife Action Plans especially attractive to corporate land managers who may want to steer clear of attracting protected species with the political and regulatory complexity they bring. Working with an NGO partner, the site-based team can review the State Wildlife Action Plan for priorities it can adopt, and align its conservation actions accordingly.

The two assessment approaches—using BMPs and aligning with existing external conservation plans—are designed not to meet the needs of the conservation community but the needs of the corporate conservation team that is trying to implement a project that connects value on the ground to meaning in the C-suite. The approaches do not align with the preferences of conservation professionals, but they are not offered to meet those particular needs. The search for the holy grail of biodiversity metrics will continue, but as we wait, we need to use what we already have in terms of BMPs and existing conservation plans and priorities.

Recognition and Verification

If corporate conservationists are to measure their efforts using these simple approaches, external verification and recognition becomes an important aspect of value recognition and reporting.

There are many reasons for the private sector to seek verification or recognition of its local efforts. When a company receives a national or international corporate award, the sites where operations occur and value is made rarely share in the glory. Yet recognition at the local level secures a sense of ownership. Sites that are directly recognized for their conservation efforts feel a real sense of pride that will in turn support long-term investment in the project. The power of recognition, whether through standards and certification or awards and honors, is a potent driver in all aspects of the private sector.

Recognition also provides meaning at the corporate level when the company can aggregate locally appropriate actions to be globally relevant and recognized. The best recognition provides for scaling so that even though each project is "owned" locally, the corporate office realizes value across its multiple facilities, business units, or subsidiaries. If each quarry in a region is going beyond compliance in its land-management efforts and is being recognized for this, the message to the regional office will be about the number of programs going above and beyond, not just a single site implementing conservation action. If every operation in a power company, from the generation station to the transmission lines and the substations, is engaged in conservation, the message will be meaningful to employees who feel part of a larger group effort and to customers who will recognize the commitment.

Recognition drives competition, which in turn drives engagement and change. It is very hard to overstate the importance of competition in the corporate world. Our entire capitalist system is built on competition for resources, for customers, and for being the top in any given field. Anyone who has ever intersected with the corporate community knows that within and across industry sectors, competition is a powerful force. Employee-driven, employee-owned competition that increases corporate success in an area like voluntary conservation is a powerful tool. Companies do not enter into benchmarking exercises to be seen at or below the benchmark. Most, especially publicly traded companies, seek to exceed the benchmark and show leadership in subsequent benchmarking exercises. With respect to voluntary conservation efforts, the inclusion of an element of competition can be the difference between a standard conservation exercise and an outstanding one.

As discussed earlier, biodiversity metrics do not meet the needs of the conservation community or the corporate community for a variety of reasons—but recognition and competition can. If a company is investing resources, time, and money in voluntary conservation efforts, it must be able to report value. Companies may decide to enter into recognition or certification systems and adopt the metrics of those systems as their key performance indicators for their conservation efforts.

Voluntary Sustainability Standards

Some recognition systems bestow a seal of approval that customers understand, but many private-sector institutions do not have a public face and therefore do not need to satisfy a retail consumer. A mining company selling metals to a processing company that will sell the final product to a parts manufacturer who will, in turn, sell to a consumer-electronics company has a different need for a seal than the consumer-electronics company selling its device to the public. But all private corporate entities have customers of some sort, and these customers, whether individual consumers or large industrial buyers, demand transparency about the source of the goods and the location in which they are being produced. Efforts to increase transparency and accountability in the supply chain are growing across all industry sectors, raising fascinating questions about how attributes of a commodity can be assigned and communicated from the site of extraction to the customers' hands and, in the case of the circular economy, beyond. The majority of these concerns start with human rights and labor practices, but increasingly they are moving beyond human rights and into land use and land management. Having a seal, a certification, or a standard associated with lands-management activities provides the industrial landowner with a way to leverage and communicate the value from the work. A seal of approval or certification provides a shorthand and a credible way to talk about the effort.

Recognition also enhances reputation, which is increasingly important for a corporate entity in today's world where a company's doings, both wrong and right, can be easily seen and communicated. Good reputation enhances a company's financial performance. A good reputation, in fact, is a priceless commodity, because its intangible nature makes it hard for competitors to copy it.[10]

Corporate recognition can range from a seal of approval, a certificate with specific requirements or an award, and depending on the power of the recognition, it can act as an incentive for a company to continue its conservation efforts. Within the conservation community, giving a company an award for their conservation activities can be contentious for a number of reasons. For many activists, every aspect of a company today is colored by the actions of the past or inactions to address present-day issues, which renders the entire company ineligible for any recognition of good behavior. But this is changing. Younger generational attitudes toward the corporate world are less informed by missteps that occurred in the past and more informed by how the company is rated today as a corporate citizen and how it is rated as a good place to work.

To be trusted by consumers and other certifications, seals and other third-party recognitions should adhere to a set of stated design principles and hold up to external verification. Awards, to be credible, must have a posted set of criteria. The best voluntary sustainable standards should be transparent and accessible; stakeholder-informed; credible yet impartial; and able to drive change within and across industry sectors.

In the private sector, external verification through adoption of voluntary sustainability standards and certifications is a massive industry across all aspects of environmental management, corporate responsibility, and accountability. These standards can be associated with products and the processes that create them. Voluntary sustainability standards have evolved from being used in early attempts to indicate good practices to now being required by customers along the supply chain. Auditing firms are increasingly involved in ensuring that these standards are credible, moving outside their traditional remits of reviewing financial structures to increasingly auditing performance of a nonfinancial nature such as performance in the arenas of social responsibility, environmental stewardship, and corporate governance. If corporations are making claims to meet customer or investor needs, these claims must be verified. Today there are many initiatives that will do so.

There are many different originators for these standards. Industry associations develop environmental management systems (EMS) to create common frameworks for benchmarking or for meeting requirements from vendors or other industry groups. The National Ready Mixed Concrete Association (NRMCA) launched the Environmental Product Declaration to meet the needs of customers to demonstrate the environmental performance of products used in a building seeking Leadership in Energy and Environmental Design (LEED) certification. The growth of EMS has been shown to improve the environmental performance of the facilities that embrace them and have also been shown to impact aspects beyond what the EMS is managing.[11]

Government and nonprofit groups have also launched certifications or seals of approval such as Energy Star or other ecolabels. Knowledge of these programs is important, since many operations will be required to adhere to the principles so that the company can retain its particular certification, or a specific operation may seek certification, especially in the case of the International Standardization Organization's (ISO) 14001 standard for assessing environmental management performance, a site-specific designation. Many companies will have a mandate from head office that all their operations seek and maintain ISO 14001, which is becoming the dominant standard. Not all ISO 14001–certified facilities report the same performance outcomes, but facilities that integrate environmental performance into everyday operations show the best outcomes from their certified management programs.[12] Working with industry, conservation practitioners will find that many industry associations have their own recognition and awards programs advancing best environmental management practices, and these can be the best frameworks for reporting conservation outcomes. Working with these industry standards, conservation partners may find a common language with the site and may be able to advance conservation implementation more easily if it can be done to meet the needs of an existing certification or management system.

Who Certifies the Certifiers?

It is important to be able to assess a certification scheme and what it purports to show. The rapid increase in third-party certifications has led to a proliferation of initiatives. Some are more robust than others. It has also led to a proliferation of critics of the schemes; some critics have valid and sincere objections while others do not.

Into this fray we see the certification of certification schemes through a process that is content-neutral and that does not itself certify but provides a methodology to assess the development, governance, and other aspects of any standard. One such initiative also from ISO is its 14020 series, which provides guidance and certification for the development of declarations of environmental performance for ecolabels.

Many certification programs or voluntary sustainability standards are focused on commodities such as palm oil, forest products, or cotton. Some are focused on end-use such as jewelry, golf, etc., while others seek to drive change on practices like child labor and fair-trade issues. With an increasing number of sustainability standards, the ISEAL Alliance has emerged as a group that looks not at the content of what is being certified but the process through which the certification is developed and governed. Compliance with ISEAL Alliance best practice and guidance on standard choice has become an important part of the verification conversation.

The ISEAL Alliance looks at the management of standards, standard-setting, and compliance with the standards (also known as assurance). While the language used by ISEAL is dense and academic, the approach is quite simple. It highlights the need for robust management systems, results-oriented learning, and, most importantly, transparency along the process from standard-setting to management, compliance, and standard revision.

Any standard that does not embrace transparency should be treated with caution. Any site or operation that seeks a conservation-based standard and yet does not adhere to the principles of transparency, stakeholder engagement, and process governance may end up securing a certification or recognition that can be called into question by customers and others.

At the end of the day, implementing a strategic corporate conservation plan across a company will face many more difficulties than implementing a conservation plan developed for single species or for lands that are designated for conservation action. A company's lands may be in different parts of the country—or, indeed, the world—and may have different conservation needs or opportunities. The lands may have differing potential to contribute to a conservation goal.

Operations will be working under widely varying budgets, different available resources, and different sets of regulations. At every site, conservation knowledge will vary widely. Implementation may be fully resourced or not. Monitoring will always be under-resourced. And the corporate office will have needs for information that may defy logic but are critical to fulfill.

By taking a pragmatic approach to monitoring, the almost-universal challenges of measuring outcomes can be addressed. By collecting data to meet different needs across the company, the value of the effort will be enhanced. Using this data will also secure recognition for the conservation effort, the local site, or the company overall. The need for conservation data to meet a number of different corporate needs is unique to corporate conservation and, when done well, can be immensely valuable.

07 EDUCATION

—

I believe that it's vital for children and teens to be educated, to be given information to help them understand the impacts humans are having on our water, soil, and air.

—JAYNI CHASE, CONSERVATION EDUCATOR

When Bridgestone Americas built a new truck tire manufacturing plant in Warren County, Tennessee, the company planned to make it the most advanced tire plant in the world. Tim Bent, the former director of environmental affairs for Bridgestone, explains that the plant had progressive management for energy efficiency, operational teamwork, advanced maintenance, and self-management, all of which were the norm and not the exception. The plant manager was, in Tim's estimation, one of the best leaders ever. He inspired his staff and supported innovation. Under this leadership he created an enlightened workplace across all aspects of operations and nonessential activities. When it came to introducing nature-based efforts at the plant, the existing enabling environment fostered the development of an award-winning educational program that met a critical community need.

The Bridgestone plant is located in one of the poorest counties in one of the poorest states in the United States. The school district has few resources for essentials, let alone extracurricular activities. Leadership at the plant, aware of the needs of their community, was inspired by the work of other companies that connected conservation programs on their lands with education in their communities. Encouraged and supported by a local teacher, they teamed up to add an educational aspect to ongoing natural-resources management efforts at the plant and created BEECH—the Bridgestone Environmental Education Classroom and Habitat.

Since 2008, BEECH has been a model resource for the community. Every child in the Warren County School District visits BEECH at least once, learning about the natural environment through hands-on lessons both indoors and outside, exploring environmental management through reduction, reuse, and recycling and learning basic science concepts. The facility has a full-time educator, and employees at the tire plant volunteer their time to lead groups through the learning experience. There is no cost for schools to attend, the educator at the facility is an employee of Bridgestone, and the program's budget is part of the annual operations budget for the plant.

BEECH is an example of a company combining its corporate citizenship values with environmental education and community enrichment. Not every company will be willing to make such an investment in education, and, indeed, not all Bridgestone operations have a BEECH. But the effort is inspiring and shows how the private sector can supplement existing educational and community resources, and leverage its lands to benefit community members of all ages.

Using corporate lands for education can be the primary objective of a strategic corporate conservation plan or contribute to a broader plan. Just like conservation action itself, education using corporate lands has many manifestations. This chapter will explore how corporate conservation plans can easily and meaningfully include education efforts and bring value to communities.

Corporate Lands as Education Locations

Companies can use their lands for education in many ways, from hosting informal annual Earth Day events to providing access to their lands for postgraduate research students. The decision to open corporate lands to education and the final design of any education offering will depend on the business need that informs the corporate conservation strategy, as well as a number of other factors such as the availability of land, proximity of people and community, and the commitment and interests of leadership.

Toyota, the global auto manufacturing company has adopted six environmental challenges for 2050. They include achieving zero emissions from vehicles, factories, and the manufacturing life cycle, and also a nature-based challenge, "Establishing a Future Society

Figure 7-1: A burrowing owl is relocated onto a specially designed corporate habitat while local school children learn about its conservation needs. (Used with permission from Freeport-McMoRan, Inc.)

in Harmony with Nature." The challenge explicitly requires that any conservation action implemented by Toyota on its own lands or in the community are done in collaboration and connection with society across all sectors. To this end, programs have been designed to involve education, both formal and informal, in locations where Toyota implements ecological stewardship projects. In Georgetown, Kentucky, the employees invite second-grade students for an annual field day to learn about the environment and give youth groups access to their ponds for fishing. At its manufacturing facility in Pakota Township, Indiana, Toyota engages over 1,000 middle school students annually in the World Water Monitoring Challenge that teaches STEM (Science, Technology, Engineering, and Math) skills about water quality and engages the students in collecting data from their area rivers to contribute to this international effort.

There are many benefits to using corporate lands for education through formal and informal methods alike. Companies leveraging their lands both for environmental and STEM education offer not only outdoor education opportunities, but also an experience of place in the community and an engaging alternative to classroom instruction. By providing access to company lands for education, a business can introduce itself to the community and show what goes on "inside the fence." It can demystify the location as visitors gain a greater sense of the operations and knowledge about the environmental management occurring on-site. Education efforts on company lands create deep local value at a site that can also be leveraged by the corporate office as part of a success story around conservation, corporate citizenship, or community engagement.

Company lands offer a learning experience that is uniquely different from what is seen at nature centers or parks. On company lands, students can view nature integrated into a working landscape, a place that is industrial or is managed for a purpose other than ecological outcomes. Nature centers and outdoor education facilities tend to follow a traditional design, with a natural area and an interpretive center focused on wild and idealized nature. Nature centers offer a common suite of interpretive exhibits and programs explaining life cycles of both plants and animals. Unintentionally, they can create a sense of distance between the students and nature, presenting nature like art in a gallery, lovely to look at but isolated from a greater context.

Corporate lands offer a different educational experience that can range from traditional nature-based activities to experiences that educate about the industrial operation, its place in the global supply chain of goods and materials, and the environmental and safety management associated with it. Combining traditional nature-based environmental education with education about operations provides a whole-world lesson and highlights the connection between natural resources and manufactured products. Increasingly, consumers don't know where the things they purchase or consume come from or how they are made. In the words of Rob Hopkins, a founder of the Transition movement, consumers can't change behavior if they can't connect the oil well in Saudi Arabia to the refinery in Yemen, the plastics factory in China, and the easily broken toy from the McDonald's Happy Meal in their own hometown.

Connecting the journey of materials from nature to component or finished product gives corporate lands a unique use in environmental education. In addition, using natural-resources stewardship programs occurring on corporate lands for education brings nature home, illustrating that nature can thrive in less pristine places and nature engagement need not be limited to parks or preserves.

Another benefit of using corporate lands for natural-resources stewardship and environmental education is that the programs on these lands can reach learners in school districts and communities that have limited resources and little access to outdoor classrooms or nature centers. Like BEECH, corporate lands can become a valuable asset for underserved communities.

Many studies have shown racial and income disparities when it comes to exposure to nature. Youth living in poorer communities have reduced access to national parks, trails, and even sports facilities, while youth of color are less likely to access their public parks than their white counterparts.[1] Youth in poor urban areas express fear of public parks in their areas due to gangs and crime.[2] One way to connect urban youth and those from underserved communities to nature is through educational partnerships with outdoor classrooms, whether on protected lands or elsewhere.[3]

Since transportation costs remain a barrier to access outdoor classrooms, corporate lands that are located in a community may represent a cost-effective option for many school districts. Historically, the relationship between corporate facilities and poor communities has been fraught. Inequities in siting hazardous waste and other facilities in poor communities spurred the creation of the environmental justice movement in the 1970s and '80s, which resulted in President Clinton's Executive Order 12898 in 1994, compelling federal agencies to consider community burden when approving permits for industry to operate. Today, many corporate locations in poor communities are seeking to repair their relationships with the community and are finding that they can provide outdoor, hands-on learning experiences for students that are unavailable to them elsewhere. Whether in rural areas where extraction in quarries and mines take place, or in urban areas where distribution, manufacturing, or waste management facilities are located, an industrial operation can, in an unlikely fashion, serve a community that lacks easy access to the outdoors. A good example of corporate lands being used as an educational resource for underserved communities is in River Rouge, Michigan, a small city with an outsized burden of environmental challenges.

As is obvious from its name, the city River Rouge sits on the Rouge River. The small city is bounded on two sides by the city of Detroit. On its northernmost boundary is Detroit's sewage-treatment plant and the infamous Zug Island, one of the densest collections of heavy industries in the country, which has consistently noncompliant air quality. In the small city of River Rouge itself, there are about fifty-two industrial locations within a three-mile radius. The school district's per-pupil spending is just below the state's average, and the school district offers a program for homeless youth as well as a summer meal program. On EJScreen, the Environmental Protection Agency's (EPA's) Environmental Justice Screening and Mapping Tool, River Rouge scores high for most environmental contamination indicators and environmental justice indices such as proximity of Superfund sites, the amount of daily vehicular traffic, and the levels of ozone in the air.

In such a challenged urban area in a heavily industrialized city, a power plant has created a resource that gives students in the local school district and nearby universities access to lands for environmental education, real-world learning opportunities, and hands-on experience in many aspects of ecological stewardship.

On the banks of the Rouge River, DTE, Detroit's electric utility, maintains a power plant that also happens to be a quality environmental learning center. Over recent decades, DTE and its employees at the power plant have implemented a number of ecological restoration projects as part of the company's commitment to improved environmental outcomes across its territory. Employees and conservation partners at the plant reengineered the river frontage to soften the edge of the river, which is 99 percent "hardscaped." The employees also created artificial nesting habitat for the common tern (listed as endangered by the state of Michigan) on unused ship-mooring cells in the river. To create opportunities for education, the plant converted five acres of lawn and restored it to a small wooded prairie for use as a nature center and outdoor education classroom for local students and others.

Youth from the neighborhood have worked to help the employees with the ecological restoration efforts. A group of young people identified as "at risk" uses the site for hands-on experiential learning.

They have designed and installed a native wildflower demonstration garden and they monitor a variety of aspects of the project, including benthic macro-invertebrates in the pond on-site. Local teachers are invited to the site to learn how to align site-based learning with the Michigan Grade Level Content expectations using lesson plans developed by the employees of the plant and an educational partner. The ecological stewardship project is used as a demonstration site for students from nearby Wayne State University to learn about planning and implementing an ecological restoration project. The site is also the location of a PhD study researching the movement of coyotes in an urban area. In addition to the formal education programs, non-school-based youth groups like the Scouts and the Girl Guides use the natural areas at the power plant to earn merit badges in both wildlife conservation and bird study. This five-acre patch of nature in an urban industrial landscape gets heavy use across the educational spectrum.

Another contribution that corporate lands can make to education is by acting as an outdoor laboratory like the River Rouge plant does for the coyote study, answering research questions related to habitat and species' response to operations, ecological remediation, or reclamation activities. The unique active nature of corporate lands also provides a contrast for studies being conducted on protected preserved lands.

Former Superfund and brownfield locations with ongoing monitoring or treatment for remediation and site cleanup are perfect laboratories for research in the ever-evolving field of restoration ecology. All corporate lands provide great locations for longitudinal research that can provide a student or cohorts of students with data sets for school projects and provide a company with the information they need to illustrate compliance or conservation outcomes.

Warms Springs Pond is a single remediation site within the larger Anaconda Mine remediation complex in Clark County, Montana. The project is a series of constructed wetlands managed by the Atlantic Richfield company. This wetland complex has become a premier birding destination overseen by the state of Montana as a Wildlife and Recreation Management Area. It is also a water-treatment facility for surface water impacted by historical mining pollution. The site's split personality as a destination for avian life and a mitigation site for past waste mismanagement makes it a perfect outdoor laboratory to study ecotoxicology. The Montana Osprey Program, a research project of the University of Montana, studies the ospreys in the region, measuring the levels of toxins in their blood as a way to determine how the environment is responding overall to the cleanup efforts in the Superfund complex. These studies provide students with access to wildlife and data that has a very practical outcome, which will be to direct further actions by Atlantic Richfield and the agencies overseeing the cleanup.

Where a company has a portfolio of contaminated sites in populated areas, on-site education programs can be a great way to provide a valuable resource to the communities and to repair community relations. BASF, the chemical giant, uses education and community outreach to change community minds at remediation sites such as Fighting Island in the Detroit River, Renselaer in upstate New York, and an infamous site of mismanaged toxic waste in Tom's River, New Jersey. Across its remediation portfolio, the company creates partnerships with schools promoting multi-grade approaches for using the land. It subsidizes transport and works to secure external funding and partnerships to support the programs.

Many of BASF's educational programs, like the one on Fighting Island, are so popular that interested schools must enter a lottery to participate. Fighting Island sits in the Detroit River on the Canadian side of the international border and is part of the town of LaSalle, Ontario. The island of just over 1,500 acres was so named because of the many skirmishes between the English and French which occurred there over the years, thanks to its location on an international border. In 1918, the island was bought by industrialist John B. Ford, who created the Michigan Alkali company. He used the island as a waste site for the distillate byproduct of an industrial soda ash operation. The waste was deposited on the island in three lagoons across 900 acres. The silt-like waste, containing chlorides, coke ashes, and unreactive limestone, was not incorporated into the environment in any way. With a high pH, high salt concentration, and no organic matter, the lagoons became inert places that could not support any life and proved to be a nuisance as well as a threat to human health as the waste, once dried, blew across the river into the homes and gardens along the Canadian banks of the river.

Responsibility for the site has passed to BASF, and in the 1980s the company began a multiyear effort to restore the soil and bring nature back to the island. Because of the nature of the material in the settling lagoons, the best way to restore the island is to radically lower the pH by adding shredded organic material to the distillate and over the years rebuild the soil through composting. In the beginning, 25,000 bales of straw were used every year to try to build up the organic layer and act as windrows to protect from blow-off. Today lawn and leaf waste collected from the residents of LaSalle are removed to the island and ground up and spread for use in rebuilding the organic layer.

Through the restoration, the island is becoming revegetated, although at present the lagoon restoration is limited primarily to the establishment of phragmites—an invasive yet opportunistic plant that can survive in challenging soil conditions. Beyond the lagoons, though, the island is host to a variety of wildlife, from charismatic species like a resident pair of bald eagles and over 140 deer to smaller species like butterflies, toads, and bats. In the shadow of the island an artificial sturgeon reef is the location of the first successful sturgeon egg-laying in the Detroit River in decades.

At Fighting Island, BASF has invested in two classroom buildings to provide place-based environmental education to the Greater Essex School Board District that encompasses Windsor and LaSalle Ontario. The program is described by BASF and the teachers that use it as a living, breathing textbook. The island does not have a permanent educator, so every year a competition in the school district selects a number of teachers to be the Fighting Island educators, ensuring fresh energy for the project year after year and making the project cost-efficient for the school district and the company. Schools must enter a lottery to secure a place for their students at Fighting Island, and the classes fill quickly every year. To date, 3,000 school children have visited the island for grade-appropriate lessons in the laboratory and outside.

The students arrive at the island by boat—a first-time experience for many students. They do hands-on environmental education activities such as seining the ponds, identifying plants, building bug hotels, learning about beaver dams and osprey nests, and even building their own eagles' nest. The students enjoy state-of-the-art technology in the classrooms that allows them to test water, look at macroinvertebrates, understand identification keys, and more. Both teachers and students have a memorable time on the island. The school board supports the effort by freeing up the teachers chosen through the competition to spend the year on the island, and BASF supports the project by providing the classrooms and the equipment, as well as access to the island.

What was once a community health concern and a blight is now a community asset. The island is not yet a fully recovered and functioning ecosystem—that result will take decades to achieve—but during those decades the residents of LaSalle can look across the river and see an award-winning education facility and not the source of windborne pollution. This is a deliberate strategy by BASF to have productive use of its remediation sites while the cleanup is under way so that communities can realize the benefits as quickly as possible. Because these education efforts are taking place at a contaminated site on an island, the company ensures that all precautions are taken and is strict in its adherence to health and safety protocols.

As BASF shows, education programs based on industry lands can achieve multiple benefits for both company and community, whether as a resource to an underserved community, an outdoor laboratory to study the effects of ecological remediation, or a way to repair community relations. Such programs can sit within the corporate citizenship initiatives and the community relations function, or integrate with operations and cleanup work. There are so many options for using lands for education that a company must design carefully to make sure that the outcomes benefit the community but also contribute to the business reason.

Programming Decisions

Before any company designs a program or seeks to secure educational partners, and especially before it opens its lands to education, it must answer a number of key questions about what sort of education will meet the business goal. It should consider different op-

Table 7-1: Considerations and Options for Designing Strong Education Programs

Considerations	*Options*
Frequency of activity	One-off—an annual event Ongoing—multiple events over a year
Alignment with curriculum	Formal—delivering curriculum value Informal—delivering broad educational value
Targeted age group	Students—structure around educational levels Community—inclusive of all ages
Connectivity across multiple locations	Linked—one approach across multiple sites Replicated—same program, same delivery Unique—designed specifically for the site
Type of education	Outdoor—on corporate lands Place-based—connecting to community Environmental—focused on awareness Hands-on—building or experimenting STEM—integrated with the environment

tions and understand the consequences and tradeoffs of the decisions it makes.

Table 7-1 sets out the options that the company and its partner must consider.

ONE-OFF OR ONGOING

The options for educational programs are not exclusively either/ or. They can be combined to offer a variety of educational opportunities to different communities of learners. When a company decides to open its lands to the community for education, one of the most important first choices is whether it wants to welcome learners throughout the year or just once. This decision will drive budgets and other resource needs.

The choices will range from a one-off open house for employee families to an effort that brings students to the site week after week during school time. A single educational activity like an open house or science fair may be an attractive proposition from the point of view of staff resources, but it will have limited value and meet the business objective once only or just once annually. An ongoing activity such as a relationship with a school district may take up more employees' time but is more likely to realize greater value for both the company and the participants.

However, a one-off event can become part of the fabric of the community when it is repeated with common elements. At CRH America's Marcus Autism Center Trail, the community program in Atlanta, Georgia, an annual open day is attended by families of clients at the center, employees of CRH, and neighborhood residents. This open day has been repeated for six years and has now become integrated into the community. It is well known and well attended and brings value to the same community again and again. This repetition of the event and the ongoing investment by CRH greatly increases its value as a corporate investment and a community resource—but it has taken time and consistency to achieve.

An ongoing educational activity sees the same community, school district, or educational partner engaged in repeat visits over a period of time. The activities can be an annual field trip to a specific corporate operation that welcomes a single grade level, or multiple grade levels over the course of a school year. It can be designed for one grade level to be on-site multiple times during a school year, or for multiple grade levels to visit multiple times. At BASF's Fighting Island, children from one specific grade across multiple schools get to visit the island every year. The investment has been long term and is now delivering results. The children who attended the island's educational programs in the early years are now sending their children to participate in the program, weaving the program into the fabric of the community and securing community relations through ongoing education.

The consequences of the choice between a one-off event or an ongoing series lie in the amount of resources and employee time that will be needed for the effort. It may appear on the surface that an ongoing effort will be more resource-intensive than a one-off event, but that is not necessarily the case. An Earth Day event, fair, or family day will, if targeting community members and the general public, require vendors with materials and giveaways and entertainment. An Earth Day event may also require tents and other infrastructure, such as portable toilets, and food trucks or other food vendors. All of these aspects cost money.

For an educational effort that engages learners in the environment, water-testing kits and similar materials will not be as expensive as the one-off event. Once the initial investments are made, it will get less expensive every year. A fair or open house will require fewer employee hours than a series of lessons in the landscape. Usually a one-off event is managed by a single employee or committee investing significant planning, and a broader group to act as volunteers at the event. A series of learning activities may consume a smaller amount of staff planning time but many more hours in delivery and assessment.

The trade-offs of this decision will determine the ease and speed with which value is realized. A one-off activity will have a big initial impact if a large number of community members participate. It will also receive attention from local media. The value may be short-lived unless it becomes an annual, highly anticipated activity. A one-off event that is a regular occurrence, embedded in the community,

Figure 7-2 : An activity like making bee-nesting structures from coffee cans and bamboo can be carried out during an Earth Day fair or open house event. (Used with permission of Wildlife Habitat Council.)

has greater value and contributes more to the business goal. An ongoing effort will return value quickly but to a smaller group—the students and education partners. As with a one-off event, value increases year after year, but more slowly since school groups will be smaller in size and the impact limited to families with children in the participating schools. An ongoing activity will need a sound communication strategy for the company to realize value through the students' engagement.

FORMAL OR INFORMAL

Informal education happens outside the structured curriculum, while formal education is aligned with an official curriculum and any other standards that teachers must adhere to. The decision to engage in formal or informal education will be linked to the decision to offer a one-off event or an ongoing engagement. A one-off event that engages the general public is informal education, while a multi-year engagement with multiple grade levels can be either.

The decision to offer formal or informal education will depend on factors like the proximity of schools and also the business reason for starting the educational program in the first place. An operation that seeks only to connect to community, improve community relations, and secure social license to operate through education may find informal education the best option, while a corporate conservation strategy that seeks to impact future workforce development through targeted STEM education on corporate lands may decide to adopt formal programs.

The consequences of deciding between informal or formal approaches will mainly be seen in the need for external partners. A strong education partnership is necessary if the educational program is to be formal. Employees are unlikely to have the knowledge of curricular requirements and alignments. A more robust design approach with external partners will be needed to ensure that the activities align with the standards, whether state or federal. For example, at the DTE River Rouge plant, the education programs align with Michigan state standards, and one of the programs offered at the site helps teachers map the standards to their environmental education efforts beyond the River Rouge plant by providing template lesson plans they can adapt for their own locations and students.

For formal education efforts, a program that clearly aligns with standards and requirements will be infinitely more attractive than one that offers immersion in environmental issues without any alignment to the curriculum. Teachers in schools adhering to state or federally mandated standards cite limited resources and limited time for extracurricular offerings, as they are increasingly teaching to a set curriculum. A formal effort has greater appeal to an overstretched teacher, as it will have the co-benefits of providing curricular content in an off-campus location for an enhanced learning experience.

ELEMENTARY, HIGH SCHOOL, AND BEYOND

The type of education program (formal or informal / one-off or ongoing) will inform decisions on the age of the audience for the program. Other information that will inform this decision will focus on ease of access, the nature of the lands, and how rustic the outdoors experience is. Younger students will require more shelter and more bathroom facilities. It will be important to understand whether the operation itself—open pits or large machinery, for example—presents a risk to younger students.

This decision will drive the choice of education partner. More resources and infrastructure are required for lower grade levels and should be factored into the decision. A consequence of engaging post-secondary students will be that fewer students will come on-site at any time. It's also important to keep in mind that those students are not necessarily community members, so specific community value will not be realized.

At Waste Management's Bucks County landfill in Pennsylvania, education efforts connect the landfill, local schools, and a local senior group through the Intergenerational Pollinator Partnership Project. With project partner Bucks County Audubon, three pollinator gardens have been installed, one at each location: the senior center, the Pen Ryn School, and an almost 6,000-square-foot pollinator garden at the landfill itself. Bucks County Audubon educates all three groups—the employees at the landfill, the students at the school, and the senior citizens—about how best to align their efforts and how to design and maintain the gardens so they will have maximum benefit for biodiversity. In addition to this effort, another team at the nearby GROWS/Tullytown Landfills connects with the Pennsbury School District to help three local schools create and manage pollinators on their own properties. Employees from the landfills help each school with design and then give tours of the landfill's composting area, native gardens, and the William Penn Forest, a small woodland on the landfill site. The small team of employees led by the ever-energetic Judy Archibald, who was formerly head of public affairs for the landfill for many years and is now coordinating the community and education efforts as her "retirement" job. She has long provided educational opportunities to teachers by hosting an annual teachers workshop that helps teachers learn how to incorporate sustainability in their lessons.

UNIQUE, LINKED, OR REPLICATED

If a company is seeking to build a network of programs across its operations, it will want to consider whether each program should be unique in terms of audience, effort, and alignments, or whether all the programs should be linked in ways that allow for metrics to be consolidated for a specific success story. While ecological stewardship projects are strongest when they reflect the conservation context at the site, education programs have their greatest value to corporations when they are linked across a theme regardless of location and are using the same curriculum, the same types of education partners, and focusing on the same audience. The decision to link or not will depend on the business reason for engaging in education, the story the company wants to tell, and the metrics it has developed.

General Motors' formal education efforts are offered under GM Global Rivers Environmental Education Network (GREEN), which connects GM employees with local schools and conservation groups to mentor students through water-related education and engagement activities. To ensure quality and consistency, GM's education nonprofit partner, Earth Force, provides the training and management for 3,200 GM staff members as mentors and 150,000 students. By partnering with one education partner, independent of location, GM not only ensures quality but also establishes a system that allows the program to easily increase its impact across GM sites in North America and Canada.

However, if a corporation exercises control over its education offerings to such an extent, it may weaken local ownership of the effort, which could hamper the effort's success. By designing a program that engages employees in the delivery, GM minimizes the potential impact of weaker ownership. The GM approach to use one provider for its environmental education efforts requires higher levels of upfront energy and oversight. Unique local efforts, on the other hand, may realize substantial community value but may not realize the same value for corporate success. Unique programs will enjoy greater ownership at the location, while replicated programs will tell a stronger story overall and ensure quality control. Replicated programs with existing materials and templates for onboarding are easier to implement and may be adopted by employees for that reason.

Pedagogy Decisions

Nontraditional education is generally defined as "educational programs that are offered as alternatives within or outside the formal educational system and provide innovative and flexible instruction, curriculum, grading systems, or degree requirements."[4] Nontraditional education programs can be offered for a variety of reasons, such as providing options for different learning styles, alleviating delinquency or truancy, or merely augmenting traditional approaches. Outdoor, place-based, hands-on environmental and STEM education can all be offered within nontraditional education approaches. Corporate lands can be effective locations for nontraditional education efforts that seek to transmit knowledge outside of the formal structure of a school classroom.

There are so many opportunities for nontraditional education approaches on company lands that options beyond those which meet the business objective for investing in education may easily appear. But, if the business reason is part of the discussion as the education effort is designed, the resulting program can satisfy the business need and make securing corporate support easier.

ENVIRONMENTAL EDUCATION

Environmental education can exist along the continuum from traditional to nontraditional education. At its most basic, environmental education teaches about the natural world: the web of life and the processes (from geological to microbial) that contribute to the web of life. Traditional education may teach photosynthesis or the hydrologic cycle in isolation, but environmental education goes further by integrating these concepts. Environmental education looks at the interconnectedness of humanity and nature and also advances practices and behaviors that have a positive impact on the planet. Environmental education takes the more formal lessons of biology and applies them to the real world.

Environmental education as a discipline has many progenitors, stretching back to Goethe, Rousseau, and Humboldt. In more recent times it found its way into the mainstream and onto curricula through the various paths and evolutions of the study of nature and conservation education. The International Union for the Conservation of Nature (IUCN) embraced environmental education at its founding in 1948. Today, the longest-standing committee in the IUCN is the one that advances education about the environment all around the world. Environmental education is intertwined with outdoor education, hands-on or experiential learning, and place-based education. It is also a perfect integrating framework for STEM education.

While environmental education has been around for a long time, the argument in favor of it received a sharp boost in the late twentieth and early twenty-first centuries when research identified a growing gap between children and the natural world as kids from suburban, urban, and even rural places spend less time in nature; and even when in nature, engage mostly in structured activities with time limits as well as geographical limits. This absence of exposure to the natural world has impacts on physical and mental health and well-being as well as on the next generations of leaders. The collective wisdom agrees that without an understanding of nature and empathy for environmental concerns, there will be no advocates for protecting and restoring nature in the future. In the late twentieth century, exposure to nature to combat what the author Richard Louv called nature-deficit disorder, became a rallying cry for child-development professionals, environmental advocates, and others.

The publicity surrounding these studies, including Louv's seminal work, *Last Child in the Woods*, and other communications around this issue, has resulted in a marked increase in interest in the outdoors and an increased awareness of the value of environmental education to the future health and well-being of society. In the United Kingdom, the Forest School program saw membership in its network jump from 200 practitioners in 2013 to over 2,000 in 2018.[5] The global Eco-Schools program overseen by the Foundation for Environmental Education saw its enrollment almost double from 10 million students in 2010 to 19 million in 2017. This increased awareness in the importance of environmental education has also encouraged the corporate world to embrace the approach as an investment in the citizens of the future and an efficient use of existing resources.

OUTDOOR EDUCATION

Outdoor education is, as the name implies, education that is conducted outside of the typical classroom. This education can take

Figure 7-3: Children learn differently in the outdoors and gain a real sense of place through active participation in an activity like sampling water for macro-invertebrates or other biota. (Used with permission of Bruce Power.)

place in a school yard, a local park or at a corporate site. Outdoor education is not wedded to any scholarly discipline but merely uses the fact of students being outside to change attitudes, perspectives, and focus.

In addition to environmental education offering an antidote to nature-deficit disorder, outdoor classrooms with or without environmental education have also proven to be very effective teaching tools for different learners. Outdoor education promotes cooperative learning and civic responsibility, and is proven to improve academic achievement.[6] Companies that are seeking meaningful engagement with the communities in which they operate will easily see the link between providing quality outdoor education opportunities and enhanced relationships with the community.

PLACE-BASED EDUCATION

Place-based education focuses both on the natural and cultural world of the individual. It seeks to create a sense of, and connection to place. These efforts could incorporate lessons from environmental education but also include teaching on civic engagement, and they can take place in both natural and constructed environments.[7]

Most company efforts are place-based, as they are generally offered in the community where the learners live. By opening the gates of a factory or power plant to students, the company shows what's inside the fence and demystifies the operation. In Brazil, a conservation effort by Bayer seeks to reconnect two fragments of Atlantic Forest, one of the most threatened biomes on the planet. To connect the community with this effort and educate about the importance of the Atlantic Forest region, Bayer invites local school children to its factory site to learn about the importance of the restoration and the species that depend on the forest, and then invites them to take action by planting seedlings. It also involves local community members during family days at the plant and provides updates on the restoration effort to all employees. This place-based education helps gain community support for the restoration project and the Atlantic Forest biome, increasing sense of place and connection to this important habitat.

HANDS-ON LEARNING

We know that not every learner thrives in a formal classroom setting and that not every learner absorbs knowledge through a theoretical approach. Hands-on learning, whether indoors or outdoors and whether for environmental education, engineering, homemaking skills, or any other subject with a practical application has been shown to be an effective teaching tool for all sorts of learners, especially those who do not thrive in a formal educational setting. One of the easiest places to provide hands-on learning is in nature because of the ease of access, the lack of specialized equipment needed for nature-based learning, and the proliferation of quality environmental education curriculum from organizations ranging from the United Nations Educational, Scientific, and Cultural Organization (UNESCO) to the US Forest Service, which is free and easily available to educators.

STEM EDUCATION

Integrated STEM education has grown in popularity in recent years as the number of students electing careers in engineering and math has decreased even as the need for a workforce literate in science and technology has increased or remained steady.[8] STEM education is an approach to teaching science, technology, engineering, and math through real-life examples and in an integrated manner that creates connections beyond the classroom and illustrates the many applications of science and technology in today's world. The availability of STEM jobs is likely to increase in the future and make up more of available jobs. Today many companies cite lack of a qualified workforce as a serious risk to future growth.

While STEM careers are typically promoted with scenes of happy people in white coats working in a laboratory seeking a cure for cancer, or in Silicon Valley striving to be the next Steve Jobs, potential career opportunities are much more diverse and interesting. Science and technology jobs abound in the extractive industries, the manufacturing industries, and the chemical industries. However, these jobs are less attractive to graduates, who increasingly seek to work in companies that do not have complicated land-use legacies or produce goods and services that are perceived to be more environmental friendly.

There is a sound body of research that shows that interest in STEM can be generated through exposure to STEM activities, so many private-sector companies are investing in activities that promote STEM to students as a way of investing in the workforce of the future. Typical STEM activities include science fairs, invention competitions, and PR campaigns that promote such careers as achievable and interesting. Many companies promote STEM through competition. Shell Oil's Eco-marathon brings teams of high school students together to compete to build the most efficient race car. Google's science fair promotes STEM to students around the world who submit projects that propose solutions to global problems in health, energy, the environment, and transportation. These examples, however, make heavy demands on corporate resources, as they cost a lot of money and staff time to implement and promote. A less intensive approach involves using corporate lands and the environment as an integrating framework for STEM, in which companies are increasingly connecting their philanthropic corporate STEM investments to practical STEM programs on their lands and within their operations.

A company with a corporate STEM goal looking to leverage its lands for education may choose to use the environment on its lands as an integrating concept for STEM. A company that can provide students with access to its operations can also deliver place-based STEM learning that can have a powerful environmental and operational message, teaching students where the materials they encounter on a regular basis come from, and how they are manufactured and managed. It is easy to insert an environmental and conservation lesson into any of these approaches.

By using the environment as an integrating concept for STEM education, a company will realize many benefits. It can link its operations to its own particular land use. It can show how STEM education is needed for extraction, materials testing, manufacturing, or waste and water management. Companies making this investment will realize the co-benefits of helping to create an environmentally literate population and develop a STEM workforce. Companies making these connections can become a respected resource in the community and a stepping-stone to employment in a variety of positions.

Site Considerations

Once a company makes the decision on what types of education efforts can satisfy its business need and who is the ultimate stakeholder and how such efforts can contribute to the success story, operational considerations once again come into play. Some of these operational considerations may be hard to overcome, and, for others, adjustments will have to be made. While perhaps frustrating and time-consuming, consideration of operational restrictions underscores why the planning process is so important.

Corporate lands are significantly different from parks or other public lands, in particular because they are not designed or built for young people. Industrial operations can be loud and dangerous places. Research and technology offices can be off-limits to the public. The lands around a site may be well maintained in a pastoral aesthetic, maintained under a regulated regime, or left wild and rugged. Access to a corporate location may be heavily controlled by security or wide open to anyone at any time. All of these factors are important when choosing education programs and partners.

Many years ago, I was visiting a defense contractor's offices to discuss their possible support for a conservation effort. We had to meet in the lobby since I wasn't able to enter the offices, as I was not a US citizen at the time. There are many corporate locations where security clearance must be given in advance, and these requirements may or may not be waived for students and their teachers. A corporate location that is heavily restricted may decide to contribute to the corporate education goal by going to the classroom instead of inviting students onto the lands. Some locations may be closed completely during times of peak operations or other cycles that prevent access for non-employees.

Safety considerations can also impact the ease of access or usefulness of corporate lands. Safety is a big concern for most industrial operations where strict guidelines and standards are established to promote and protect worker safety. Many locations mandate safety training in advance of access. Most will require protective clothing to be worn by all regardless of the activity being engaged in and the proximity of the activity to operations. Entering into the safety-first world of corporate operations can be a culture shock for many NGO partners and educators, and while some aspects of access may be negotiable, safety almost never is.

The relationship between a corporate location and the community it sits in will be different from location to location, even within the same company. Every community will have different needs. Since education programs are designed to bring community value, it is very important that the site respond to community need when making decisions on education programs.

If a company builds a program that duplicates or replaces an existing effort, such as building a nature center when one already exists or one that does not meet the needs of the community in any way, the program will not be well used by community members and will ultimately fail. By understanding the needs of the community, the company builds a stronger program that will have high rates of use. Operations with an active and honest stakeholder-engagement program can easily understand community needs. Alternately, facilities that maintain a distance from the communities in which they operate may decide to engage first with a trusted local partner to help identify an education need and satisfy it.

An easy way to establish community need through formal education is to align with existing education and conservation priorities. By seeking to align the education efforts with state education curricula or standards like the Next Generation Science Standards in the United States, potential education partners can easily envision a fit with the project. Many local conservation plans such as State Wildlife Action Plans or local watershed plans contain education priorities around local ecosystems, rivers, or special plant and animal species. The Montana State Wildlife Action Plan, for example, seeks to educate residents about living with bears, identifying species of interest properly, knowing the threats posed by the pet trade to reptile and amphibian populations, and understanding the biology of reptiles and amphibians, especially the importance of nest and den sites. Thus, a corporate site in Montana can design an education project focused around these objectives.

The Watershed Action Plan for the Elizabeth River Project in Virginia lists a number of education priorities, including the creation of a curricular continuum that will engage across grades for a multiyear progression of education about the river and solutions for cleaning it up. A corporate landowner on the Elizabeth River in Virginia could align its efforts with this existing conservation education goal and develop a multiyear curriculum that engages students in healthy waterways and shows them how a corporate landowner manages its waterfront real estate for ecological health.

In addition, there are many existing curricula created for nature-based learning—for example, those offered by Project WILD, a conservation education program about wildlife that seeks to build awareness of the links between humans and the wild world. The program is built for early-childhood learning through to higher grade levels. It is context-sensitive and adapts to the resources and location of the schools that offer it. Project WILD is also a network of educators helping their peers bring nature into the classroom and the classroom into nature. Project Learning Tree trains teachers in environmental education and provides resources to make outdoor learning engaging and fun. Project Learning Tree touts the ability of environmental education to be multidisciplinary, teaching hard skills like math and science and softer skills like civic engagement and leadership. A company can invest in its employees by supporting them to train as Project WILD or Project Learning Tree educators and establish its own company-wide network.

The natural and human resources on a corporate site will influence program design. Bridgestone's Woodlawn remediation site (described in chapter 2) provides school groups with wetlands to do water-quality testing, a woodland trail with wildlife observation areas, a meadow area, a pollinator garden, a pavilion for outdoor classes, and bird boxes, raptor perches, and a bat box to attract species to the site. The site is used formally by school groups as an outdoor classroom for environmental education and informally by youth groups such as the Scouts, including an Eagle Scout candidate who recently built a vegetated roof for the pavilion.

Human resources are also important. While Bridgestone's Woodlawn site has extensive natural resources, there are no employees at the site, so school programs are designed and led by school personnel or volunteers. Bridgestone's BEECH program has a full-time educator on-site. At a CEMEX sand mine in Florida, employees are heavily involved. An educational committee of CEMEX employees and local educators have developed a cross-disciplinary curriculum specific to the location that aligns with Florida's state standards and has trained employees in Project Wet and Project Learning Tree so they can deliver the education to the students who visit the site.

A Successful Program

What describes success for a nature-based educational program hosted by a company? Is it the number of individuals engaged, the number of times the education activity is offered, or some metric designed to evaluate knowledge and perception before and after the event? Metrics for education are just as tricky as biodiversity metrics, and like biodiversity metrics they must be considered as the program is being designed. The metric of success for an education program on corporate lands will differ according to the business need, focusing on the reason the company is making the investment in education.

All effective nature-based education and outreach programs on corporate lands share some common elements. When these aspects are present, both the site and the company can realize their goals and continue their investments over a long time. The best formal education programs forge strong relationships among professional educators, schools or colleges, and the company. For informal education, an annual event like a monarch release or a fishing derby helps embed the event into the community's memory. For both types of education, a dedicated budget is essential. Unlike conservation activities that can happen on a shoestring budget and can be maintained during tight budget seasons, education efforts must be supported properly. A clear communication strategy that connects the dots between the effort on-site and the corporate goal ensures that the local program has value at the corporate level.

All companies are located in communities. Most communities welcome contributions to the educational needs of community members. Smart companies will see that they can leverage their lands and their employees to contribute to these communities and achieve one or more business goals at the same time. Employees will also gain from the experience of working with education programs by acquiring knowledge about the natural world, learning new skills such as bird identification or water and soil testing, and working with groups they don't normally connect with in the course of their work.

There are infinite opportunities for conservation-based education and community engagement partnerships with corporate locations, and infinite benefits from well-designed, thoughtful programs.

08 CLIMATE CHANGE

—

The science is settled. Climate change is real.

—FROM EXELON'S CORPORATE SUSTAINABILITY STRATEGY

It's simple. Industrial processes have caused the planet's climate to change, impacting nature in many different and complex ways. A lot of energy and money has been put into denying and ignoring environmental change, but industry is slowly changing this approach in a variety of ways. The corporate world has a schizophrenic relationship with climate change. Many of the big emitters of greenhouse gases are implicated in understating and downplaying the impacts they have long known were imminent. Corporate leaders have actively lobbied against the federal regulations needed to curb carbon emissions and transition to a carbon-free economy. Even now, companies are being shown to undervalue their financial risk in a climate-changed world.[1]

At the same time, many companies have established and published goals related to reducing carbon emissions. Many are retooling, researching, or investing to bring products and processes into compliance with a low-carbon future. Many companies are dependent on government action to support a transition to a low-carbon economy, although many are also dependent on government *in*action to allow things to continue as they are.

In the corporate sphere of influence, the majority of climate action is focused on climate mitigation. The climate commitments of the largest companies are varied but do have one aspect in common: they are all focused on reducing their emissions of greenhouse gases and transitioning to a carbon-neutral business model. Car companies such as Toyota and General Motors have posted zero-emissions goals for their fleets and their factories, moving to electrify their products. But an electric car is only as "green" as the electricity that charges it. The move to electrification shifts the burden of decarbonization to the energy sector. In the energy sector, Exelon, stating that "the science is settled, climate change is real," plans to reduce its carbon emissions by 15 percent by 2022 by retiring its coal-fired plants and growing its investment in a clean-energy portfolio. In Ontario, the provincial government introduced the Clean Energy Act, which impelled and supported companies like Ontario Power Generation (OPG) to transition to clean energy. OPG's transition caused the largest provincial impact on carbon emissions in Canada. It retired all of its coal-powered facilities, and today no coal is burned in Ontario. But this was not a painless transition. Consumers keenly felt its impact and cost, and in 2018 a new provincial leader swept into office on the promise to repeal the Clean Energy Act and halt over 700 clean-energy contracts previously awarded for wind and solar projects. The road toward a carbon-neutral world is winding and difficult, as easy wins are prioritized over longer-term goals and political shifts swing from inaction to action and vice versa.

One easy area to shift business-as-usual thinking, is for industry to leverage its own lands to help with climate mitigation, restoring lands to maximize their potential as carbon sinks and for adaptation, managing lands to enhance their resilience for both humans and nature. Using the power of nature for climate action is relatively simple, but it's not commonly done, especially on corporate lands. Lands management can complement existing corporate climate transition efforts and offer benefits beyond climate concerns. While it's important to be clear that lands-management efforts won't make the most significant contribution to addressing a single company's impact, they can also create positive outcomes for biodiversity, and empower employees and community members to take action on an issue that they may view as too big and too complex for their individual contributions to make a difference.

Cape May, New Jersey, is a famous location for nature lovers, known as one of the top birding spots in the world. In fact, many consider it to be the center of the birding universe. Almost half of all North American bird species have been recorded in Cape May. But this county in the extreme southern end of New Jersey is also important for species beyond birds. It is where many southern species of wildlife reach the northern extent of their ranges. Cape May County and indeed the entire state is classic edge habitat, as northern and southern species' ranges overlap. Edge habitat allows range-restricted animals to move as their ranges expand or contract with mean-temperature increases. It is critical for biodiversity health in a changing climate.

In Cape May, the eastern tiger salamander (an endangered species in New Jersey) is living close to the edge of its range, and in habitat that is under threat from rising sea level. The eastern tiger salamander is an "obligate" species, meaning that it depends on certain conditions for survival. (An obligate aerobe cannot survive without oxygen; an obligate carnivore cannot survive without meat. A polar bear is an ice-obligate species.) Some species of salamanders, such as eastern tiger salamanders, are "vernal pool"–obligate species.

A vernal pool is an intermittent wetland, dry for much of the year but filled with water during the spring, when the salamander needs to lay its eggs. The intermittent nature of the wetland means that few, if any, predators threaten egg development. When not in breeding season, salamander populations live in proximity to these ponds, carving out mini–migration corridors from the upland woods where they overwinter to the wetlands where they lay eggs.

Of fifteen breeding ponds available to the salamander in Cape May County, one third are at risk of sea-level rise. Without a way to expand its range farther inland, the eastern tiger salamander is destined for extinction in New Jersey. In 2010, a partnership effort between local electric utility, Atlantic City Electric (ACE), a subsidiary of Exelon, the state's Division of Fish and Wildlife (NJ-DFW), and a local nongovernmental organization (NGO), the Conserve Wildlife Foundation of New Jersey (CWF), found a way to use utility rights-of-way to help the eastern tiger salamander adapt to climate change.

Under ACE's utility lines through Cape May, the partners worked to establish a succession of vernal pools, moving northward and away from the coast, to provide the salamanders with the habitat they needed to successfully reproduce and survive. They made depressions on the rights-of-way that could fill with rainwater during the late spring, when salamanders would lay their eggs. They removed some eggs from existing ponds and, in partnership with the Cape May Zoo, kept them safe from predators in order to increase survivorship and then placed the eggs in the new vernal pools, successfully establishing new communities of this population of salamanders.

This example shows the potential of partnerships between company lands and conservation professionals to help species adapt to—and, hopefully, survive—a world transformed by climate change. And yet approaches like this have been consistently overlooked in the conversations about climate action. Indeed, nature-based solutions have been largely ignored until the "nature for climate" movement launched in 2018, bringing a much-needed voice to the discussion. The result of the absence of nature-based solutions from the climate conversation is that corporate landowners lack guidance about how they can use their nonoperating lands for nature-based climate mitigation and adaptation.

This chapter will explore how corporations can and should leverage nature within a changing climate. It will start by outlining possible impacts of climate on biodiversity. It's important to understand the impacts of climate change on nature in order to better inform approaches for corporations to engage in strategic and meaningful nature-based climate mitigation and adaptation. The chapter will also highlight the various frameworks whereby companies are already connecting with climate so that NGO conservation partners can frame their recommendations to fit with existing corporate efforts.

Having an understanding of frameworks like the CDP (formerly the Carbon Disclosure Project) or the various industry-specific efforts can help NGO partners craft a persuasive argument for integrating lands management into corporate climate efforts. This chapter will also present strategies for encouraging corporate landowners to view their lands as having potential to make a contribution to climate-mitigation or climate-adaptation pathways and engage employees and community members in action and conversation around climate. (Because there is already much written on the subject, this chapter will not address agribusiness, the impacts of commodities like palm oil or soy, or the past complicity and future responsibilities of the oil and gas industry.)

There is an enormous body of scientific research on the future impacts of climate change and how we might both reduce the impacts in the future and adapt to those impacts we can't mitigate. The connections to the corporate world are crystal clear. The operational and financial impacts on industry are becoming real: from the lines for gas that formed in the northeast United States after Superstorm Sandy shut down refining capacity in 2012; to the Houston, Texas, area where Hurricane Harvey caused flooding, fires, and toxic releases from an underprepared chemical facility; to California's largest electric utility, Pacific Gas and Electric (PGE), entering bankruptcy protection in 2019 to shield itself from liability for one of the deadliest forest fires in the state's history. According to the *Wall Street Journal*, the PGE action could be viewed as the first climate-related corporate bankruptcy in the United States.

Impacts of Climate on Companies and on Biodiversity

The Task Force on Climate Disclosure asks companies to report on two main types of risk with respect to climate change. The most aggressively addressed risk is called the "transition risk," which involves potential changes in law, policy, technology, and markets related to the transition to a lower-carbon energy supply. It is also an easier risk to report on, as it blends with the usual strategic planning and "future-casting" that companies do as a matter of course.

Less aggressively or publicly assessed are the physical risks from climate change, which include damage to fixed assets such as buildings, property, and land, or supply chain disruptions.[2] With increasing storms and other weather events, the physical risks are already occurring and the impacts are being felt by companies. Estimates of the impact of climate change on the market value of global financial assets places the risk between US$2.5 trillion and US$24.2 trillion.[3]

When it comes to the natural world, the main risks to biodiversity are more indeterminate. Predicted change to natural communities will not happen equally across the world or in the same direction for all species. While much is uncertain, we do know that existing relationships in nature will break down and new ones will be formed. How and when these changes will happen is as yet unknown. It's important to understand the variety of impacts to biodiversity to know the limits of certainty in any actions promoted to corporate landowners.

Biodiversity and Climate Change

Biodiversity is already facing the existential threat called the sixth mass extinction, which is caused by human impact on the landscape.[4] It is an impact so forceful and so profound that some scientists believe it should be classified as a new geological epoch called the Anthropocene, defined as a geological period dominated by human activity.[5] According the World Wildlife Foundation's "Living Planet Report," this biodiversity collapse is caused primarily by agriculture, land conversion, and overexploitation of species. From the report: "Of all the plant, amphibian, reptile, bird, and mammal species that have gone extinct since AD 1500, 75 percent were harmed by over-exploitation or agricultural activity or both."[6] The global assessment from the Intergovernmental Platform on Biodiversity and Ecosystem Services (IPBES) painted a stark picture, saying

> Nature across most of the globe has now been significantly altered by multiple human drivers, with the great majority of indicators of ecosystems and biodiversity showing rapid decline. Seventy-five percent of the land surface is significantly altered, 66 percent of the ocean area is experiencing increasing cumulative impacts, and over 85 percent of wetlands (area) has been lost. While the rate of forest loss has slowed globally since 2000, this is distributed unequally. Across much of the highly biodiverse tropics, 32 million hectares of primary or recovering forest were lost between 2010 and 2015.[7]

In addition to land clearances and overharvesting of marine species, invasive species, pollution, and climate change are all driving the biodiversity crisis. Climate change is just one driver of biodiversity loss, but it is having an increasing impact at the ecosystem, species, and genetic levels.

Biodiversity loss, because of its complexity, is not easy to quantify in a climate-change scenario. Organisms and natural communities do not respond to "average" scenarios, and there are many inputs into the system. The ability to attribute a specific reaction in a species, ecosystem, or population to climate change is not simple, but despite uncertainty, research shows many possible impacts of climate change on biodiversity at all levels.

There are two main ways that climate change impacts biodiversity. The first and most easily studied are the impacts driven by the increase in the mean global temperature.[8] The less studied impacts are those from increased and unpredictable climate conditions like droughts and violent weather events. This unpredictability is known as the "variable climate effect."

The responses of most species to future climate scenarios are not understood well enough to estimate extinction risks or survival chances based solely on mean-temperature-shift scenarios, projections of movements, or reductions in range areas.[9] Biologically speaking, plants and animals exist in geographic ranges that are limited by temperature, altitude, physical barriers, and other factors. As temperature changes, ranges will change too. How or how much each species' range will change is not yet known. Some studies suggest that changing temperatures will have a greater impact on species in more temperate climates because higher latitudes have warmed more than the lower latitudes in the last century.[10] Other studies suggest that species in the tropics and equatorial regions face greater pressure because they contain more endemic species with niche habitat needs that have less tolerance for even the smallest changes in temperature. Yet even more studies tell us that species in the poles and at high elevations will see the biggest impacts because of the physically restricted nature of their ranges.[11]

The effect of climate change has already been seen in animals and plants for over a decade,[12, 13] with some studies from as early as 1945 showing range shifts in butterflies in Europe in response to summer warming trends.[14] A study of 1,598 species has estimated that 41 percent of all species have been impacted by climate change already.[15]

Species and habitats on corporate lands can be impacted by climate change in a number of different ways. Awareness of these impacts can help in assessments of corporate lands for climate-related conservation purposes.

1. CHANGES IN RANGE

Climate change will cause geographic ranges for species to shift. Providing a way for the species to shift with them is key. Global meta-analyses have documented significant range shifts averaging a 6.1 kilometer shift per decade toward the poles.[16] This means that species will be forced to move poleward or to higher latitudes or see their natural ranges become smaller if movement is not possible. These changes in range will impact genetic diversity and species interactions. Two connected species may react in different ways—a bird species may migrate farther north, while the plant it depends on for food may shift its blooming time earlier but will remain in position.

Ranges that are already limited—such as those at the poles and high altitudes, or those limited by physical barriers both natural, such as mountain ranges, or man-made, such as roads and cities—may be lost completely. For species that cannot move or that have nowhere to move to, such as the eastern tiger salamander on the Cape May peninsula, or populations that are disjunct, cut off from others of their species that they can breed with, the impacts will be the most severe.

Connecting ranges to allow movement is key to reducing impact on biodiversity. Land managers concerned with range shifts should learn about the species present on their lands and overlay their current and likely future ranges to create a map showing where connectivity exists or can be created. A lands manager can focus on those species that are existing at the "top end" of their ranges and manage to both strengthen the populations and provide for movement if possible. Roads and other linear infrastructure on corporate lands can be obstacles to species movement. Wildlife crossings that don't impact operations are a great tool to manage movement. These structures, which cross roads as underpasses or overpasses, have been developed and deployed in many jurisdictions to allow wildlife movement and in many cases reduce collisions between cars and animals; now the crossings can serve species responding to range shifts.

2. CHANGES IN PHENOLOGY AND ECOLOGICAL INTERACTIONS

We don't call it the "web of life" for purely poetic reasons. Every species on the planet is connected to other species, dependent in so many different ways for food, shelter, and other biological processes. Because these interdependent species do not adapt to climate change in the same way, the connections in the web of life becomes tenuous, and the links in the web weaken and ultimately break. In a climate-change scenario, the absolute change is less important than the relative change, which can break the connections between predators and prey, pollinators and the flowering plants that depend on them, insects and parasites, and the species they need as hosts to complete their life cycles.[17] Species' interconnections are what make ecosystems.

Phenology is the timing of natural events such as flowering or egg laying. Today, spring events such as emergence from hibernation are occurring on average 2.3 days earlier than normal.[18] Many plants are flowering and fruiting significantly earlier,[19] which impacts species that depend on them for food. Migratory birds are impacted if food sources along migratory routes shift peak production to before or after the birds arrive. An example of this change in species interaction has been found in Colorado, where a 1.4°C rise in local temperature caused the yellow-bellied marmot to emerge twenty-three days earlier from hibernation but snow melt and plant flowering did not follow suit, resulting in very cold and hungry marmots encountering conditions in which survival was difficult.[20]

Land-management actions to protect species interactions depend on knowing the life cycle needs of the species in the ecosystems. Actions that a corporate land manager can take include adjusting plant choice to ensure season-long blooms for pollinators or other species that depend on such plants. There may be a short-term benefit to providing food for early-emerging species, although this could lead to challenges in the future if the species become dependent on the food subsidy over the longer term. Understanding the dependencies and connections at the site of action is important in order to inform a climate-smart conservation action. The National Phenology Network's Nature's Notebook project connects citizen scientists to local

Figure 8-1: The relationship between butterflies and the blooming time of the plants on which they depend may be in danger as the global mean temperature continues to rise. (Used with permission of Exelon.)

phenology groups that record the timing of bud appearance, flowering, fruiting, pollination, and leaf fall. Corporate land managers can create a local phenology group on-site and engage employees and community members to collect this information and contribute it to the national effort that collates data from across the country and provides maps and visualization tools at no charge.

3. CHANGES IN PRIMARY PRODUCTIVITY AND MORPHOLOGY

If temperatures increase, the ability of plants to convert energy into food increases. Plants will grow faster. Animals may also grow faster. In fact, changes in temperature under any climate-change scenario will directly impact developmental rates in many animals and rate of growth and tissue makeup in many plants.[21] In the United States, the pine beetle has altered its life cycle in response to warmer temperatures, shortening the pest's generation to one year instead of two, resulting in large population increases and subsequent damage to the pine forests in the Rocky Mountain West and elsewhere.[22]

Changes in primary productivity and morphology will increase the rate of invasion from nonnative species that are already a threat to biodiversity. Already, the global economy that moves goods around the world is causing the spread of nonnative species and diseases that, in less mobile times, would have been confined to their historic ranges. Under climate change, the ability of nonnative species to establish in new places increases. If humans facilitate species movement, climate change facilitates their becoming established.[23]

Unfortunately, corporate lands are perfect for spreading invasive species as goods are moved in and out of manufacturing and processing facilities, and linear infrastructure offers highways for invasives' propagation. To prevent this, land managers can institute vehicle cleaning at their facilities or adopt other process changes to minimize the spread of species. They can also manage for invasive species by understanding which species are already present, preventing the spread of existing invasive species and the establishment of new ones with a variety of management techniques. Local NGOs make perfect partners for invasive-species actions and can form rapid response teams to help stop new species from taking hold.

Changes in primary production also impacts carbon sequestration. Future warming may likely increase plant growth, which in turn will remove more carbon from the atmosphere. But climate variability may undermine increased sequestration as droughts and heatwaves lower primary productivity, as occurred when the European heatwave of 2003 reversed the effect of four years' net ecosystem carbon sequestration.[24] Likely increases in the number and intensity of forest fires will also reverse any increased carbon sequestration.

Corporate land managers implementing climate-focused conservation on their lands should consider that maintenance schedules will shift if plant productivity increases. For example, meadows may need to be managed earlier and more often. Trees should be planted if the goal is to absorb the most carbon. The ideal tree for sequestration is one that grows most quickly and lives longest. These two attributes are rarely found in a single tree species, so corporate land managers should plant the best tree for their location and seek input from NGO partners of the US Forest Service (USFS) when choosing trees to sequester carbon. The i-Tree tool, a suite of software from the USFS, can quantify carbon storage in trees, which can then provide a valuable metric to allow climate-focused conservation to contribute to corporate carbon reporting.

4. THE IMPACTS OF CLIMATE VARIABILITY

Studies have found that climate variability is a more potent force on some species than the mean global temperature increase. Heatwaves and flooding have been shown to have stronger impacts on plant physiology than changing mean climate because plants react more to extreme rather than average conditions.[25] In another aspect of how reactions can become drivers, drought and extreme precipitation have been shown to impact carbon turnover, evapotranspiration, and evaporative cooling, which in turn leads to additional warming of an ecosystem.

Forest fires can wipe out acres of forests. Hurricanes can cause flooding and wind damage can destroy habitats and impact species. In 2017, a forest fire in southeastern Arizona wiped out 86 percent of the remaining population of the Mount Graham red squirrel and left the remaining thirty-five individuals with no food stores for the winter. After superstorm Sandy in 2012, beach-nesting bird habitat on Delaware Bay and Atlantic coastal beaches were destroyed, and while some of the habitat was rebuilt by conservation partners, many beaches still remain damaged and unsuitable as habitat for these species. In January 2019, the United Kingdom saw wildfires in some of its most pristine places. In the Philippines, the IUCN has determined that a single natural catastrophe could wipe out the Philippine tarsier, a small primate endemic to the country, after typhoon Haiyan caused destruction in one of the species' last strongholds, resulting in a severely reduced population density of 36 individuals per square kilometer, down from 157 individuals per square kilometer before the storm.[26]

While it is impossible to protect against or even predict these climate-related storms and fires, it is possible to manage species, habitats, and ecosystems for resilience so that they can easily recover following a destructive event. Corporate land managers assessing their lands for risk of climate variability may be able to adapt existing land-management processes (or adopt new ones) to be climate-smart in order to increase resilience and strengthen the capacity of systems to rebound.

Natural Climate Solutions

Nature-based climate action, *climate-smart conservation*, *natural climate solutions*, and *ecosystem-based adaptation* are all terms for an underused yet cost-effective tool for addressing climate change. These nature-based climate actions fall into two main approaches— climate mitigation (i.e., reducing atmospheric carbon) and climate adaptation (i.e., building resilience).

Natural climate solutions that address climate mitigation are those land-management activities that increase the amount of carbon being stored or that avoid adding to greenhouse-gas emissions. These solutions can be applied on all lands, but they are most effective on forested lands, wetlands, and grasslands.[27] The same solutions, while confronting climate change, will have multiple co-benefits for biodiversity, soil health, flood protection, and other aspects of ecosystem services. Regreening the planet for climate is one of the most cost-effective, simple, and yet underutilized mitigation solutions.

Natural climate solutions that address climate adaptation increase the resiliency of ecosystems for both biodiversity and humanity, and they also increase connectivity for species movement. Nature-based climate adaptation can occur on all lands, especially those at the intersection of nature and the built environment.

In the book *Biodiversity and Climate Change*, editor Tom Lovejoy points out that ecosystem restoration has yet to emerge as a global priority vis-à-vis climate change. He likens the potential of natural climate solutions to the victory gardens of World War II, which had both practical and psychological impact. In the United Kingdom and the United States, victory gardens were installed in small backyards and large public parks to increase food production during the war. The gardens reduced pressure on food supply, but crucially they also engaged groups and individuals in action toward a shared national goal during a global emergency. Corporate lands of all types can easily become victory gardens for climate change, where every employee or community member can take action on

Figure 8-2: Ecosystem restoration on properties like this quarry can be designed to be climate-smart to maximize both mitigation and adaptation opportunities. (Photo by author.)

a corporate climate-conservation project that contributes to mitigation or adaptation.

Corporate Climate Conservation

Company lands can be used for natural climate solutions. Companies reporting against carbon-reduction goals or toward zero-carbon targets can assess the potential of their lands to contribute to these efforts. Strategic conservation planning can be done with climate change as the business reason and the reported goals as the ultimate stakeholder. For companies not driven by corporate carbon goals or carbon-accounting, existing and future conservation efforts should be assessed through the lens of climate change to see if different strategies should be adopted to increase the value of the conservation action for climate mitigation or adaptation, or to secure the conservation investment against possible future climate scenarios.

The National Wildlife Federation and a number of conservation partners published a practical guide to conservation-focused climate adaptation in 2014.[28] It set out a framework for what it called climate-smart conservation. This framework has been adopted by many and can easily be adapted by corporate lands managers. The framework is set out in the following table:

Table 8-1: Climate-Smart Conservation*

Climate-Smart Conservation Framework	Corporate Considerations
Link actions to climate impacts.	For large-scale conservation projects, whether reclamation or remediation, consider options for end-state contribution to climate mitigation or adaptation. Consider whether these actions can become part of corporate reporting on climate.
Embrace forward-looking goals.	Design ecological adaptation strategies with future landscapes in mind and help others understand that the beloved landscapes of today may require too much management to maintain in a changing climate.
Consider broader landscape context.	Consider whether the project can contribute to range shifts or specific ecosystem adaptation needs outside of the corporate operation. Think about connecting across fence lines to support species movement. Consider connected infrastructure or supply chains as possible landscape-scale contributors.
Adopt strategies robust to uncertainty.	Understand that weather events may have greater impacts than mean-temperature increase, and design with storm resiliency in mind. Consider whether shorelines can be softened at ports and terminals. Can impervious surfaces be reduced for better stormwater management?

Table 8-1: Climate-Smart Conservation* (*continued*)

Climate-Smart Conservation Framework	Corporate Considerations
Deploy agile and informed management.	Create SOPs and BMPs that will incorporate the latest climate trends and allow for adaptation of practice across all lands management, from landscaping at facilities to remediation and reclamation efforts. Insert a climate contingency in contracts.
Minimize carbon footprint.	Design and implement conservation projects that will not require machines that emit carbon. Consider low-maintenance landscaping regimens for all facilities.
Account for climate influence on project success.	Identify risk of climate change, whether from mean temperature rise but more likely from storm events, on investments in conservation. Understand that immediate success will be harder as the predictability of ecosystem adaptation declines in a variable-climate model.
Safeguard people and nature.	Climate-related ecosystem adaptation that is focused on human communities can also benefit natural communities if designed with this in mind. When deploying nature-based efforts, ask how biodiversity and community can also benefit.
Avoid maladaptation.	Consider all projects designed for adaptation for chances of maladaptation—a project that results in increased vulnerability to climate variability and change, directly or indirectly, or that significantly undermines populations' capacities or opportunities for present and future adaptation.

* Adapted from: Bruce A. Stein et al., Climate-Smart Conservation: Putting Adaptation Principles into Practice (Washington, DC: National Wildlife Federation, 2014).

For corporate conservation efforts, landowners should start by assessing their lands for both vulnerability to climate change and potential to address it through mitigation or adaptation. Vulnerability assessments are increasingly being used to help better understand the risks from climate change to natural and built environments. The assessments gather the current science and modeling, engage stakeholders for input, and help identify priority actions or areas. They don't offer prescriptions for action but help identify where action may be necessary or possible. Assessments of mitigation potential are not yet fully developed, but corporate land owners can, with stakeholders and science, make a broad estimate of whether forests, grasslands, or wetlands can be created or better managed as carbon sinks or adaptive infrastructure.

Once assessments have been done, a corporate conservation plan can be developed that integrates the finding of the assessment with the previously identified business reason for conservation. Climate action in a corporate conservation plan will strengthen the plan and may also contribute to the business reason. If a business reason for implementing conservation action is, for example, to secure social license to operate, adding climate conservation will support the effort and show that the company is thinking beyond the short term for results and beyond the fence line for impacts. If corporate conservation is being deployed to contribute to STEM education goals, climate assessments and subsequent climate conservation action will be an innovative contribution to any STEM lessons.

There are many ways that a corporate landowner can include climate strategies in corporate conservation plans. Different industry sectors will have different opportunities according to their landholdings, but every industry or corporate location can contribute a climate conservation action.

In the extractive and building materials industries, reconsider remediation, reclamation, or closure plans to assess the potential to reforest surplus, legacy, or spent landholdings worldwide. Adopting and implementing a corporate-wide goal to assess and address all degraded lands for climate conservation could be a powerful act from leading companies in the mining and quarrying industries. Not all lands will be suitable for reforestation. Some remediation sites may have remedies that require the contaminated areas to be capped, which may make reforestation a difficult sell to regulators. On other sites with contaminants in the soil, reforestation may cause the contaminants to enter into the food web if they are absorbed by the trees and then eaten by other species. Choosing the appropriate trees or augmenting the soil with biofertilizers and amended composts may address this issue.[29] Sending a message to communities living with blighted industrial properties that these sites will now be contributing to climate mitigation is a powerful way to change a liability into an asset. Companies with large land liabilities can also count the carbon sequestration as contributing in a small way to their carbon goals.

Energy-industry companies with linear infrastructure can manage their rights-of-way for climate adaptation for both resilience and connectivity. Pipelines and electricity transmission and distribution networks can fragment habitats and impact species movement for mammals and reptiles. Designing new installations that will allow rather than hamper species movement, or adding crossings and other structures to existing rights-of-way can contribute to species connectivity and the resilience of local populations. With better design, these rights-of-way can themselves reconnect habitats. Managing the lands for resiliency by reducing the broadcast use of chemicals and adapting mowing and other maintenance activities to species' life-cycle needs can create healthier populations that will bounce back from storm events and cope with range shifts or broken ecological interactions.

All industries can consider all lands as potential grasslands, including formal landscaped properties at headquarters, closed landfills, remote server farms, solar arrays, and other locations that cannot be reforested. Imagine how thinking about managed-landscape aesthetics would shift if high-visibility corporate campus settings became grasslands. A "carbon meadow" in front of a gleaming glass office location communicates commitment to climate action more clearly than a report on gigatons of carbon. Such a meadow is the victory garden of today's global climate emergency.

Another action that all corporate landowners can take is adopting the main tenets of climate-centered conservation, including approaches to restore soil health. Healthy soil captures carbon. While most soil-health efforts are focused on agricultural lands, there are many actions that corporate landowners can take. Repairing and restoring riparian corridors and engineering stormwater-mitigation efforts can minimize soil erosion and restore soil health. Existing grounds- and lands-management efforts can be redirected across all corporate lands to consider soil health as an outcome.

Companies with infrastructure along the coasts have seen increased flooding from both storms and sea-level rise. Rebuilding marshes and coastal wetlands with nature instead of hardening the shoreline provides better climate outcomes. Healthy marshes can absorb more stormwater and support more biodiversity. By rebuilding marshes using nature, companies can address the threats to their coastal infrastructure and increase the productivity and resiliency of the marsh ecosystem itself.

The Mississippi River Delta is a living landmass, a massive wetland that accrues and loses land as the flows of water seek and find the fastest routes to the sea. Human intervention on the delta has fundamentally altered its processes and profile, with over 100,000 acres of land lost in the last sixty years, some of it to natural processes but most through human-caused impacts from the restriction of the river flows, maintenance of navigation canals, and mineral exploration.

Today, natural subsidence threatens much of the infrastructure on the delta, including an extensive network of oil and gas pipelines that gather crude oil from the Gulf of Mexico into the refineries of Louisiana. Critical infrastructure such as this is at risk from climate-change-induced sea-level rise that exacerbates wetland destruction, as well as increased violent storms and storm surges, which are also climate-related. Shell oil has extensive infrastructure in this region and a business reason to secure it against storm surges that may impact it and cause ecological damage from oil spills in addition to financial damage from lost revenues. It also has a community engagement interest, as many of its employees are residents of the delta. Because of these interests, Shell is helping to rebuild the delta, restoring it as an original climate-smart solution.

In recent years, Shell has partnered with an NGO, the Coastal Conservation Association, and its Building Conservation Trust program and also with Martin Ecosystems, a creative environmental consultancy designing nature-based, climate-smart solutions for the delta. Martin Ecosystems builds floating islands to kick-start land development in the delta. The islands are installed in the water with 300 or so plants whose roots will eventually grow to adhere to the bottom and begin the process of extending the coastline or building new lands. Nearly 200,000 square feet of new marsh has been built in this way, with some of the artificial marshlands outperforming the natural ones in terms of erosion control. The project provides an intersection point to education too, as local schools are invited to build the islands and deploy them.

This is, by any and all measures, a small and concentrated effort in the fight against global climate change, but it is illustrative of climate-smart thinking that is also being deployed by Shell on specific infrastructure investments in its nature-based engineering approach to protect the Ship Shoal Pipeline, also in the delta. This pipeline carries 200,000 barrels of crude oil a day to feed into the global economy. The pipeline must be protected from the increased risk of climate uncertainty. A natural-engineering approach has deployed baskets filled with sediment and coir logs that are designed to *adapt* to the natural processes of the delta, in contrast to the common hardscaping approaches that seek to conquer these processes.

This project was designed for Shell in consultation with the Nature Conservancy, exemplifying recent findings that a key need for companies adopting ecosystem-based or natural approaches is the type of expertise that an NGO can bring. Most company decision makers are more comfortable with engineered solutions than nature-based approaches. Most successful corporate ecosystem adaptations and climate-smart programs have engaged NGO or government partners.[30] There is clearly a need for the corporate world to view such partnerships as a necessity and not a luxury, and for the NGO community to seize the opportunity afforded by their expertise and aggressively advance the idea and practice of climate conservation to the corporate world.

It's difficult for a conservation NGO to openly work with a corporation on climate-smart conservation without accusations of complicity from their advocacy colleagues, but, if we agree that action on climate on every front is necessary to restrict warming to 1.5°C, then we should agree that we're better off enabling robust climate-smart conservation on corporate lands than condemning it. By integrating these actions with existing corporate reporting efforts on carbon-reduction goals, we can bring essential transparency to the effort.

The Corporate Response

Today, there is a confusing array of initiatives to track company commitments or actions around climate, but they are largely focused on reducing emissions through changes in products and processes. This focus leaves little room for considering nature-based options with biodiversity co-benefits, but the field of climate reporting is new and rapidly evolving.

The Science-Based Targets joint initiative lists 515 companies adopting targets for direct and indirect carbon-emission reductions, with 164 targets deemed to be science-based (i.e., in line with existing climate science and focused on holding global warming to 2°C or lower). CDP (formerly the Carbon Disclosure Project) looks across a broader spectrum of corporate action and lists and scores companies for a variety of environmental, social, and governance topics around climate. CDP grades 7,000 companies from A to D–, with the A List of top companies published every year. CDP's vision is to focus investors, companies, and cities on taking urgent action by measuring and understanding their environmental impact.

America's Pledge on Climate and We Are Still In collect the actions of US cities and companies in the face of the withdrawal of the US from the Paris Agreement on climate action in 2017. This initiative serves as a consolidation point for all the climate commitments and actions to see whether individual city and company commitments will, when consolidated, meet the 2025 goals that the United States initially agreed to in the Paris Agreement in 2015.

A relative newcomer to the field is the We Mean Business Coalition, another partner initiative with the CDP listing 850-plus companies that have climate-related commitments across a suite of actions. The current and only nature-based option on the list is a goal for removing commodity-driven deforestation from the supply chain. There is an obvious opening for more additions to the reporting world for corporate aspiration and action at the three-way intersection of business, biodiversity, and climate. All of these frameworks can drive change by promoting nature-based solutions and encouraging climate-smart conservation pledges and actions. Such an addition to the reporting world would be an inspiration or incentive for companies to view their own lands as having potential to help them meet climate goals.

It is very difficult to find any company currently connecting biodiversity and climate. Where nature-based investments are happening toward a climate goal, they are being made as offsets, paying for projects elsewhere that will have a positive climate impact. This isn't surprising. Biodiversity loss is not considered a material risk in a climate-change scenario for many businesses, and any company that has committed to science-based targets will find it difficult to align a biodiversity commitment with a science-based target. The science remains complicated, and the metrics (as discussed in chapter 7) remain elusive.

All across the corporate world, there are too many cross-sectoral or industry-specific initiatives to keep up. To read company websites is to see, at first glance, a world where industry is hard at work to address these issues, but where a deeper dive leaves the reader wanting more. On close examination, most corporate climate commitments fall along the vaguely worded lines of reduced greenhouse gases (GHGs), increased efficiencies, and supporting supply chains toward reduced GHGs and increased efficiencies. It doesn't seem to matter what the company's specific impact is—the collective response is to reduce GHG emissions and to help others to do so as well.

Corporate climate commitments are still in their infancy. CDP was founded as recently as 2000, and the financial standards for carbon accounting are still being developed through the Task Force on Climate-Related Financial Disclosure (TCFD). There remains a big opportunity to frame corporate lands management as a contribution to a climate solution. The carbon- and climate-reporting community can drive conservation action for climate that will also benefit biodiversity, whether the action is designed to sequester carbon as a mitigation effort or to manage for climate adaptation and resilience. NGO partners can help companies by showing corporate landowners what is possible, credible, and necessary.

Climate change can be a strong enough business reason to propel the private sector to conservation action. Climate concerns can also feed into corporate conservation plans developed for other business reasons, as climate conservation offers many co-benefits for biodiversity, community resilience, education, and corporate reputation. Climate conservation is also very cost-effective—but it has not been broadly adopted on either private or public lands. One of the barriers in the private sector is likely to be that biodiversity-focused climate science is complicated. Corporate lands managers as well as sustainability and corporate citizenship officers are not experts in it. Another barrier is that climate action usually occurs elsewhere in most companies—in product innovation and financial and strategic planning for transition to carbon-neutral business models. It's hard to connect the dots between a climate-smart reforestation effort and the development of a carbon-neutral product or process.

NGO partners can help connect the dots and play a role in moving the private sector toward climate conservation. They can help dispel the myths that nature-based climate action is complex and can communicate the science in a clear and locally appropriate way. They can engage in a positive conversation around climate vulnerabilities and the potential of corporate lands to play a positive role. As the struggle to develop policies and regulations to meet the Paris Agreement goals continues at global, national, and subnational levels continues, climate conservation action can start to quietly engage corporations and communities to act and make a difference.

09 BUILDING A CULTURE OF CORPORATE CONSERVATION

—

The world is moved along not only by the mighty shoves of its heroes, but also by the aggregate tiny pushes of each honest worker.

—HELEN KELLER

All around the world, ecological stewardship efforts on corporate lands are restoring habitats for species both common and rare, providing environmental education value for communities of learners and implementing lands management in new and different ways, all focused on conservation outcomes. The fundamental difference between these efforts on corporate lands to those on protected lands is that the driver for action will always be business, not biodiversity. Because of this business-first focus, the culture in the company, more than budget or passion, will dictate the speed of the effort and likely the chances of success. Every organization has a culture founded on the values it adopts and the philosophies it adheres to. In many organizations, the corporate culture is spelled out and specific; in some it is unspoken and innate. Either way, it can be a potent force, with significant impact on performance, organizational strategy, and the ways that strategy is implemented.[1]

Imagine two large multinational companies that, like many others, have established their American headquarters in Houston, Texas. The first company is in a sleek new building in the suburbs. The lobby is like a museum, a quiet and reverent place. Employees move about in orderly groups and ascend escalators in a line, each person holding the rail. Nobody walks and talks on a phone at the same time. Indeed, if someone were to do this, any employee is within their rights to step up and stop this unsafe behavior. On the other side of town, the second multinational company's headquarters building is a bit disheveled. It is in a constant state of refurbishment, which means packing crates line the walkways and temporary signs point to meeting rooms with a numbering logic that nobody can understand. The lobby is full of noise and bustle, with walking meetings and never-ending motion. While the employees in the first headquarters have all adopted a corporate "uniform" of khakis and plaid shirts for both men and women, the employees here have a much more varied style.

These two companies sell the same product to the same customers and are generally interchangeable in the minds of the general public. In fact, though, they couldn't be more different. One company is safety-first, risk-averse, and process-oriented. The other is chaotic and creative. Conservation efforts within these two companies will proceed along completely different routes. For the orderly company, a conservation strategy will be developed first, and an implementation plan will follow soon after. A process will be then be developed to onboard new projects. The resources will be secured and committed before implementation begins. In the other company, a strategic plan will be discussed but never delivered and conservation action will be sporadic. But the company will also, when the planets align and timing is right, create conservation action that will be big, innovative, and impactful.

One thing all corporations, regardless of culture, have in common, however, is the need to engage with experts. The most successful corporate conservation projects are those done in partnership with nongovernmental organizations (NGOs) or government agencies. Sharing expertise allows a corporate manager to identify a business need and an NGO partner to overlay a conservation opportunity onto it. Partnerships will encourage alignments with the best conservation plan to meet all objectives and ensure that the correct best management practices (BMPs) are followed. An NGO partner can also provide resources for monitoring and feed that data into larger citizen-science efforts, thus extending the value further. An NGO partner can bring an authentic voice to support corporate efforts that may push against the bounds of regulations, as in the case of an environmental reclamation project in Spain (described in chapter 5) where the Lafarge Group's nature-focused plan for site closure received government approval thanks to a respected conservation partner's agreement with it.

When an NGO partner engages with a company, it is important to see the cultural differences, to understand who you are working with and what their main motivation is vis-à-vis nature and business. Be clear. Be honest. Keep linking back to the business need and the success story. Companies need NGO partners for their expertise and will appreciate a straightforward approach from them.

From the partnership point of view, a common mistake that conservation NGOs make when working on corporate lands is arriving with their own ideas of what conservation programs should be implemented. These ideas are formed from their personal passion, their professional knowledge of the conservation context, and the mission of their NGO. Nevertheless, it's important to understand the interests of the site and the drivers for conservation before presenting implementation ideas. Support for conservation objectives will be secured more easily through listening than through talking.

The second common mistake is that the project proposed by the NGO partners comes with a large price tag for expensive and complex work that requires specialized equipment or costly materials. Misaligned expectations represent one of the most common causes of failure to implement conservation projects at a corporate site. For example, in 2017 a utility company in the Midwest wanted to implement a simple monarch conservation project on a small site in order to contribute to the National Pollinator Strategy. It had no more than an acre of land available for the project at the time. As part of its stated corporate strategy, the company wanted to work with local NGOs and sought a cost estimate from a specific group, asking them to detail the costs of designing and planting the monarch conservation area.

The wildlife team at the company was shocked to receive a cost estimate of $80,000 for the planting work alone, based on containerized plants purchased at premium rates rather than the seed mixes that are much more affordable. The NGO offered no alternative and refused to compromise. To date, this small program has not been implemented. Corporate budget managers expect to pay for goods and services, but they are very sensitive to cost and cost-saving opportunities, especially in locations operating with low margins. NGOs seeking to work on corporate lands should be realistic in their estimates and not expect that a local operation has access to unlimited funding. All too often, NGO development or fundraising staff are directed to manage the relationships with corporate connections for sponsorships and contributions. Building connections with conservation action and program implementation may have better and longer-term outcomes.

Partnerships will vary according to the business need of the company and the lands available for action. ConocoPhillips and Phillips 66 (once the same company) are both engaged in conservation efforts that could be the metaphorical bookends to the range of actions that companies can take in their engagement with nature. In 2012, ConocoPhillips created a new company called Phillips 66. This new company would assume responsibility for what is called the "downstream" business of refineries and gas stations, while Conoco Phillips would retain responsibility for the "upstream" business of exploration and production. With different types of landholdings and different business needs, the two companies have engaged in two very different approaches to advancing natural-resources stewardship.

ConocoPhillips is one of the largest owners of wetlands in the United States, with over 600,000 acres of wetlands in the state of Louisiana. This land is managed by a subsidiary, the Louisiana Land Exploration Company, for environmental purposes—mainly for biodiversity but also to provide protection against storm surges. Conoco Phillips has partnered with a national conservation NGO, Ducks Unlimited, for help managing the wetlands and has contributed $1 million to support their wetland-restoration and species-management efforts in one of the world's most productive estuarine systems.

At the other end of the spectrum, Phillips 66 is promoting conservation action to almost 3,000 gas stations across the United States and the United Kingdom. Starting with its California stations, the company, through its Habitat and Conservation Education Initiative, developed and distributed regional planting guides for gas station owners that provide detailed information on the local plants suitable for the growing zone in which the gas station is located. Each guide, created in partnership with the Wildlife Habitat Council, gives a list of plants with common names, scientific names, bloom time, and color. It allows the gas station owner to easily find what zone they are in. The program was rolled out to gas station owners through the company's marketing department, with an incentive that purchases of approved plants would be reimbursable. The effort was so successful that Phillips 66 expanded the campaign beyond California to all of its US gas stations and to its Jet stations in the United Kingdom. It spread the effort across its summer intern program and into its university recruitment efforts. It surveyed recipients of the guides and was able to measure change in attitude and likely change in behavior that would lead more gas station owners to plant native species and allow small interpretive signs be installed in order to educate customers.

ConocoPhillips, with over 600,000 acres, and Phillips 66, with almost 3,000 gas stations, both illustrate what can be done with resources but also with commitment and imagination. ConocoPhillips' support for wetland restoration has a huge impact on biodiversity and

Figure 9-1: A small pollinator garden in an office location could be the extent of a company's effort—or the starting point for a much larger project. (Used with permission of the Wildlife Habitat Council.)

on the communities and businesses across eight parishes in Louisiana that are better protected from storm surges by more resilient wetlands. Phillips 66's conservation education effort is impacting a large number of small lands but connecting to a significant number of people. While ConocoPhillips' efforts are concentrated in a subsidiary, Phillips 66's program reaches across much of the company. With these two initiatives, each effort brings value to the company and the environment but in completely different ways.

While most conservation NGOs dream of the $1-million corporate contribution, the likelihood of it happening is rare. Many corporate conservation engagements will be much more modest. But an opportunity to work on corporate lands should be embraced, because if a small effort is successful, like the pollinator garden shown in fig. 9-1, it could lead to further projects, such as the grassland restoration shown in fig. 9-2, and it could eventually result in the development of a corporate conservation strategic plan to be rolled out across all the company's lands.

Figure 9-2: Waste Management's project at Kirby Canyon in Northern California sees 600 acres of serpentine grasslands managed to recover the bay checkerspot butterfly, a federally protected species. (Used with permission Waste Management.)

By embracing the business need, local conservation NGOs have a real chance to work with the companies in their communities to make a difference on the ground. By understanding the opportunities afforded by nature and reaching out to the conservation community, the private sector can address a business need and learn from those who are knowledgeable and passionate about their local biodiversity.

Throughout this book, many of the successful conservation projects on corporate lands described as examples have only been successful through partnerships. They have all impacted the people involved as much as the habitat. At Boeing's Santa Susanna Field Laboratory, John Luker, once a critic of the project, is now its biggest cheerleader. In Warren County, Tennessee, Bridgestone Americas' partnership with the school district has impacted thousands of young minds and exposed them to environmental education and opportunities for science, technology, engineering, and mathematics (STEM) careers. In the city of River Rouge in Michigan, DTE's restoration and education project has touched many groups and individuals. All around the world, GM has made conservation a connector into communities wherever it has manufacturing facilities.

There is a huge potential out there for more conservation partnerships between the private sector and civil society. There is also a huge need for it. As we face the biggest environmental challenges of our time, we need to take action on all fronts to restore ecosystems and protect biodiversity. Like the victory gardens of World War II, conservation efforts on corporate lands can achieve results at both institutional and personal scales through restoration or ecological stewardship efforts both large and small. These conservation efforts can realize benefits for biodiversity as well as empower employees, community members, and NGO partners to take action. By mainstreaming nature into planning and operations, the corporate world can improve its relationship with the land and the communities in which they operate.

I like to imagine a future journey along the urban/rural transect from densely populated cities through suburban towns to sparsely populated countryside and wilderness. Along this journey, industry's impact is no longer seen as one of dominance over nature but instead as a comprehensively designed integration with nature. In this future, the anonymous offices in central business districts sport green walls and green roofs that provide habitat for pollinators, birds, and other species dwelling in the city or just passing through. Buildings are darkened at night as a matter of course to protect migratory species. Urban industrial areas are managing their buffer lands for biodiversity. Suburban office parks are meadows, corporate campuses are forests, and smaller corporate locations such as gas stations, shopping malls, and shipping depots manage for nature not purely for aesthetics but also for ecological functionality. When the journey ends in rural or wilderness areas, the impact of industry on the landscape has a bigger footprint in mines and quarries. But in this greener future, the old scars on the land are no longer visible, thanks to ecological remediation and dynamic reclamation, while current operations integrate nature in new and innovative ways.

This future can be realized if corporate landowners and conservation partners take the time to plan and build programs that will bring long-term benefit to business, biodiversity, and community. And if we all—leaders and actors in both the corporate and NGO worlds—can adopt the elements of the successful approaches laid out in this book and build on them, we can be proud of our role in this future landscape where nature is mainstreamed and integrated and we all thrive.

ACKNOWLEDGMENTS

—

Thelma Redick, this was all your fault/idea.

Mike, thank you from the bottom of my heart for keeping our little ship calm and moving in the right direction.

Thank you to: The board, staff, and leadership at the Wildlife Habitat Council for giving me the space to write and allowing me access to your stories, especially Josiane Bonneau, whose words I have shamelessly stolen; Colleen Beatty and Monica Keller, who have both made me a better writer; Daniel Goldfarb, who understands the power of a great story to inspire; Dan Litow (in advance), who will ensure that this book gets into many hands; and Chuck Adkins and Emily Voldstad, who achieved great things despite my mental absences. Prue Addison, Tim Bent, Sue Kelsey, John Luker, Jim Rushworth, and Steve Shestag for talking to me about your experiences. The Urban EE Collective on Facebook for inspiration about quotes. Laurie Davies Adams who helped me frame the climate-change chapter. Liz Johnson for giving me clarity on sperm-stealing salamanders. My family in Ireland and elsewhere for helping me across the finish line: my mother for the blazing fires and a quiet place to work, the Berube-O'Gorman clan in Dublin for giving me a place to perch and a companion for cocktails, the Stapletons in Birr for keeping me company and feeding me pizza during the last stretch, and the Gill-O'Gorman family for the welcome distraction last December. The employees at Atlantic City Electric, Arcelor Mittal Burns Harbor, Ash Grove Midlothian, BASF Fighting Island, Bayer Camçari, Boeing Santa Susana Fuel Laboratory, BP Warm Springs Pond, Bridgestone BEECH, Monterrey and Woodlawn, Cemex Florida, Covia Tamms/Elco, CRH Americas Marcus Autism Center and Milton Quarry (Dufferin Aggregates,) DOW Freeport, DTE River Rouge and Navitas House, Exelon, ExxonMobil in Spring, Texas, FCA Auburn Hills, Freeport MacMoRan, General Motors, LafargeHolcim, Lehigh Hanson, Owens Corning Granville, PPG Pittsburgh, Shell USA, Toyota North America, Vulcan Calica

Quarry and Grandin, and Waste Management GROWS/Tullytown, whose stories fill this book. I wish I had room to include all the great corporate conservation efforts I have either visited or heard about. I wish I had the skill to translate the incredible passion of corporate conservationists into the pages of this book.

Thank you to Island Press for taking a chance on a book that says something positive about the corporate world, especially Courtney Lix, whose advise and direction I will happily take any day, Elizabeth Farry for the last mile, Sharis Simonian for clear guidance, Mike Fleming for obtuse reading, and Rachel Miller for sales support.

Every Act of Conservation Matters.

NOTES

—

Chapter 1

1. The Indiana Writers Program, *The Calumet Region Historical Guide* (Gary, IN: Garman Printing Co., 1939).
2. Howard R. Bowen, *Social Responsibilities of the Businessman* (New York: Harper, 1953).
3. Linda Forbes and John Jermier, "The New Corporate Environmentalism and the Symbolic Management of Organizational Culture," in *The Oxford Handbooks of Business and The Natural Environment,* ed. Pratima Bansal and Andrew J. Hoffman (Oxford: Oxford University Press, 2011), 556–71.
4. Michael Porter and Mark Kramer, "Creating Shared Value," *Harvard Business Review* 89, nos. 1/2 (2011): 62–77.
5. Ibid.
6. Thomas Singer, *Sustainability Matters 2014: How Sustainability Can Enhance Corporate Reputation,* Research Report R-1538-14-RR, Conference Board of the USA, 2014.
7. P. F. Addison, J. W. Bull, and E. J. Milner-Gulland, "Using Conservation Science to Advance Corporate Biodiversity Accountability," *Conservation Biology* 33, no. 2 (2019): 307–18, http://doi.wiley.com/10.1111/cobi.13190.
8. Pierre Legagneux et al., "Our House Is Burning: Discrepancy in Climate Change vs. Biodiversity Coverage in the Media as Compared to Scientific Literature," *Frontiers in Ecology and Evolution* 5 (2018): 175, https://doi.org/10.3389/fevo.2017.00175.
9. Sristi Kamal, Malgorzata Grodzinska-Jurczak, and Gregory Brown, "Conservation on Private Land: A Review of Global Strategies with a Proposed Classification System," *Journal of Environmental Planning and Management* 58, no. 4 (2015): 576–97.

Chapter 2

1. "Key Characteristics of Prominent Shareholder-Sponsored Proposals on Environmental and Social Topics, 2005–2011," Investor Responsibility Research Center Institute (New York: Ernst & Young, 2013).

2. Dr. Kate Brauman (Coordinating Lead Author), "Selected Findings from the IPBES Global Assessment on Biodiversity and Ecosystem Services" [*Nature in Crisis: Biodiversity Loss and its Causes*], House Committee on Space, Science, and Technology, June 4, 2019, https://science.house.gov/imo/media/doc /Brauman%20Testimony.pdf.

3. "Guidance Note 6, Biodiversity Conservation and Sustainable Management of Living Natural Resources," International Finance Corporation (IFC), November 15, 2018, https://www .ifc.org/wps/wcm/connect/a359a380498007e9a1b7f3336b93d75f /GN6_November+20+2018+.pdf?MOD=AJPERES.

4. US Sustainable Remediation Forum, "Sustainable Remediation—Integrating Sustainable Principles, Practices, and Metrics into Remediation Projects", *Remediation* 19 (2009): 5–114, doi:10.1002/rem.20210.

5. J. Prno and D. S. Slocombe, "Exploring the Origins of 'Social License to Operate' in the Mining Sector: Perspectives from Governance and Sustainability Theories," *Resource Policy* 37, no. 3 (2012): 346–57.

6. Kathleen Wilburn and Ralph Wilburn, "Achieving Social License to Operate Using Stakeholder Theory," *Journal of International Business Ethics* 4 (2011): 3–16.

7. Elizabeth Holley and Carl Mitcham, "The Pebble Mine Dialogue: A Case Study in Public Engagement and the Social License to Operate," *Resources Policy* 47 (2016): 18–27, ISSN 0301-4207, https://doi.org/10.1016/j.resourpol.2015.11.002.

8. Chris Joseph, Thomas Gunton, and Murray Rutherford, "Good Practices for Environmental Assessment," *Impact Assessment and Project Appraisal* 33, no. 4 (2015): 238–54, doi.org/10.10 80/14615517.2015.1063811.

9. Daniel J. Fiorino, "Citizen Participation and Environmental Risk: A Survey of Institutional Mechanisms," *Science,*

Technology, & Human Values 15, no. 2 (1990): 226–43, www
.jstor.org/stable/689860.

10. M. L. Dare, J. Schirmer, and F. Vanclay, "Community Engagement and Social Licence to Operate," *Impact Assessment and
Project Appraisal* 32, no. 3 (2014): 188–97, doi.org/10.1080/14615
517.2014.927108.

11. Roger Fisher and William L. Ury, *Getting to Yes* (London: Pen-
guin, 1981).

12. Tony Schwartz, "How Employee Engagement Hits the Bottom Line," *Harvard Business Review*, November 8, 2012, https:
//hbr.org/2012/11/creating-sustainable-employee.

13. "2012 Engagement at Risk: Driving Strong Performance in a
Volatile Global Environment," Willis Towers Watson, https:
//www.towerswatson.com/Insights/IC-Types/Survey-Research
-Results/2012/07/2012-Towers-Watson-Global-Workforce
-Study.

14. Global Environmental Management Initiative, "Engaging
Employees in Sustainability," 2015, http://gemi.org/solutions
/solutions-quick-guides/engagingemployeesinsustainability/.

15. M. Garbuzov, K. A. Fensome, and F. L. W. Ratnieks, "Public
Approval Plus More Wildlife: Twin Benefits of Reduced Mowing of Amenity Grass in a Suburban Public Park in Saltdean,
UK," *Insect Conservation and Diversity* 8 (2015): 107–19, doi.org
/10.1111/icad.12085.

16. S. Du, C. Bhattacharya, and S. Sen, "Maximizing Business Re-
turns to Corporate Social Responsibility (CSR): The Role of
CSR Communication," *International Journal of Management
Reviews* 12 (2010): 8–19, doi.org/10.1111/j.1468-2370.2009
.00276.x.

17. F. Bowen, A. Newenham-Kahindi, and I. J. Herremans,
"When Suits Meet Roots: The Antecedents and Consequences
of Community Engagement Strategy," *Journal of Business Ethics* 95 (2010): 297, https://doi.org/10.1007/s10551-009-0360-1.

18. Karen Maas et al., *Investors and Companies' Biodiversity and
Natural Capital Reporting and Performance* (Breukelen, the
Netherlands: Sustainable Finance Lab, 2017), https://www.
netwerkfan.nl/uploads/da86192432293156bccdca5380246fba
.pdf.

Chapter 3

1. Ontario Environment and Energy Ministry, "Jefferson Sala-mander and Jefferson-Dependent Unisexual Ambystoma Re-covery Strategy," https://www.ontario.ca/page/jefferson -salamander-and-jefferson-dependent-unisexual-ambystoma -recovery-strategy.
2. Albert Charlier and Helene Soyer Nogueira, "Protection of Biodiversity: Companies Need to Take Action as Scores Re-main Quite Limited," Vigeo Eiris, May 2019, http://www.vigeo -eiris.com/wp-content/uploads/2019/05/VigeoEiris-UN-Biodiv -day-22-05-19.pdf.
3. C. Schmitz-Hoffmann et al., *Voluntary Standards Systems* (Ber-lin: Springer-Verlag, 2014).
4. Ben Phalan et al., "Avoiding Impacts on Biodiversity through Strengthening the First Stage of the Mitigation Hierarchy," *Oryx* 52, no. 2 (2018): 316–24, https://doi.org/10.1017/S003060 5316001034.
5. S. Clare et al., "Where Is the Avoidance in the Implementation of Wetland Law and Policy?" *Wetlands Ecology and Manage-ment* 19 (2011): 165, https://doi.org/10.1007/s11273-011-9209-3.
6. J. W. Bull et al., "Biodiversity Offsets in Theory and Practice," *Oryx* 47, no. 3 (2013): 369–80, https://doi.org/10.1017/S00306053 1200172X.
7. Hugo J. Rainey et al., "A Review of Corporate Goals of No Net Loss and Net Positive Impact on Biodiversity," *Oryx* 49, no. 2 (2015): 232–38, https://doi.org/10.1017/S0030605313001476.
8. Robert Costanza et al., "The Value of the World's Ecosystem Services and Natural Capital," *Nature* 387 (1997): 253–60.
9. George Monbiot, "The UK Government Wants to Put a Price on Nature—but That Will Destroy It," *The Guardian*, May 15, 2018, https://www.theguardian.com/commentisfree/2018/may /15/price-natural-world-destruction-natural-capital.
10. Sandra Díaz, Josef Settele, Eduardo Brondízio, "Global Assess-ment Report on Biodiversity and Ecosystem Services," Inter-governmental Panel on Biodiversity and Ecosystem Services, 2019, https://www.ipbes.net/global-assessment-biodiversity -ecosystem-services.

11. Paolo Nunes and Jeroen van den Bergh, "Economic Valuation of Biodiversity: Sense or Nonsense?" *Ecological Economics* 39, no. 2 (2001): 203–22, https://doi.org/10.1016/S0921-8009(01)00233-6.

12. See the Global Environmental Facility website on natural capital and ecosystem service valuation: https://www.thegef.org/topics/natural-capital-and-ecosystem-services-valuation.

13. T. Smith, P. Addison, M. Smith, and L. Beagley, *Mainstreaming International Biodiversity Goals for the Private Sector: Main Report & Case Studies*, JNCC Report no. 613 (Peterborough, UK: JNCC, 2018), http://jncc.defra.gov.uk/pdf/Report_613_Full-Report_Final_v2_WEB.pdf.

14. Ibid.

15. Governance and Accountability Institute, "85% of S&P 500 Index Companies Publish Sustainability Reports in 2017," https://www.ga-institute.com/press-releases/article/flash-report-85-of-sp-500-indexR-companies-publish-sustainability-reports-in-2017.html.

16. Giovanna Michelon et al., "CSR Reporting Practices and the Quality of Disclosure: An Empirical Analysis," *Critical Perspectives on Accounting* 33 (2014), https://doi.org/10.1016/j.cpa.2014.10.003.

17. Smith et al., *Mainstreaming International Biodiversity Goals*.

18. Ibid.

19. Ibid.

Chapter 4

1. F. Zafara et al., "Strategic Management: Managing Change by Employee Involvement," *International Journal of Sciences: Basic and Applied Research* 13, no. 1 (2014): 205–17.

2. Michael Beer and Russell A. Eisenstat, "The Silent Killers of Strategy Implementation and Learning," *Sloan Management Review* 41, no. 4 (Summer 2000): 29.

3. Kit Fai Pun and Anthony Sydney White, "A Performance Measurement Paradigm for Integrating Strategy Formulation: A Review of Systems and Frameworks," *International Journal*

of Management Reviews 7 (2005): 49–71, https://doi.org/10.1111 /j.1468-2370.2005.00106.x.

4. Christopher Gresov et al., "Organizational Design, Inertia, and the Dynamics of Competitive Response," *Organization Science* 4, no. 2 (1993): 181–208, https://doi.org/10.1287/orsc .4.2.181.

5. Achilles A. Armenakis and Arthur G. Bedeian, "Organizational Change: A Review of Theory and Research in the 1990s," *Journal of Management* 25, no. 3 (1999): 293–315, https:// doi.org/10.1016/S0149-2063(99)00004-5.

6. Bernard Burnes, *Managing Change*, 7th ed. (Harlow, UK: Pearson, 2017).

7. R. Edward Freeman, "Strategic Management: A Stakeholder Approach," *Journal of Management Studies* 29 (1984): 131–54, http://doi.org/10.1017/CBO9781139192675.

8. Amy J. Hillman and Gerald D. Keim, "Shareholder Value, Stakeholder Management, and Social Issues: What's the Bottom Line?" *Strategic Management Journal* 22, no. 2 (2001): 125–39, http://www.jstor.org/stable/3094310.

9. Ian Wilson, "Realizing the Power of Strategic Vision," *Long Range Planning* 25, no. 5 (1992): 18–28, https://doi.org/10.1016 /0024-6301(92)90271-3.

10. Manuela Pardo del Val and Clara Martínez Fuentes, "Resistance to Change: A Literature Review and Empirical Study," *Management Decision* 41, no. 2 (2003): 148–55, https://doi.org /10.1108/00251740310457597.

Chapter 5

1. "Mergers and Acquisitions 2018—The 10 Biggest Corporate Consolidations," *USA Today*, December 10, 2018, https://www .usatoday.com/story/money/business/2018/12/10/mergers-and -acquisitions-2018-10-biggest-corporate-consolidations/38666 639/.

2. Steven N. Handel et al., "Restoration of Woody Plants to Capped Landfills: Root Dynamics in an Engineered Soil," *Restoration Ecology* 5 (1997): 178–86, https://doi.org/10.1046/j .1526-100X.1997.09721.x.

3. See: https://www.hemmings.com/magazine/hcc/2011/04/Don-t
-Let-the-Facts-Get-in-the-Way-of-a-Good-Story/3697871.html.
4. Louise A. Mozingo, *Pastoral Capitalism: A History of Suburban
Corporate Landscapes* (Cambridge, MA: MIT Press, 2011).
5. Santiago Saura, Örjan Bodin, and Marie-Josée Fortin,
"Stepping-Stones Are Crucial for Species' Long-Distance
Dispersal and Range Expansion through Habitat Networks,"
Journal of Applied Ecology, October 1, 2013, https://doi.org/10
.1111/1365-2664.12179.
6. R. Cottle, "Linking Geology and Biodiversity," English Nature
Report 562, 2004, https://www.cbd.int/doc/pa/tools/Linking%
20Geology%20and%20Biodiversity%20(part%201).pdf.
7. J. Beneš, P. Kepka, and M. Konvicka, "Limestone Quarries as
Refuges for European Xerophilous Butterflies," *Conservation
Biology* 17 (2003): 1058–69, https://doi.org/10.1046/j.1523-1739
.2003.02092.x.

Chapter 6

1. David Lindenmayer et al., "Improving Biodiversity Monitoring," *Austral Ecology* 37 (2011): 285–94, https://doi.org/10.1111/j
.1442-9993.2011.02314.x.
2. Dirk S. Schmeller et al., "Advantages of Volunteer-Based
Biodiversity Monitoring in Europe," *Conservation Biology* 23
(2009): 307–16, https://doi.org10.1111/j.1523-1739.2008.01125.x.
3. Pierre Yves Henry et al., "Integrating Ongoing Biodiversity
Monitoring: Potential Benefits and Methods," *Biodiversity and
Conservation* 17 (2008): 33–57, https://doi.org/10.1007/s10531
-008-9417-1.
4. Jesús Jiménez López and Margarita Mulero-Pázmány, "Drones
for Conservation in Protected Areas: Present and Future,"
Drones 3, no. 10 (2019).
5. Samantha L. L. Hill et al., "Reconciling Biodiversity Indicators
to Guide Understanding and Action," *Conservation Letters* 9
(2016): 405–12, https://doi.org/10.1111/conl.12291.
6. Philip Bubb et al., *National Indicators, Monitoring, and Reporting for the Strategy for Biodiversity 2011–2020* (Cambridge, UK:
UNEP-WCMC, 2011).

7.   Henrique M. Pereira and H. David Cooper, "Towards the
     Global Monitoring of Biodiversity Change," *Trends in Ecology
     and Evolution* 21, no. 3 (2006): 123–29, ISSN 0169-5347, https:
     //doi.org/10.1016/j.tree.2005.10.015.

8.   UNEP-WCMC and the Proteus Partnership, *Biodiversity Indi-
     cators for Extractive Companies: An Assessment of Needs, Current
     Practices, and Potential Indicator Models* (New York: United
     Nations Environment Programme, 2017).

9.   Scott Bearer et al., "Environmental Reviews and Case Studies:
     Evaluating the Scientific Support of Conservation Best Man-
     agement Practices for Shale Gas Extraction in the Appalachian
     Basin," *Environmental Practice* 14, no. 4 (2012): 308–19, https:
     //doi.org/10.1017/S1466046612000385.

10. Peter W. Roberts and Grahame R. Dowling, "Corporate Repu-
     tation and Sustained Superior Financial Performance, *Strategic
     Management Journal* 23 (2002): 1077–93, https://doi.org/10.1002
     /smj.274.

11. Steven A. Melnyk et al., "Assessing the Impact of Environ-
     mental Management Systems on Corporate and Environmen-
     tal Performance," *Journal of Operations Management* 21, no. 3
     (2003): 329–51, ISSN 0272-6963, https://doi.org/10.1016
     /S0272-6963(02)00109-2.

12. Haitao Yin and Peter J. Schmeidler, "Why Do Standardized
     ISO 14001 Environmental Management Systems Lead to Het-
     erogeneous Environmental Outcomes?" *Business Strategy and
     the Environment* 18 (2009): 469–86, https://doi.org10.1002
     /bse.629.

Chapter 7

1.   Susan Strife and L. Downey, "Childhood Development and
     Access to Nature," *Organization and Environment* 22 (2009):
     99–122, https://doi.org/10.1177/1086026609333340.

2.   Ibid., 13.

3.   "Connecting Youth to Nature Survey," National Recreation
     and Parks Association, 2018.

4. Janice L. Woodhouse and Clifford E. Knapp, *Place-Based Curriculum and Instruction: Outdoor and Environmental Education Approaches* (Charleston, WV: ERIC Clearinghouse on Rural Education and Small Schools, 2000).

5. See, for example: Anna Leach, "Improving Children's Access to Nature Starts with Addressing Inequality, *The Guardian*, March 1, 2018, https://www.theguardian.com/teacher-network /2018/mar/01/improving-childrens-access-nature-addressing -inequality-bame-low-income-backgrounds.

6. Strife and Downey, "Childhood Development and Access to Nature," 8.

7. Woodhouse and Knapp, "Place-Based Curriculum and Instruction."

8. Yi Xue and Richard C. Larson, "STEM Crisis or STEM Surplus? Yes and Yes," *Monthly Labor Review* 138, no. 5 (2015), https://doi.org/10.21916/mlr.2015.14.

Chapter 8

1. Allie Goldstein et al., "The Private Sector's Climate-Change Risk and Adaptation Blind Spots," *Nature: Climate Change* 9, no. 1 (2019): 18–25.

2. See, for example: "Climate-Related Financial Disclosures," C2ES: Center for Climate and Energy Solutions, n.d., https: //www.c2es.org/content/climate-related-financial-disclosures/.

3. Simon Dietz et al., "'Climate Value at Risk' of Global Financial Assets," *Nature: Climate Change* 6, no. 7 (2016): 676–79.

4. Gerardo Ceballos et al., "Biological Annihilation via the Ongoing Sixth Mass Extinction Signaled by Vertebrate Population Losses and Declines," *Proceedings of the National Academy of Sciences* 114, no. 30 (2017): E6089–96, https://doi.org/10.1073 /pnas.1704949114.

5. Will Steffen et al., "The Anthropocene: Are Humans Now Overwhelming the Great Forces of Nature?" *AMBIO: A Journal of the Human Environment* 36, no. 8 (2007): 614–21.

6. World Wildlife Foundation, "Living Planet Report—2018: Aiming Higher," 2018, https://c402277.ssl.cf1.rackcdn.com /publications/1187/files/original/LPR2018_Full_Report _Spreads.pdf.

7. Sandra Díaz, Josef Settele, Eduardo Brondízio, "Global Assessment Report on Biodiversity and Ecosystem Services," Intergovernmental Panel on Biodiversity and Ecosystem Services, 2019, https://www.ipbes.net/global-assessment-biodiversity -ecosystem-services.

8. Terry L. Root et al., "Fingerprints of Global Warming on Wild Animals and Plants," *Nature* 421 (January 2003): 57–60.

9. H. R. Akçakaya et al., "Use and Misuse of the IUCN Red List Criteria in Projecting Climate Change Impacts on Biodiversity," *Global Change Biology* 12 (2006): 2037–43. https://doi.org 10.1111/j.1365-2486.2006.01253.x.

10. Root et al., "Fingerprints of Global Warming."

11. Camille Parmesan, "Ecological and Evolutionary Responses to Recent Climate Change," *Annual Review of Ecology, Evolution, and Systematics* 37, no. 1 (2006): 637–69, https://doi.org/10.1146 /annurev.ecolsys.37.091305.110100.

12. Root et al., "Fingerprints of Global Warming."

13. Gian-Reto Walther et al., "Ecological Responses to Recent Climate Change," *Nature* 416 (March 2002): 389–95.

14. Parmesan, "Ecological and Evolutionary Responses."

15. Ibid.

16. Ibid.

17. Ibid.

18. Ibid.

19. Eva M. Morton and Nicole E. Rafferty, "Plant–Pollinator Interactions under Climate Change: The Use of Spatial and Temporal Transplants," *Applications in Plant Sciences* 5, no. 6 (2017), https://doi.org/10.3732/apps.1600133.

20. David W. Inouye et al., "Climate Change Is Affecting Altitudinal Migrants and Hibernating Species," *Proceedings of the National Academy of Sciences* 97, no. 4 (2000), doi:10.1073/pnas.97.4 .1630.

21. Lesley Hughes, "Biological Consequences of Global Warming: Is the Signal Already Apparent?" *Trends in Ecology and Evolu-*

tion 15, no. 2, (2000): 56–61, ISSN 0169-5347, https://doi.org/10
.1016/S0169-5347(99)01764-4.

22. Parmesan, "Ecological and Evolutionary Responses."

23. Walther et al., "Ecological Responses to Recent Climate
     Change."

24. Philippe Ciais et al., "Europe-Wide Reduction in Primary
     Productivity Caused by the Heat and Drought in 2003," *Nature*
     437 (2005): 529–33.

25. Christopher P. O. Reyer et al., "A Plant's Perspective of
     Extremes: Terrestrial Plant Responses to Changing Climatic
     Variability," *Global Change Biology* 19 (2013): 75–89, https://doi
     .org/10.1111/gcb.12023.

26. Sharon Gursky et al., "Impact of Typhoon Haiyan on a Philip-
     pine Tarsier Population," *Folia Primatologica* 88 (2017): 323–32,
     https://doi.org/10.1159/000479404.

27. Bronson W. Griscom et al., "Natural Climate Solutions," *Pro-
     ceedings of the National Academy of Sciences* 114, no. 44 (October
     2017): 11645–50, https://doi.org/10.1073/pnas.1710465114.

28. Bruce A. Stein et al., *Climate-Smart Conservation: Putting
     Adaptation Principles into Practice* (Washington, DC: National
     Wildlife Federation, 2014).

29. R. van Herwijnen et al., "Remediation of Metal-Contaminated
     Soil with Mineral-Amended Composts," *Environmental Pollu-
     tion* 150, no. 3 (2007): 347–54, ISSN 0269-7491, https://doi.org
     /10.1016/j.envpol.2007.01.023.

30. Goldstein et al., "The Private Sector's Climate-Change Risk."

Chapter 9

1. Abdul Rashid et al., "The Influence of Corporate Culture and
    Organizational Commitment on Performance," *Journal of
    Management Development* 22, no. 8 (2003): 708–28, https://doi
    .org/10.1108/02621710310487873.

INDEX

—